Harm and Responsibility

Thomas J. Miceli

Harm and Responsibility

The Economic Factors Controlling the Extent of Civil and Criminal Liability

palgrave
macmillan

Thomas J. Miceli
University of Connecticut
Storrs, CT, USA

ISBN 978-3-031-74830-1 ISBN 978-3-031-74831-8 (eBook)
https://doi.org/10.1007/978-3-031-74831-8

This Palgrave Macmillan imprint is published by the registered company Springer Nature Switzerland AG
The registered company address is: Gewerbestrasse 11, 6330 Cham, Switzerland

Preface

Risk is an ever-present element of life in a complex world, and so an important challenge for any orderly society is to manage that risk in a just and efficient way. This includes determining how responsibility for any resulting harm should be assigned. The original plan for this book was to examine that question from an economic perspective, focusing especially on how the assignment of responsibility would affect people's incentives to refrain from causing unnecessary harm, whether by accident or intent. The argument would emphasize how responsibility for harm functions to mitigate risky behavior in the most efficient way; in other words, how it achieves optimal deterrence. At the outset, this seemed like a fairly straightforward task that would involve using the tools of economics to examine various doctrines in tort and criminal law. The first order of business, however, was to define in a precise way the meaning of both "responsibility" and "harm," and that turned out to be a more difficult, but also a more interesting, task than I had anticipated.

First, as to responsibility, the dictionary defines it in two ways: as "moral, legal, or mental accountability," and as "something for which one is responsible; a burden." Presumably, the first of these definitions follows as a consequence of the second. That is, one first takes on a burden or duty, either as part of the normal course of things (e.g., one's actions naturally lead to certain outcomes in a causal sense), or has it given to them (e.g., one is charged with carrying out a task). Then, as a result of that burden, one expects either to reap the rewards for carrying it out successfully, or to bear the consequences for failing to do so. In the latter event, the consequences may be self-imposed (guilt or shame), externally imposed (liability or punishment), or both.

The main (though not exclusive) focus here will be on externally-imposed (legal) responsibility—both the form that it takes and how it influences incentives. As already noted, our main interest will be what assignment of responsibility achieves optimal deterrence in the presence of risk. Secondarily, we will be concerned with justice in whatever way that concept is defined. We will see that in some cases, justice aligns with efficiency, whereas in others it does not. Formal laws most likely arose from pre-existing social norms, often in the form of religious beliefs, which had evolved over generations, and so they oftentimes embody sensible (efficient) solutions, refined by experience, to pervasive social problems. This includes the management of risk. To the extent that justice involves adherence to these social norms, efficiency and justice will generally align. However, when the two values diverge, we will argue that economics can still be useful for prescribing the most efficient means of achieving a just outcome.

From a modern legal perspective, the principal areas of law by which responsibility for harm is assessed are tort law, which determines the assignment of liability for accidental harms, and criminal law, which imposes punishment on offenders for intentional harms. There exist vibrant economic theories of both of these areas of law, and the current volume will draw heavily on those literatures. One important insight that has emerged from an economic approach to these areas is that intent is not necessary for assigning responsibility for harm in an efficient way. What matters more is causation—those who caused harm (whether intentionally or accidentally) should be held responsible for it. In one sense, this is a desirable feature of law because causation is more easily observed than intent. And yet the manner in which the law actually assigns responsibility is more complex than that—although causation is surely relevant, other factors sometimes matter.

For example, negligence law shields injurers from responsibility for harms that they accidentally caused provided that they took reasonable steps to prevent those harms. And criminal responsibility is only relevant for harms that an injurer intentionally caused. On the other hand, the law sometimes expands responsibility beyond those who caused harm, as in the case of vicarious liability and various forms of collective responsibility, a concept that was more prevalent in historic legal traditions but persists in various forms in modern law. As these examples reveal, causation is neither a necessary nor a sufficient condition for imposing liability for harm. One purpose of the current study is to offer coherent economic explanations for these departures from a strictly causal basis for assigning legal responsibility.

I said above that defining harm also turned out to be more difficult than expected. This is not because of different possible meanings of the word. It is, rather, a consequence of what we will call the "reciprocal" nature of causation in situations involving external harm, an insight first noted by the Nobel-Prize winning economist Ronald Coase. This has to do with the direction of the "arrow of causation" in situations involving harm. Often, that direction will be intuitively obvious, as when A punches B in the nose, and so the conclusion that A should be held responsible for B's harm will be universally acknowledged. In other cases, however, the direction of the arrow will be less clear. For example, if A operates a garbage dump that emits foul odors, and B knowingly moves next to it, can we not justly say that B is at least as much a cause of the harm as A? And if the remedy is for A to shut down, can we not say that there is a real sense in which A suffers harm?

As another timely example, suppose A utters statements or engages in behaviors that offend B, and B responds by taking measures to prevent A from engaging in those actions. What is the nature of harm in this case—is it A's initial actions that offended B, or B's effort to restrain A from being free to take those actions? The answer depends on how rights are assigned: Does A have a right to engage in the offending actions, or does B have a right not to be offended? These questions can only be answered with reference to an existing definition of legal rights. The point is that when rights are inherently in conflict, someone has to suffer a harm. Current debates about "cancel culture" epitomize this issue.

In light of this argument, I will conclude that economic theory cannot offer any special insights into how legal rights should be assigned in these circumstances. At most, it can prescribe an efficient mechanism for enforcing and exchanging rights once they have been put in place. This reflects the view that, while economic theory is useful for understanding a broad array of legal issues and doctrines within a common framework, the determination of how rights should be defined is ultimately a moral or political question.

The ideas expressed here are the product of over thirty years of research and thought about criminal justice from an economic perspective. My views on this topic have changed considerably over that time, due both to my personal journey as a scholar and to the untold influences of a multitude of other scholars, past and present. I would like to acknowledge some of the more prominent of those influences here. I owe my introduction to law and economics to my first teacher on the subject, Richie Adelstein, whose knowledge and enthusiasm enthralled me and ultimately inspired me to pursue a scholarly career. I can't thank him enough for the influence he has had on my life, both professionally and personally. I have also derived tremendous benefits from two colleagues and long-time collaborators, Kathy Segerson and Metin Cosgel. Kathy is the best economist I know, and Metin brings a unique multi-disciplinary perspective and multi-varied skill set to any problem. Both are also trusted friends. Two other valued collaborators throughout my career have been the late C.F. Sirmans and Matt Baker. Of course, all of the above are absolved of responsibility for any of the views expressed here.

I also want to thank my editor, Bronwyn Geyer, who expressed enthusiasm for this project from the beginning and ably assisted me through the production process. Finally, and most importantly, I want to acknowledge my family, my wife Ana Maria and my sons Tommy and Nick, whose enduring support and love make everything I do worthwhile.

Summer 2024 Thomas J. Miceli

Contents

List of Figures

List of Tables

CHAPTER 1

Introduction

When a public figure is found to have committed a misdeed or an embarrassing act, it is not uncommon for him or her to respond by admitting guilt and accepting "full responsibility." This is often a hollow admission, however, because both the speaker and the listeners know that actual consequences are unlikely to follow. It is as if the admission alone were sufficient atonement for the sin. In many instances, this no doubt reflects the privilege of the powerful or well-connected, but a less cynical reaction is that it bespeaks an ethic of forgiveness—the idea that wrongdoers deserve a second chance. Animating this view, which is pervasive in modern society, are two competing though not necessarily contradictory objectives. One is the idea of redemption, representing restoration of a wrongdoer to a position of good standing in the community. The other is reform or rehabilitation, representing the hope that offender will have learned his or her lesson and will therefore refrain from committing future transgressions. The first of these reflects a moral judgment regarding one's past behavior; the second concerns the prospect of better behavior in the future.

A sharply different concept of responsibility underlies the belief that wrongdoers should bear actual punishment for the harm they caused. This reflects the Aristotelian concept of corrective justice, which demands

T. J. Miceli, *Harm and Responsibility*,
https://doi.org/10.1007/978-3-031-74831-8_1

retaliation for wrongdoing[1]; in other words, that punishment should be visited upon the offender in proportion to the harm he or she has inflicted. This ethic embodies a causal basis for responsibility: A imposed harm on B, and so A should be held responsible for it. This conception also furthers two objectives—retribution and deterrence—which again embody, respectively, a backward-looking moral judgment and a forward-looking instrumental goal.

These contrasting views (and their associated rationales) regarding the determination of responsibility for harm reflect the complexity of the issue, both its appropriate form and its social purpose. The first view, which we might associate with a Christian ethic as epitomized by Jesus Christ's vicarious acceptance of responsibility for the sins of humanity, emphasizes forgiveness following admission of guilt. It therefore represents a view of human nature that centers on the optimistic belief that people are generally well-intentioned and will strive to do the right thing once shown the error of their ways. The second view, which we might associate more with an ancient, vengeance-driven ethic, reflects the belief that humans are fundamentally sinful, and so need to be continuously steered in a socially desirable direction by the threat of punishment. Consequently, some atonement must be offered as recompense for any harm they inflict, both to punish and deter.[2]

These vastly different perspectives on the role of responsibility for controlling harmful behavior reflect contrasting perspectives on human nature—that people are inherently good, straying only occasionally from the proper path on one hand, or that they are purely self-interested, continually weighing the benefits and costs of their actions on the other. In reality, most people are a mixture of these types—a combination of Dr. Jekyl and Mr. Hyde—and so it is not surprising that the concept of responsibility is similarly fluid, being lenient and forgiving in some instances, and harsh and punitive in others. The question of how and when society should impose punishment on those who cause harm is therefore a difficult one that mirrors the complexity of human nature and involves a combination of moral, ethical, and political considerations. The focus of this study will be to examine what light economic theory can shed

[1] See, for example, Posner (1990, Chapter 11).

[2] The idea of law as embodying a quest for revenge is a theme in Holmes (1881).

on the problem of assigning responsibility for harmful acts—including its nature, magnitude, and scope.

On its face, causation (as that concept is commonly understood) would seem to be the most natural, and to many the most morally defensible, way to assign responsibility for harm. The standard economic approach to controlling harm—the theory of externalities—is in fact based on this causal linkage because it prescribes that individuals or businesses that impose harm on others should be held liable for the victims' losses, thereby creating incentives for injurers to prevent or mitigate risk, and secondarily, to compensate victims. In this view, responsibility serves the primary purpose of internalizing the harm for purposes of encouraging deterrence. The economic theories of both tort and criminal law are based on this forward-looking perspective with respect to legal liability.

A review of various doctrines in tort and criminal law reveals, however, that the law is more complicated than that, sometimes exempting from responsibility those who caused harm, and sometimes holding responsible those who did not. We will see that there are many reasons for these departures from a strictly causal linkage, but one is that causation is itself not a well-defined concept. It is, indeed, one of the central insights of the economic approach to externalities that causation is reciprocal in nature, meaning that both an injurer and a victim must be present for harm to materialize. And as a consequence, we will see that harm is also a mutable concept that depends on how conflicting rights are legally defined.

As an example, consider the concept of negligence, which governs the assignment of liability in most areas of tort law. Under a negligence standard, defendants are only responsible for harms that result from their failure to take reasonable precautions to avoid risk. Injurers are therefore exempted from liability for that portion of the harm that would have occurred even if they had taken reasonable precautions. In other words, they are only responsible for the harm that their *negligence* caused. Any residual harm therefore remains with victims. Similarly, injurers are only responsible in criminal law for harms that they intentionally caused.

In thinking generally about how the actions of party A contribute to the risk of harm to some party B, some reflection reveals that negligence and intent are merely two points on a causal continuum ranging from a purely accidental connection at one end to malicious intent on the other. In between are varying degrees of linkage, the progression of which reflects, one supposes, an increasing degree of moral culpability. The policy question is where to set the threshold that triggers *legal responsibility*. That will ultimately depend on the objective that the imposition of such responsibility is meant to achieve—whether it is to deter harm, compensate victims, punish or rehabilitate wrongdoers, reflect moral outrage, or some combination of these goals.

Besides economic efficiency, the norm most commonly associated with the assignment of legal responsibility is justice, which is closely associated with a moral theory of law. Because both justice and morality are subjective concepts, however, their application is susceptible to circular reasoning. For example, if we say, "A caused the harm to B and so it is just for A to be held legally responsible for it," we are in effect defining justice in terms of causation rather than defining it independently. And, as we have already noted, causation itself is not a clearly defined concept.

By contrast, the use of economic efficiency as a norm for evaluating law is objective in the sense that it can be defined independently of the particular circumstances or contexts to which it will be applied. As we have noted, it is to assign responsibility for harm so as to minimize the expected costs, or maximize the expected benefits, associated with the risky activity. The resulting prescription may or may not align with particular notions of justice, depend on the intent of injurers, or reflect any particular causal linkage. For these reasons, some critics, particular those wedded to a moral basis for law, object to the use of economics as a norm for evaluating law. One of the goals of this book will be to argue that a strength of the economic approach is its ability to offer a coherent perspective on a wide array of rules and doctrines pertaining to the assignment of legal responsibility for harm, both accidentally and intentionally caused. As part of this effort, the analysis will seek to explain why the law sometimes relies on concepts like causation, negligence, and intent, but at other times does not.

The argument is organized into four parts. Part 1 reviews the institutional structure of law enforcement, principally tort and criminal law, with a particular focus on the economic approach to these areas. The essential assumption underlying the economic theory of law is that people are, for the most part, rational decision-makers who respond to legal incentives in the same way that they respond to prices in the marketplace.[3] As we have noted, this approach is based on the economic theory of externalities, which are unwanted harms that one party imposes on another party

[3] See Posner (2003) for a comprehensive survey and defense of this theory.

or parties. Consistent with this approach, the economic theory of both tort and criminal law views the function of liability, in whatever form it takes, as assigning responsibility for these costs to the party that caused them, thereby creating incentives for the latter to refrain from causing the harm, or at least to take reasonable efforts to mitigate its effects.

In advancing this argument, I will acknowledge that pursuing efficiency is not the only objective of the law. As I have noted, justice and morality are also important, if less clearly defined, goals. Indeed, I will suggest that law likely emerged from moral precepts, founded in religious beliefs, which predated the emergence of the state, and that secular laws, as they emerged, often codified these precepts as part of the general historical trend toward greater secularization. Nevertheless, I will argue that law has not completely crowded out moral responsibility as an important mechanism for maintaining social control, particularly in those areas where actions are unobserved and among those individuals who retain strong religious beliefs.

The main focus of the current study, however, will be how tort and criminal law deal with the problem of unwanted harms. Chapter 2 provides the theoretical foundation for this viewpoint, while Chap. 3 describes both how the law is designed to function in assigning responsibility, and how it actually functions. The usual distinction is that tort law concerns accidental harm while criminal law deals with intentional harm. As noted, the analysis is founded on the causal linkage between a potential injurer's decisions and the possible consequences of those decisions. According to the theory, it is the threat of legal responsibility in the form of a "price" for those consequences which create incentives for efficient harm avoidance. However, imperfections in the enforcement of both tort and criminal law—due to litigation and enforcement costs, legal error, and other factors—impede the law's ability to assign responsibility according to this ideal. The result is that some actual injurers escape responsibility while others are erroneously held responsible. These are unavoidable errors in the operation of the legal system, though I will argue that its procedural structure is designed, in part, to minimize their effect.

Chapter 4 concludes Part 1 by reviewing and assessing the causal basis for legal responsibility. It particularly considers the question of whether causation is a *necessary* or a *sufficient* condition for imposing responsibility for harm. If only a necessary condition, then everyone held legally responsible in fact caused harm, but some others who caused harm may escape responsibility. Conversely, if causation is only a sufficient condition, everyone who caused harm is held responsible, but some who did not may also be held responsible. Only if causation is both necessary *and* sufficient does the set of responsible individuals exactly coincide with the set of those who caused harm. This distinction sets the stage for next two parts of the book, which examine various doctrines in both tort and criminal law that depart in both directions from a strictly causal basis for responsibility. Unlike departures due to imperfections in enforcement (as discussed in Chap. 3), however, these are policies that purposefully limit or expand liability relative to the casual benchmark.

Part 2 first considers departures in the direction of shielding some injurers from responsibility for harms that they caused, or at least limiting their liability for it. Chapter 5 considers tort doctrines that limit an injurer's liability for accidental harms. These principally consist of proximate cause, which limits an injurer's responsibility to reasonably foreseeable risks; and negligence, which limits injurers' liability to those harms that result from their failure to take reasonable precautions. Both limitations take the form of "threshold rules" that specify a standard of behavior beyond which an injurer is shielded from liability. We will argue that this threshold feature of liability has very desirable incentive properties, particularly in those accident settings in which the actions of both injurers and victims contribute to risk. Indeed, I will contend that this insight explains the pervasiveness of these fundamental elements of tort law.

Chapter 5 goes on to discuss various extensions to the standard theory of negligence, such as contributory negligence, comparative negligence, and last clear chance. It then turns to issues related to responsibility for accidents involving dangerous products (products liability), with an emphasis on how the existence of a market relationship between injurers and victims affects the assignment of responsibility. The discussion concludes by examining the problem of insolvent injurers (the judgment-proof problem), and statutes of limitations on tort claims, both of which limit injurer liability.

Chapter 6 turns to various criminal law doctrines that limit an offender's liability. The chief of these, of course, is criminal intent, which is a *sine qua non* for criminal conviction. The economic theory of crime, however, reveals that intent is not an essential requirement for achieving optimal deterrence, and so much of the discussion in this chapter suggests reasons—some based on efficiency and some not—as to why there exists a distinct area of law for dealing with intentional harms. The chapter also discusses various procedural safeguards for criminal defendants that effectively limit their liability, including, most notably, the rule against self-incrimination, and the exclusionary rule. It also discusses various defenses against criminal prosecution, including whether or not there should be immunity for failed attempts, entrapment, and mistaken beliefs on the part of injurers.

Chapter 6 concludes by considering the treatment of repeat offenders. It is a pervasive feature of criminal codes that penalties are harsher for repeat offenders, and although this seems like an intuitively appealing policy, it turns out to be rather difficult to explain on purely economic grounds. If the goal of criminal punishment is deterrence, why not set a high penalty for the first offense rather than reserving it for repeat offenses? One explanation is that some offenders are ignorant of the law, and a lenient initial punishment is meant to be "educational." This argument, which seemingly violates the axiom that ignorance is not a defense, reflects the so-called expressive function of law. The problem is that a low "initial price" will invite crimes by knowledgeable offenders who would have been deterred by a high initial sanction. I will show, however, that if the uneducated form a large enough fraction of potential offenders, the rising sanction structure minimizes the overall costs of crime (including enforcement costs).

A very different perspective on a rising sanction structure is the idea of redemption. This is based on a belief that a first offender, even one who *knowingly* committed the offense, can be reformed. In this vein, I show that a lenient initial punishment, coupled with a harsh punishment for future offenses, can create an incentive structure that induces offenders to refrain from committing future crimes. This reflects the economic concept of marginal deterrence. The downside, again, is that such a structure invites initial crimes. The parable of the Prodigal Son serves as a motivation and illustration of this trade-off. I conclude by relating the insights from the discussion of redemption to modern law enforcement issues like the debate over three-strikes laws.

Part 3 turns to departures from causal responsibility in the direction of expanding responsibility to individuals who were *not* the cause of any harm. While this idea may seem particularly objectionable to many readers, especially when it is part of a conscious policy, I will argue, first, that there is some economic justification for it, and second, that such policies are not restricted to historical contexts in which law enforcement lacked the ability to detect offenders.

Chapter 7 considers tort doctrines that expand responsibility, beginning with situations in which the identity of the actual injurer is unknown, or where there are multiple possible injurers. In these circumstances, the law faces the question of how to assign responsibility among multiple suspects. One solution is to pick one particular suspect to bear all of the harm; another is to spread it out among several suspects. Both solutions are capable of achieving efficient deterrence (provided that they are structured to create the appropriate *expected* punishment), but they obviously entail a different degree and scope of actual responsibility. And both entail the possibility of holding innocent individuals responsible. Another solution is to impose prospective responsibility—that is, to assess liability for *risk* rather than for actual harm. The prototypical examples of this strategy are safety regulations and fines for speeding.

Chapter 8 turns to criminal law doctrines that expand responsibility beyond causation. One example is the felony murder rule, which holds a defendant liable for murder if he or she participated in a felony that resulted in a murder, even if the actual murder was committed by someone else. Another example is preventive law enforcement, which, like liability for risk, involves apprehending individuals before they have committed, or while they are in the act of committing, an actual offense. These examples introduce the concept of "collective responsibility," which involves holding an entire group of people liable for an act committed by one member of the group. We will argue that, purely from a deterrence perspective, this approach to the assignment of responsibility can be part of an efficient law enforcement strategy, principally because it saves on the costs of detection. However, most people find the practice objectionable on moral grounds because they associate it with ancient legal traditions that centered on vengeance, particularly when that involved punishing the innocent. I will nevertheless offer examples of its persistence in modern legal practice. Chapter 8 concludes by relating collective responsibility to the familiar concepts of insurance and risk-spreading.

The first three parts take as given the existence of some harm; Part 4 turns to the fundamental question of what is meant by "harm." Chapter 9 begins by arguing that harm is not a uniquely defined concept, an insight that is a consequence, as noted above, of the reciprocal nature of causation in settings involving external harms. For example, a factory that emits pollution is only harmful when people reside next to it and breathe the unhealthy air or drink the dirty water. In other words, both an "injurer" and a "victim" are necessary for harm to occur. The definition of harm in this context therefore amounts to answering the question: Does the factory have a right to emit the pollution, or do the residents have the right to be free of pollution? The answer depends on how legal rights are defined.

This point may seem pedantic, particularly when describing situations where the direction of causation is clear, as when one person punches another person in the nose. Obviously, both the injurer and victim must be present for the harm to occur, but is it reasonable to attribute equal responsibility to them? Obviously not in this case, where most would agree that the injurer's right to swing his arm ends at the victim's nose. However, Chap. 10 points out that the issue is more complicated in other cases. For example, where is the line between free speech and hate speech? And, when is it permissible to limit one person's freedom to express his or her identity if that expression offends others? The answers to these questions will vary with time and place, depending on changing attitudes and mores, and the definitions of harm and responsibility will evolve accordingly. Current debates about civil disobedience, cancel culture, and victimless crime are all manifestations of this ever-changing notion of rights and harms.

The conclusion that we will ultimately draw from this argument about the nature of harm is that economic theory cannot uniquely define a neutral point for defining legal rights. At most it can provide a framework for facilitating the efficient exchange of rights—a "pricing scheme"—once a particular starting point has been put in place. However, some other mechanism must be used to choose that initial point—whether a political process, a judicial ruling, or some other means. Only then can legal responsibility for harm, defined to be a departure from that starting point, be assigned.

References

Holmes, O.W. 1881 [1963]. *The Common Law*. Boston: Little Brown.

Posner, R. 1990. *The Problems of Jurisprudence*. Cambridge, MA: Harvard Univ. Press.

Posner, R. 2003. *Economic Analysis of Law*, 6th ed. New York: Aspen Publishers.

PART I

Assigning Responsibility: Values and Institutions

"The law threatens certain pains if you do certain things, intending thereby to give you a new motive for not doing them. If you persist in doing them, it has to inflict the pains in order that its threats may continue to be believed."

Oliver Wendell Holmes (1881 p. 40)

CHAPTER 2

Values

Part 1 of this book discusses preliminary issues related to the question of how the law controls behavior and what economics has to say about it. This chapter begins by describing the economic approach to the regulation of risk, which is based on the theory of externalities, or unwanted harms. The principal criterion for the analysis is efficiency, which in most instances involves minimizing the costs associated with risky activities. Some provision is also allowed, however, for pursuing other objectives, like justice, in conjunction with efficiency. Chapter 3 turns to a discussion of institutions charged with the pursuit of these objectives, focusing specifically on tort and criminal law, with an emphasis on how their operation, both ideally and in practice, affects the allocation of responsibility.

Efficiency as the Basis for Evaluating Law

The economic analysis of law is based on the application of economic tools, and particularly the concept of efficiency, to the study the law.[1] This endeavor represents an example of the general expansion of economics to the analysis of decision-making in areas outside of the traditional market

[1] See Posner (2003), Shavell (2004) for overviews of this theory.

T. J. Miceli, *Harm and Responsibility*,
https://doi.org/10.1007/978-3-031-74831-8_2

setting, reflecting the idea that economics is defined by its methodology—rational choice—rather than by its subject matter—the study of markets.

Law is an ideal subject matter for economic analysis because both disciplines are fundamentally concerned with how people respond to incentives, whether in the form of prices or threats of punishment. In order to accept economics as the basis for evaluating law from this perspective, however, one must first acknowledge the fundamental premise that people generally behave rationally in their various endeavors, not just in those areas traditionally associated with economic activity. The current study is especially interested in circumstances where people's decisions potentially bring them into contact with the law. In this context, economists who study the law presume that people decide whether or not to obey the law in the same way that they make any other decision—by weighing the benefits and costs. In this view, law is devoid of moral content but instead represents a system of prices aimed at guiding behavior in socially desirable directions (which usually involves obeying the law). This approach allows economists to predict how people will behave in the face of certain laws (positive analysis), and also to recommend how those laws might be improved to better achieve the desired outcome (normative analysis).

As noted, the principal norm, or value, that economists use to judge behavior is efficiency, by which we mean the optimal use of scarce resources. In most practical situations this amounts to maximizing the value, or minimizing the cost, associated with the relevant activity.[2] Critics of the economic approach to law, and indeed most people when first exposed to the idea of evaluating law from an economic perspective, will object that justice or morality is the appropriate criterion. The problem with these concepts is that they are hard to define. Although most people know *in*justices when they see them, and believe that the object of law should be to prevent such occurrences, when asked to define justice, they will invariably give different answers. The benefit of efficiency is that it offers an objective standard for evaluating law—one not dependent on the particular circumstances of a given case or the identities of the parties involved. This would seem to be a desirable objective if the law is truly meant to be "blind."

[2] The specific criteria for judging efficiency in economics is Pareto optimality, or its relaxed version, Kaldor-Hicks efficiency, which, in all relevant contexts, is equivalent to wealth maximization. See Mercuro and Medema (2006).

To be sure, in many cases efficiency and justice will prescribe the same outcome, as when someone who has caused an injury, particularly if it was done intentionally, is held legally responsible for the resulting harm. A lawyer would call this just because it accomplishes retribution, or proportional punishment; an economist would call this efficient because it deters this injurer and others from committing the same act in the future. Such a confluence is not always attainable, however, thus setting up a potential conflict between the two norms. In those circumstances, one or the other will have to predominate. But even in cases where justice is taken to be the guiding principle, economic analysis can be useful in prescribing the least-cost way of achieving that objective. That being said, an important theme of this book will be that much of the law can be understood as an effort to achieve efficiency.

In the end, though, we will reach the conclusion that, owing to the relative nature of harm, efficiency alone cannot prescribe the content of the law. At most it can offer an efficient pricing structure for enforcing the law once its content has been determined by some other means. Somewhat ironically, therefore, economic reasoning turns out to be self-limiting in its ability to fully describe the nature of the law. I will argue, however, that this is a strength of the economic approach because it allows it to adapt to changing conceptions of justice or morality.

The Economic Theory of Externalities

I have said that the conventional economic approach to law, particularly tort and criminal law, is to internalize harmful externalities. An external harm is defined to be a harm that one entity, a person or business, imposes on others but for which there is no pre-arranged mechanism by which the injurer is required to seek the consent from, or to compensate, the victim.[3] The prototypical example is a polluting factory whose emissions cause harm to nearby residents, but all torts (accidental harms) and crimes (intentional harms) fall under the heading of externalities.

According to economic theory, externalities of this sort cause market failure in the sense that producers of the harm do not fully account for their actions and so over-engage in the harmful activity. The objective here is not necessarily to prevent the harm altogether, but to induce the party

[3] Externalities can also be beneficial, but our focus will be exclusively on harmful ones.

causing the harm to take all cost-justified steps to produce less of it. Thus, polluting factories should use the most efficient technology to limit the pollution, motorists should use reasonable precaution to reduce the risk of an accident, and criminals should (generally) refrain from committing crimes. Economic efficiency therefore does not necessarily prescribe zero harm, but rather that it should be limited to the point where the benefits of the harmful activity are balanced against the cost.

The example in Table 2.1 provides an illustration of this situation in the context of the polluting factory example. The first column shows the factory's output, the second column shows its profit as a function of output, and the third column shows the external harm. The factory's profit is maximized at an output of four, but the *socially optimal* output—that which maximizes the net social benefit (= profit – external harm)—is three, as shown in the fourth column.

The conventional remedy that economists propose for this problem is a tax on output—called a "Pigovian tax"[4]—in an amount equal to the external harm, the purpose being to force the factory to include that cost along with its other production costs. The optimal tax rate in this case would be $2 per unit of output, which equals with the marginal harm. The resulting revenue of $6 at the optimal output level of three could then be used to compensate those people who continue to be harmed by the pollution. It is important to emphasize, however, that the effect of the tax on the behavior of the factory (its incentive effect) is unrelated to the actual use of the revenue raised from the tax (i.e., whether or not it is used to compensate victims). In other words, other uses of the tax revenue would not interfere with its principal purpose of internalizing the harm.

Table 2.1 Polluting factory example

Output	*Profit*	*External harm*	*Net social benefit*
1	$7	$2	$5
2	12	4	8
3	15	6	9
4	16	8	8
5	15	10	5

[4] See Pigou (1920).

Other remedies for the above externality are possible. These include setting a limit on the factory's output (a quantity regulation), and allowing victims to pursue a tort claim for the harm caused by the pollution. We will discuss tort liability in detail later; here we will simply point out how it would differ from the tax approach just described. Both take the form of financial liability for the factory, and so they have identical incentive effects on its behavior. That is, both achieve optimal deterrence of the harmful activity if properly calibrated to the harm. Again, this does not mean completely shutting down the factory; it means limiting its output to the point where the marginal benefit equals the full marginal cost.

There are, however, two important differences between the tax and tort approaches. The first is that under the tort approach, the victim(s) of the harm rather than the government must initiate the action against the factory by filing a lawsuit. This potentially creates problems because of the cost of bringing a legal action, as will be discussed in Chap. 3. The other key difference is that under the tort approach, any monetary liability assessed against the factory *must* be paid to the victims as compensation. In this way, tort liability necessarily links the *incentive* element of financial responsibility with its *compensatory* function, something we said was not required under the tax approach. (We will return to this difference between taxation and tort liability in the discussion of negligence law in Chap. 5.)

Finally, it is important to note that both the tax and tort approaches rely on a *causal connection* between the injurer (factory) and the victim(s) (nearby residents). This reflects a concept of causation that is referred to in tort law as *cause in fact*, or *necessary* causation (Keeton et al., 1984; Shavell 2004, pp. 249–250). The applicable test, called the "but-for" test, asks: "would the harm to residents have occurred but for the activity of the factory?" If the answer is yes, then the factory is said to be a cause-in-fact of the harm.[5] This causal linkage assumes that the factory has some control over the harm, and this justifies holding it legally responsible for that harm. We will return to this conception of causation at various points throughout this study.

[5] We say *a* cause because there can be multiple such causes—see the discussion of uncertainty over causation in Chap. 7.

Incorporating Constraints

The Pigovian—also called the utilitarian—approach to determining responsibility for harm is based on the objective of maximizing aggregate net benefits, or more generally, of producing the greatest social good. As I have noted, this reflects the standard economic approach to both tort and criminal law. I have also observed that other values play a role in the determination of legal responsibility, and these may conflict with efficiency. This section addresses the question of how the economic approach to law can accommodate these competing values.

One of the characteristics of the utilitarian approach to harmful activities is that all costs and benefits, including the benefits of those who cause harm, are counted in social welfare. In other words, the rights of those who engage in activities that potentially cause harm, even if done intentionally, are given equal weight along with the rights of potential victims of that harm. It follows that some infringement of victims' rights may be necessary to achieve the highest level of overall benefits. We saw, for example, that the optimal output of the polluting factory was not zero, which required victims to endure some harm. (We will argue later, by the same logic, that the optimal crime rate will not necessarily be zero.)

This balancing approach is controversial. A moral approach to controlling harm, particularly intentional harm, takes a different perspective. Rather than balancing benefits and costs, morality generally establishes a clear standard with respect to certain harmful behaviors, often in the form of a commandment, as in "thou shalt not…." Consequently, there are no acceptable grounds on which one can engage in the prohibited action, and if one does, some punishment ensues. This reflects the Kantian principle that no one should be forced to bear a cost as a way to save greater costs, or to produce greater benefits, for others, as is implicitly allowed in a utilitarian theory of law.[6]

Although the economic and moral approaches are very different, they are not necessarily incompatible. One way to combine them is to identify and elevate certain rights or obligations to the status of "side constraints," which would then be imposed upon the problem of maximizing aggregate welfare.[7] This constrained optimization approach is illustrated in Fig. 2.1, which graphically depicts the polluting factory example. In the graph, the

[6] See Holmes (1881, p. 37) and Nozick (1974, pp. 30–31).

[7] The current discussion follows from Nozick (1974), Chapter 3.

factory's profit is increasing in its output level, indexed here by x, but the increase is diminishing, as represented by the downward-sloping curve, labeled *MB* for marginal benefits (or profits). If unconstrained, the factory would expand its operation to the point where its profits are maximized, which corresponds to the point where marginal benefits equal zero. This point is labeled x_p in Fig. 2.1.

The external harm to residents is also increasing in x, here at an increasing rate. This is represented by the upward-sloping curve labeled *MC* for marginal cost. According to the utilitarian approach to this situation, which equally counts the factory's benefit and the residents' harm, the optimal scale of operation—the scale that maximizes net *social* rather than private gains—occurs at the intersection of the *MB* and *MC* curves, the point labeled x^*. This corresponds to the output of 3 in the above example.

One way to achieve this outcome, as discussed above, is to impose a Pigovian tax on the factory that coincides with the marginal cost. Under this policy, the factory has to pay the cost borne by the residents, and so it internalizes the full costs and benefits of its operation. The tax would therefore coincide with the marginal cost curve. An alternative approach would be to impose a regulation, or constraint, stating that the scale of the factory's operation cannot exceed x^*. Because this scale is lower than what the factory would have chosen on its own, x_p, we say that the

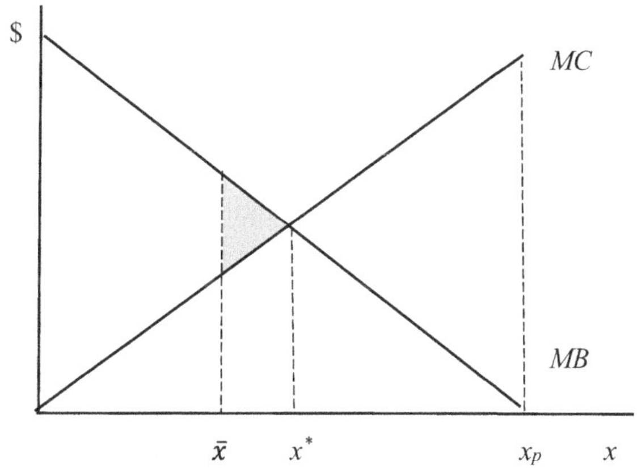

Fig. 2.1 Optimal output of the polluting factory

constraint is *binding*. Both of these approaches are able to achieve the same efficient outcome, but the constraint approach differs in an important respect; namely, the factory does not have to pay the costs that its operation imposes *up to* x^*. Thus, the residents must bear this cost, which equals the area under the MC curve up to x^*. Under the tax approach, by contrast, the factory bears that cost, and the resulting tax revenue can (in theory) be passed on to victims as compensation for the harm.[8]

Although both of these approaches yield the efficient level of operation, they reflect a different understanding of how rights and responsibilities should be assigned in the presence of the external costs. Under the tax approach, the residents in effect have the right to be free of *any* harm, and the factory has to "purchase" that right by paying the tax. It will do so to the point where its marginal profit equals the marginal tax; that is, up to x^*. In this case, we say that the external harm is "priced" by the government's tax policy. And in principle, the revenue raised by the tax is given to the residents as compensation. In this sense, an implicit exchange occurs whereby the factory "buys" the right to pollute.

Under the constraint approach, by contrast, the factory is free to operate without responsibility for any harm that it causes up to the optimal level x^*, but it is strictly prohibited from operating at any higher level. This represents a different sort of incentive mechanism: rather than pricing the harm, the regulation establishes a threshold of acceptable behavior that the factory cannot exceed.[9] In terms of the assignment of rights, under the threshold approach, the factory essentially retains the right to impose harm up to the constrained level, and so victims are forced to endure that harm. This difference highlights the importance of how rights are initially assigned—called the initial "entitlement point"—when formulating policies aimed at assigning responsibility for external harm. This will become a key issue in subsequent discussions, particularly as it relates to the problem of determining causation, and in defining harm, in externality problems.

[8] In terms of administration, the two approaches require different knowledge on the enforcer's part. The tax approach requires knowledge of the victims' harm, while the regulatory approach requires knowledge of the optimal level of output. This may be harder to obtain because it depends on both the benefit and harm.

[9] Obviously, some punishment would be threatened for exceeding the allowable point that would be set high enough to deter the factory from doing so.

The constraint approach is not limited to the control of economic costs. In his discussion of side constraints,Nozick (1974) refers to *moral* constraints. To illustrate the difference, I will consider two examples: land use zoning and criminal sentencing guidelines. Figure 2.1, suitably re-interpreted, will serve to illustrate both.

Land use zoning has a long history in the United States.[10] From an economic perspective, it is principally aimed at mitigating the spillover effects that arise when potentially incompatible economic activities exist in close spatial proximity to one another. A typical zoning ordinance will segregate different land uses so that residential users, say, are in one area and polluting factories are in another. The idea is that "similar land uses may have no (or only small) external effects on each other whereas dissimilar land uses may have large effects" (White 1975, p. 32).

Consider a landowner whose property is in a residential zone but whose highest valued use would be for industry. This situation can be represented in Fig. 2.1 by interpreting x as the intensity of land use.[11] The far left ($x = 0$) involves no uses (i.e., the land would have to be left as open space), while the far involves the most intense use. An increase in x correspondingly involves greater external costs for other owners. If there were no restrictions, the landowner in question would choose x_p to maximize profit, whereas efficient land use would dictate restricting use to x^*. Assuming that this takes the form of a constraint (i.e., $x \leq x^*$), the land user has to comply.

Historically, landowners have challenged the right of local governments to impose such constraints on the grounds that it is a taking of their property for which compensation is due under the Fifth Amendment Takings Clause.[12] The claim is that by limiting permissible land uses to x^*, the owner is deprived of profit in an amount equal to the area under the *MB* curve between x^* and x_p. Courts have universally rejected this argument, however, ruling instead that no compensation is due based on the legitimate role of local governments to prevent external costs. Thus, the landowner is not compensated for the foregone profit owing to the regulation, but nor are those landowners who are harmed by the offending activity up to the permitted use compensated for the costs they bear over

[10] See the treatise by Fischel (1985) for an economic approach to zoning.

[11] See Fischel (1985), Chapter 7.

[12] See, e.g., *Village of Euclid v. Ambler Realty*, 272 U.S. 365 (1926).

that range (i.e., between $x = 0$ and x^*). In this sense, the entitlement point established by the zoning constraint is (ideally) set at the efficient use, x^*, thereby balancing the competing interests of the two groups of landowners. In this way, responsibility for the offsetting "harms" (i.e., the foregone profit of the offending user and the external harm to other users from the permitted level of use) is shared. Each therefore bears some cost relative to their ideal point. And, given that the restriction is efficiently chosen, overall land values are maximized in the utilitarian tradition. In this example, as in the factory case, the constraint on land use is aimed exclusively at achieving economic efficiency as measured by the relevant benefits and costs.

The second example concerns criminal sentencing guidelines, which set recommended lower and upper bounds for various offenses according to the severity and circumstances of the crime.[13] Our focus here will be on the upper bound, which reflects aversion on the part of policymakers to "excessive" punishments according to the norm of retributive justice, or proportionality between crimes and punishments.[14] Figure 2.1 can be used to illustrate the impact of this constraint by interpreting x as the severity of punishment. In this view, the *MB* curve reflects the marginal deterrence benefit of increasing punishment resulting from the expected reduction in crime from harsher sentences, while the *MC* curve reflects the marginal cost of imposing more stringent punishments in the form of enforcement and punishment costs. The optimum prescribed by a strictly utilitarian approach to law enforcement would therefore dictate a severity of x^*.

Policy debates about the appropriate treatment of criminal defendants, however, generally involve difficult moral, ethical, and political considerations beyond those considered in the standard economic model. These considerations may well result in an upper bound on x that differs from x^*—most likely it is in the downward direction. This possibility is shown by $\overline{x}$ in Fig. 2.1, and the shaded triangle shows the resulting loss in welfare (in a utilitarian sense) if this restriction were implemented. In other words, it is the economic cost of implementing a policy based in part on moral or political considerations.

[13] See the fuller discussion of sentencing guidelines in Chap. 3.

[14] See Holmes (1881, pp. 36–37) and Adelstein (2017, p. 176).

As a final point (and a preview of things to come), the moral-constraint approach to the control of harm potentially runs into a problem if there are multiple side constraints that are incompatible. In Fig. 2.1, for example, competing interest groups—whether the question concerns the level of land development or the stringency of criminal sentences—may express opposing views on where x should be set. The problem is that, once the utilitarian criterion is abandoned in favor of the side constraint approach, there is no "objective" basis for arbitrating among these competing interests. In other words, there is no "right" entitlement point. Ultimately, this requires the establishment of a hierarchy of rights, which usually necessitates a political solution. Current debates about "cancel-culture" reflect this situation, as we will examine in greater detail in Part 4.

Deterrence: The Model of Precaution

This final section describes a refinement of the economic model of externalities that will be important for our study of tort law throughout this book. In the polluting factory example, the assignment of financial responsibility to the factory by whatever mechanism was aimed at inducing it to cut its output back to the efficient level. In this way, a reduction in output mitigated the harm. The factory may also have had the ability to invest in other measures specifically aimed at abating the pollution. In other words, it may have been able to invest in precautions that would reduce the harm for any given level of output. This approach reflects the so-called *model of precaution*, which economists have developed to examine the use of tort liability for controlling externalities (Brown 1973; Cooter 1985).

This model specifically emphasizes actions that injurers (and later, victims) can take, apart from their scale of activity, to reduce risk. In the case of the polluting factory, this could involve use of cleaner technology, or the installation of filters that would lower the resulting damage for each unit of output produced. These precautionary actions are costly, however, and so, like variations in output, they should only be undertaken to the point where the marginal reduction in harm equals the marginal cost of the action.

Table 2.2 provides an example involving three possible levels of injurer precaution or care: none, medium, and high. For each choice, the table shows the cost of care to the injurer, the resulting expected harm to

Table 2.2 Injurer care and accident losses

Level of care	*Cost of care*	*Expected harm*	*Total cost*
None	0	50	50
Medium	10	30	40
High	20	22	42

the victim, and the total costs (care plus harm). All values should be interpreted as being per unit of output.

Note that expected harm is decreasing with care, but at a decreasing rate—i.e., medium care reduces harm by $20 relative to no care, and high care reduces harm by only $8 relative to no care. This reflects the intuitive idea that injurers will undertake the most effective precautions first. Given that the cost of care rises at a constant rate, we see that in this example, total costs are minimized at the medium level of care. As with the factory's output choice, total elimination of harm will not generally be optimal (and indeed, may not even be possible). Imposing full (or strict) liability on the factory in this case will again induce it to invest in the efficient level of precaution (as well as output) because it will make the factory's private costs coincide with social costs.

Finally, note that the example here describes a "unilateral care" version of the model of precaution, meaning that only the injurer is able to invest in precautions to lower the risk of harm. As we will see later, in many risk settings victims can invest in their own precautions to reduce their exposure to harm, thereby creating a "bilateral care" situation. The principles regarding care by victims are exactly the same as those described for injurers. Indeed, from a purely economic perspective, the situations of the injurer and victim with respect to accident avoidance are perfectly symmetric. And, as we shall see later, the law reflects that symmetry in the various ways that liability can be assigned following an accident.

References

Adelstein, R. 2017. *The Exchange Order: Property and Liability as an Exchange System*. New York: Oxford Univ. Press.

Brown, J. 1973. Toward an Economic Theory of Liability. *Journal of Legal Studies* 2: 323–349.

Cooter, R. 1985. Unity in Torts, Contracts, and Property: The Model of Precaution. *California Law Review* 73: 1–51.

Fischel, W. 1985. *The Economics of Zoning Laws: A Property Rights Approach*. Baltimore: Johns Hopkins Univ. Press.

Holmes, O.W. 1881[1963]. *The Common Law*. Boston: Little Brown.

Keeton, W., D. Dobbs, R. Keeton, and D. Owen. 1984. *Prosser and Keeton on Torts*, 5th ed. St. Paul, MN: West Publishing.

Mercuro, N., and S. Medema. 2006. *Economics and the Law: From Posner to Post-Modernism*. Princeton: Princeton Univ Press.

Nozick, R. 1974. *Anarchy, State, and Utopia*. New York: Basic Books.

Pigou, A. 1920. *The Economics of Welfare*. London: MacMillan.

Posner, R. 2003. *Economic Analysis of Law*, 6th ed. New York: Aspen Publishers.

Shavell, S. 2004. *Foundations of Economic Analysis of Law*. Cambridge, MA: Belknap Press.

White, M. (1975) Fiscal Zoning in Fragmented Metropolitan Areas, in *Fiscal Zoning and Land Use Controls*, E. Mills, ed. Lexington, MA: Lexington Books.

CHAPTER 3

Institutions

This chapter turns to the question of how the law actually assigns responsibility for harmful activities. We will concentrate on tort law, which is concerned with accidental harm, and criminal law, which is concerned with intentional harm. Consideration will be given to the ideal functioning of these areas as well as to how they actually operate, as that determines how legal responsibility is assigned in practice. The discussion begins, however, by speculating on the relationship between morality and law, and particularly about how secular law emerged from pre-existing moral and ethical precepts regarding behavior in a social setting.

Morality and the Emergence of Law

That morality is an important source of law is, to most people, self-evidently true.[1] For example, the famous American judge and legal scholar, Oliver Wendell Holmes, asserted in this classic essay, "The Path of the Law," that "The law is witness and external deposit of our moral life. Its history is the history of the moral development of the race" (Holmes 1896, p. 49). The prominent legal philosopher, H.L.A. Hart, likewise observed that "it cannot seriously be disputed that the development of

[1] See, for example, Brague (2005) for an examination of the relationship between morality (divine) law and secular law throughout history and across religious traditions.

T. J. Miceli, *Harm and Responsibility*,
https://doi.org/10.1007/978-3-031-74831-8_3

law, at all times and places, has in fact been profoundly influenced both by the conventional morality and ideals of particular social groups" (Hart 1961, p. 181).

But law and morality are not the same thing; some laws have nothing to do with morality (e.g., traffic and tax laws), and not all violations of moral precepts are illegal (e.g., lying to or cheating on one's spouse). Nor are they enforced in the same way. Morality is enforced by internal mechanisms such as guilt or shame, usually according to some religious doctrine, while law is enforced by the threat of publicly administered punishments as prescribed by legislatures and courts.

For many people, however, law and morality are so intertwined that they view disobedience of the law per se as an immoral act, even when they are ignorant of the reasons for the law or the consequences of breaking it. It is enough that the secular authority has announced that an act is forbidden, and they have internalized a belief that laws should be obeyed. Hart again offers a clear statement of this expressive role of law: "Why are certain kinds of acts forbidden by law and so made crimes or offences? The answer is: To announce to society that these actions are not to be done and to secure that fewer of them are done" (Hart 1982, p. 6). Kahan (1998, p. 610) likewise observes that "as communities, [people] structure the criminal law to promote the meanings they approve of and to suppress the ones they dislike or fear."

A person who obeys the law reflexively once informed of its content is epitomized by James Madison's assertion in Federalist No. 51 that "If men were angels, no government would be necessary" (Madison 2008, p. 257). A clear-eyed view of human motivation reveals, however, that most people are not angels in this sense, and so it is not enough to merely assert that certain acts are socially unacceptable and expect that all or even most people will conform to that mandate. For these individuals, there must be a real threat of punishment. Such a rational decision-maker is epitomized by Oliver Wendell Holmes's "bad man," "who cares only for the material consequences which … knowledge [of the law] enables him to predict" (Holmes 1897, p. 459).[2]

Law thus plays a dual role of announcing to society what acts are unacceptable in the hope that at least some people will reflexively comply with their prohibition, while simultaneously threatening punishments to

[2] This assertion is the basis for Holmes's so-called prediction theory of the law.

those who do not conform to this expression of proper behavior. In this sense, law and religion (as the institutional repository of morality) represent alternative mechanisms for controlling behavior in society. Religion almost certainly predated law in serving this purpose, but as we have noted, law has taken over much of this function in the modern world. Morality nevertheless continues to play an important role in restraining bad behavior in certain realms and among a certain fraction of the population.

Having recognized this dual enforcement structure, it is interesting to speculate on how and why law emerged as the predominant means of controlling behavior in a society where adherence to rules is socially optimal, but opportunities exist to profit individually by breaking them.[3] The simplest way to represent this type of situation is with a Prisoner's Dilemma game, as depicted by the payoff matrix in Table 3.1. The game involves two players and two possible strategies for each: *cooperate* and *cheat*. In the current context, we will interpret cooperation as adherence to the law and cheating as breaking the law.

Table 3.1 shows the payoff to each player from the four possible strategy combinations; the left number in each cell is the payoff to player 1 and the right number is the payoff to player 2. The numbers represent some measure of well-being, such as utility or wealth, and the sum of the two represents joint (social) well-being for any outcome. The objective for both individuals and society is to maximize these payoffs. Notice that overall well-being is maximized when both players choose to cooperate (follow the rules), but an individual achieves the maximum personal well-being by cheating against a cooperator—in other words, by being a law breaker in a society of law abiders. It is the latter possibility that may entice a player to cheat. However, if both (all) players cheat, the

Table 3.1 Prisoner's Dilemma game

		Player 2	
		Cooperate	*Cheat*
Player 1	Cooperate	4, 4	0, 5
	Cheat	5, 0	3, 3

[3] The following discussion is based on Cosgel and Miceli (2019). Also see Miceli (2019, Chapter 8) and Coleman (1992, pp. 3–4).

joint payoff is lower than if they had both cooperated. Unfortunately, the outcome where both in fact cheat constitutes the equilibrium of the game if all players act rationally (i.e., in their personal interest). This is true because, if a player is unsure about what strategy the other player will select, the best choice is to cheat.

To see why, suppose player 1 expects player 2 to cooperate. The optimal strategy for player 1 is then to cheat because it yields a payoff of 5 rather than 4. Conversely, if player 1 expects player 2 to cheat, the optimal strategy for player 1 is again to cheat because it yields a payoff of 3 rather than zero. We therefore say that cheating is a dominant strategy for each player. The result is a society of law breakers. The "dilemma" is how to avoid this suboptimal outcome, which in an actual social setting would be very destructive.

Religious belief, or morality, is one solution. Indeed, several scholars have argued that the enduring nature of religious belief can be attributed in part to its role in restraining bad behavior prior to the emergence of the state. The argument is that societies that were successful in promoting religious beliefs as a way of motivating people to refrain from committing socially harmful actions gained a selective advantage over those societies that were less successful and hence fell into lawlessness.[4] Among those that avoided this bad outcome, the "incentive" to cooperate generally took the form of some sort of divine retribution for harmful acts, the detection of which could not escape the gaze of an omniscient deity.

The main disadvantage of religion in controlling behavior, however, is that it will not be effective against those who have not internalized the relevant moral sentiment (i.e., belief in the prevailing moral code). Thus, the efficacy of this means of social control will depend on society's ability to maintain a large enough fraction of believers. Secular law, by contrast, applies equally to everyone, but effective enforcement requires the establishment of an apparatus capable of detecting and punishing wrongdoers, and this is costly. This reflects the fundamental trade-off between religion and law as alternative means of social control. In the following analysis, we will conduct a thought experiment that asks what the conditions are

[4] See Wade (2006), Norenzayan (2009), and Johnson (2016) for theories of religion based on its social role in enforcing social order before the emergence of secular legal institutions. Adam Smith's *A Theory of Moral Sentiments* (1759) advanced a similar view of surveillance by God as a means of restraining bad behavior.

for secular law to emerge against a backdrop of rule enforcement purely by moral belief.[5]

Suppose that a fraction β of citizens will cooperate regardless of the material consequences (i.e., expected payoffs), while the remaining fraction, $1 - \beta$, will choose whatever strategy maximizes their payoffs. These two types correspond, respectively, Madison's "angels" and Holmes's "bad men." Our particular focus will be on the latter type, and the specific question to be asked is, under what conditions will non-believers cooperate? The first step is to show that the existence of some angels—some people who will reflexively cooperate—will *not* be sufficient to induce purely rational individuals to cooperate, no matter how large the fraction of cooperators is.

Assume that people interact randomly, and that a person's type cannot be discerned from their appearance.[6] The expected payoff from playing cooperate in this setting is 4β, while the expected payoff from cheating is $5\beta + 3(1 - \beta) = 3 + 2\beta$.[7] Thus, even if $\beta = 1$—that is, even if it is certain that one will interact with a cooperator, the payoff from cheating will exceed the payoff from cooperating. Thus, those lacking the moral sentiment to cooperate will always cheat.

Now consider the possibility of secular law enforcement in this society. Let's suppose that this requires a total (up-front) expenditure of c for the creation of an enforcement apparatus, and that this cost is equally shared among the cooperators. Thus, the cost per person is c/β. In this sense, law enforcement is a public good. Further, suppose that this enforcement mechanism will result in the certain detection of all instances where a player cheats against a cooperator, and that the penalty for doing so is that the cheater will have to disgorge the resulting payoff. This ensures that the offender can pay the "fine," and that crime does not pay. However, the fine is not handed over to the "victim."[8]

[5] Nozick (1974) offers a theory of how state monopoly of law enforcement emerged.

[6] Frank (1990) considers the possibility that people can signal their inclination to cooperate by their emotions.

[7] Specifically, note that $3 + 2\beta > 4\beta$ for any β between zero and one.

[8] Obviously, other enforcement structures, including less than certain detection and higher sanctions, could be considered. The specification here is meant to illustrate the key points in the simplest possible setting. See Furlong (1987) for a similar enforcement structure.

With this structure in place, the expected payoff to a potential cheater is now equal to $3(1 - \beta)$. Comparing this to the expected payoff from cooperating, 4β, we find that cooperating is now preferred if $4\beta > 3(1 - \beta)$, or if $\beta > 3/7$. Thus, cheating is now deterred if the fraction of cooperators is large enough. The reason is that, if would-be cheaters only expect to encounter other cheaters, there is no gain to cooperating. In this sense, the anticipation of good behavior by at least some others promotes good behavior by rational actors. Note, however, that this is not because potential cheaters have been "reformed"; it is because cheating against cooperators is no longer profitable. In other words, rational individuals reach the conclusion that "if you can't beat 'em, join 'em."

It remains to show that cooperators are willing to invest the resources needed to create this enforcement structure. If they do, the payoff per person is $4 - c/\beta$, whereas if they don't, the payoff is 4β (as in the world of religious enforcement only). Adding law enforcement is therefore desirable if $4 - c/\beta > 4\beta$. Note first that this condition can never hold if $\beta = 1$, for in that case there is no gain from enforcement because everyone cooperates. Nor can it hold if β approaches zero, for in that case the average cost of enforcement would be too high for cooperators to bear. Generally, therefore, enforcement will only be optimal for intermediate values of β, and only then if c is not too large.[9]

This conclusion suggests an interesting non-monotonic relationship between moral beliefs and the emergence of secular law enforcement institutions. At one extreme ($\beta \to 0$), law enforcement will not emerge because the fraction of believers is too small. This is due to two effects: first, would-be cheaters will not be deterred because they will most likely encounter other cheaters against whom the optimal strategy is to cheat; and second, the number of cooperators is too small for them to be willing to bear the per capita cost of enforcement. However, once the number of believers reaches a critical level, creation of laws aimed at restraining non-believers becomes a desirable strategy. In this sense, we would say that religion and law are *complementary*. Another way to say this is that existence of some minimal religious belief is a pre-requisite for secular law to emerge.

At the other extreme—i.e., a high degree of belief ($\beta \to 1$)—law enforcement will also fail to emerge because if the fraction of reflexive

[9] For example, suppose $\beta = c = .5$. The resulting inequality would be $4 - 1 = 3 > 2$, and so law enforcement will emerge.

cooperators exceeds a certain level, the benefits to cooperators of deterring cheating will not be large enough to justify the costs. This situation will primarily apply to close-knit and homogeneous religious communities where nearly everyone has internalized the moral sentiment to cooperate.[10] In this case, we would say that religion and law are *substitutes* with respect to enforcing good behavior. In other words, a high degree of religious belief makes law superfluous. Cosgel and Miceli (2019) provide some empirical evidence for this non-monotonic relationship between religion and law using data on various contemporary and historical societies.[11]

One might conjecture that in those societies where law does emerge, it will eventually "crowd out" religion by taking over its social-control function. In fact, this does not seem to have happened, at least not to the point where religion has ceased to be important in most societies. For example, religious participation did not decline in the twentieth century, despite predictions of its demise, prompting Iannaccone et al. (1997, p. 363) to observe that, "for good or ill, at home and abroad, religious belief remains widespread, religious commitments continue to shape people's behavior." This obviously reflects the wide range of functions, in addition to controlling behavior, that religion serves.[12]

But even in the latter context, moral beliefs continue to play an important role in those realms of social life where law is ineffective.Shavell (2002) offers an insightful analysis of this "division of labor" between law and morality in controlling behavior. The principal difference between the two mechanisms, as noted above, is that law employs publicly announced rules backed by the threat of punishment for transgressing them. Its effectiveness therefore relies on how much society is willing to invest in the infrastructure needed to detect, adjudicate, and punish violators, as well as on the degree to which the fear of punishment deters would-be offenders (a point to which we will return below).

By contrast, morality relies on internalized incentives such as guilt, shame, or fear of losing the afterlife. In terms of enforcement, this requires

[10] Cosgel and Miceli (2019, p. 703) cite as examples from U.S. history the Puritans in early New England, the Shakers, a communal religious group that established several thriving communities in the nineteenth and early twentieth centuries, and the modern-day Amish, another religious group.

[11] The data were obtained from Murdock and White (1969).

[12] See Iannaccone (1998) on the economics of religion.

instilling in people certain beliefs, such as existence of an omniscient deity who observes all, or at least the acceptance by members of society of a code of ethical behavior that operates through one's own conscience or fear of social opprobrium. Although morality only reaches those who have been educated in and have embraced such beliefs, among true believers, detection of a transgression is certain.

Given these differences, Shavell argues that morality alone is best at controlling actions that involve relatively small harms, such as those that arise on a daily basis in situations where people have opportunities to break promises, betray or cheat on business associates, friends, or spouses, and commit minor infractions. The costs of these harms are sufficiently small, Shavell (2002, p. 245) argues, that "it would not be socially worthwhile to append the legal system to the moral system in order to help prevent this residuum of bad things from occurring." The downside is that amoral individuals (Holmes's "bad men") will not be deterred from committing these sorts of acts because most would not be classified as crimes and hence not subject to legal redress. Thus, as the above Prisoner's Dilemma model showed, some cheating will persist among non-believers.

For more serious harms, on the other hand, Shavell argues that legal intervention is essential. This defines the realm of criminal acts. And although morality will restrain many people from committing these offenses irrespective of punishment, this is not a sufficient deterrent given the potentially serious harms that would follow from them. Thus, the threat of actual punishment must be added to deter that fraction of the population that is not dissuaded by moral considerations alone.[13]

An interesting consequence of this symbiotic relationship between law and morality, which arises as a consequence of law's expressive function, is that law is not just a mirror of morality, but is also a shaper of it. This reflects the natural affinity between law and morality, which, as we have noted, makes obedience of the law a moral imperative for many, regardless of its purpose or content. This reciprocity, however, can have cross-cutting effects. On one hand, it enhances the deterrent function of law because, as Shavell (2002, p. 255) notes, "not only does law have a direct effect on behavior through the use of legal sanctions, but it has as

[13] Shavell also recognizes a third category—those acts that are crimes but not necessarily immoral in nature. A law that coordinates behavior, such as which side of the road to drive on, is an example.

a by-product the beneficial altering of moral beliefs and of strengthening legal sanctions." In other words, morality complements and reinforces law.

On the other hand, however, it may engender a kind of moral relativism with respect to what constitutes the type of harm to which legal responsibility should be attached. As we have already noted (and will emphasize later), harm is a reciprocal concept because it requires both an injurer and a victim. The direction of causation is therefore ambiguous. And as the "culture wars" have revealed, one person's freedom of expression is another person's hate speech. Only one side can prevail in the presence of these external effects, and whatever decision emerges, and by whatever means, it will tend to shape the definition of harm and, consequently, that nature of moral beliefs. The result is an ever-changing concept of morality that can lead to a perception of arbitrariness in society's values. Part 4 elaborates on and pursues the consequences of this line of reasoning.

Tort Law and Criminal Law

We now explicitly turn to a discussion of those areas of law that principally deal with the unwanted imposition of harm: namely, tort law and criminal law. As we have noted, the usual distinction is that tort law deals with accidental harms whereas criminal law deals with intentional harms. Indeed, the demonstration of a guilty mind (*mens rea*) is a *sine qua non* for labeling an act criminal; that is, an intent to do harm. We will see later, however, that intent is a rather difficult concept to define or prove because it is a state of mind. Usually, it must be inferred from actions.

Torts and crimes also involve very different connotations regarding moral culpability. For this reason, we shall see that the two areas of law have different procedural rules and permit different sanctions. Specifically, tort actions are initiated by accident victims who file suit against injurers in pursuit of compensation for their losses, whereas criminal prosecutions are initiated and conducted by the government on behalf of society, with convicted defendants potentially facing imprisonment. For this reason, criminal defendants enjoy certain procedural safeguards that are not available to tort defendants, such as the presumption of innocence and the right against self-incrimination (i.e., the right to refuse to testify). We will specifically argue that these are responses to the nature of punishment and the stigma attached to criminal as opposed to civil conviction.

In keeping with this dichotomous legal treatment, the prevailing economic theories of tort law and criminal law have generally developed along independent lines,[14] although both are based on the economic theory of externalities as described in Chap. 2. An interesting insight arising from this common approach is that there is no clear economic need for distinct tort and criminal categories. Although a fully satisfying integrative theory remains lacking, some efforts have been made to explain their co-existence.[15] Generally, these reflect imperfections in the mechanism of enforcement, which, it is argued, make tort law alone (private enforcement) an inadequate system for controlling certain harms. The predominant imperfection is under-detection, which is particularly relevant for premeditated acts because wrongdoers have the ability to cover their tracks, thereby allowing them to reduce the likelihood of facing legal responsibility. As Sherlock Holmes observed, "Where a crime is coolly premeditated, then the means of covering it are coolly premeditated also."[16] According to this argument, intent effectively serves as a proxy for difficulty of detection.[17]

A second impediment to private enforcement is when the harm from an act is dispersed across a large number of victims, none of whom will have sufficient incentive to sue the injurer. In this case, the government needs to act vicariously for victims.[18] A third reason for criminal law is that some injurers will lack the resources to pay monetary damages and so will not be deterred from committing harmful acts by the threat of fines alone. The possibility of imprisonment or other non-monetary sanctions, which only the state can impose, is therefore needed to achieve adequate deterrence.

From a moral perspective, the explanation for criminal law is that legal responsibility is not just a means of "pricing" certain harmful acts, but of punishing those behaviors that are deemed unacceptable within a civilized society. For example, some coercive transfers of wealth may be efficient in

[14] The economic model of tort law began with Brown (1973), and the economic model of criminal law (at least its modern incarnation) began with Becker (1968).

[15] See, for example, Friedman (2000, Chapter 18), Posner (2003, pp. 215–219), and Shavell (2004, pp. 543–550).

[16] Doyle (1930) "The Problem of Thor Bridge," p. 1065.

[17] See Posner (1985, p. 1223) and Shavell (2004, p. 554).

[18] An extreme version of this argument is the need to enforce laws against "victimless crimes." See the further discussion of this issue in Chap. 10.

the strictly economic sense of transferring assets to higher valuing users, but society deems it necessary to punish such acts in order to channel them into the marketplace, where mutual consent governs exchange.[19] This argument is particularly relevant when the exchange involves a right that society has judged should never be exchanged under any circumstances. This applies, for example, to "inalienable" rights (freedom of speech, freedom of religion), and to the right to be free from bodily harm. In this view, criminal law exists because society views certain acts as being so morally objectionable that it needs to label them as unacceptable and thus wants to impose punishments on violators in a way that stigmatizes their actions. The message is that not all harmful acts are created equal, and the law needs to recognize these differences by creating a special category.

While this certainly aligns with popular perceptions of criminal law, one of the purported advantages of an economic approach to law is that it offers a unified framework for assigning legal responsibility that does not depend on subjective notions of morality. Evaluating this perspective will be one of the themes of this book. Ultimately, I will argue that the promise of a purely objective economic approach to harm and responsibility cannot be fully realized.[20] Thus, the idea that some harms are more objectionable than others in moral terms, despite the subjective nature of that determination, and therefore should be put in a different category, will re-emerge as a necessary element for defining the content of criminal law. And precisely because of its subjective nature, the moral criteria for deciding which acts to put in which category will be subject to disagreement and change. Again, I will return to this line of reasoning in Part 4.

I have already noted that dual purposes of tort law are to compensate accident victims and to create incentives for those engaged in risky activities to take all reasonable steps to mitigate the risk. The economic theory of externalities, particularly as manifested in the model of precaution described at the end of Chap. 2, places emphasis on the deterrence function, but it also reveals that compensation and deterrence can sometimes go hand-in-hand. In the case of criminal law, by contrast, compensation of victims is not an objective. In its place is the desire for retribution, or

[19] This "market-byass" theory of crime is discussed further in Chap. 9.

[20] See Miceli (2024).

revenge, which society exacts on behalf of the victim. As Oliver Wendell Holmes (1881, p. 35) argues,

> A pain can be inflicted on the wrong-doer ... for the very purpose of causing pain. And so far as this punishment takes the place of compensation, ... it may be said that one of its objects is to gratify the desire for vengeance.

Although vengeance may not strike one as an admirable objective of law, Holmes argues that it is a necessary one so as to "avoid the greater evil of private retribution" (Holmes 1881, p. 36), what we call today vigilantism. In this vein,Nozick (1974) offers a theory of the emergence of state monopoly control over the power to exact retribution for wrongful acts, thereby avoiding the costly nature of private enforcement.

The economic approach to crime, by contrast, centers on the role of sanctions as deterrents, and in this sense, its function is no different from that of tort liability. I will refer to this perspective on criminal sanctions as the "punishment-as-price paradigm." Criminologists have long debated whether deterrence or retribution is the more appropriate justification for punishing criminals.[21] Once again Holmes (1881, p. 37) frames the debate: "The main struggle lies between [these] two. On the one side is the notion that there is a mystic bond between wrong and punishment; on the other that the infliction of pain is only a means to an end." Although he cites the Kantian objection to deterrence on moral grounds because it "treats man as a thing, not as a person; as a means, not as an end in himself" (p. 37), he ultimately argues that it is the principal modern-day justification for punishment.[22]

Richard Adelstein (2017) has argued that the punishment-as-price paradigm can actually be invoked as a way to reconcile these competing rationales. This is true, he argues, because deterrence and retribution "are two sides of the same coin, different aspects of a single idea illustrated most sharply by competitive prices in explicit markets" (Adelstein 2017,

[21] Holmes also mentions rehabilitation, but dismisses it as an incomplete justification for punishment.

[22] Dostoevsky's classic novel, *Crime and Punishment*, evokes a similar conflict between the "imperatives of Christian love and the demand for more equitable social justice" on the one hand, versus the "rational Utilitarian ethic, which justifies the sacrifice of *others* for the sake of the greater good" on the other (Frank, 1995, p. 132 [emphasis in original]).

p. 160). This derives from the fact that, in a competitive market setting, the equilibrium price simultaneously serves these same two functions. On the one hand, it compensates the seller for the good or service conveyed to the buyer, thereby ensuring mutual gains for the two parties, while on the other, it discourages (deters) those transactions for which the gain to the buyer is less than the cost to the seller. As a result, only efficient (value-enhancing) exchanges occur.

It may seem perverse to extend this sort of market reasoning to criminal acts because, unlike market exchange, crimes are non-consensual. However, we noted above that consent is not a pre-requisite for efficiency. An exchange is efficient, by definition, when the gain exceeds the cost—whether or not the loser is actually compensated is purely a distributional matter. In the context of the economic model of crime, the idea of an "efficient crime" is therefore a sensible, if morally questionable, concept.

The requirement that liability payments in tort law must be handed over to victims as compensation for their losses, however, can be interpreted as an effort to approximate the outcome of a consensual exchange in the case of accidental harms. This is usually impossible for crimes, either because compensation for the harm in question is not practically possible, or because the offender is not able to pay the cost.[23] Nevertheless, the inability to achieve compensation of victims does not invalidate the idea of efficiently pricing crimes as a way to achieve optimal deterrence. In some cases, this may mean complete deterrence—the efficient level of murder or other violent acts presumably is zero—but in others it does not. Think of exceeding the speed limit, parking illegally, or breaking into a house to get shelter from a severe storm.[24]

The preceding discussion of efficient pricing of harmful acts epitomizes the standard approaches of the economic theory of both tort and criminal law. According to this perspective, all that is necessary to achieve optimal deterrence in either context is to set the "price" of an act (or the failure to act) equal to the expected harm that it causes. Further, it is irrelevant

[23] Many crimes, however, are also torts, and so victims can pursue compensation in a separate legal action.

[24] The so-called market-bypass model of crime first developed by Posner (1985) and elaborated on by Klevorick (1985) says that sanctions should be set to completely deter those acts for which a consensual mechanism for exchange is available, thereby steering them into the marketplace. (I expand on this model in Chap. 9.) Also see Hylton (2005) and Miceli (2023), who compare that model to the Becker model.

whether or not the price, once paid, is actually handed over to the victim as compensation.

An issue that *does* affect efficiency of an exchange, however, is if the purchaser believes he can avoid paying the price; i.e., that he can escape responsibility. We turn to this problem, and the way the economic model deals with it, next.

The Detection Problem and Probability Scaling

An important distinction between the standard economic models of tort law and criminal law is the problem of uncertain detection. As suggested above, in many cases this reflects the intentional nature of crimes because offenders will often make efforts, as part of their planning, to avoid detection. Victims would therefore be hard-pressed to pursue damage claims against injurers in a world without publicly-financed law enforcement.[25]

As previously noted, the economic theory of criminal law is based on the objective of optimal deterrence, which involves forcing injurers to pay for the harms that they cause. Because liability is strict for those harmful acts classified as crimes (once intent is established), criminal liability should therefore be equated to the harm from the illegal act. This will achieve the desired goal because rational offenders will only commit those acts for which the expected benefit exceeds the harm. As a result, only "efficient crimes" will be committed.

When detection is uncertain, however, holding offenders responsible for the actual harm from their acts will underdeter them because the *expected sanction*, which equals the probability of detection multiplied by the sanction, will be less than the harm. Consider, for example, an act that imposes harm equal to $100. If the fine is set at $100 but the probability of detection is 0.25 (only one in four offenders is caught), the expected fine will be $25. Thus, offenders who value the act at $25 or more will commit it, whereas it is only efficient for those who value it at $100 or more to commit it.

This problem can be corrected, however, by scaling up the sanction in inverse proportion to the probability of detection. In this example, that would require a fourfold increase of the fine to $400, which makes the

[25] Several authors have nevertheless examined the private enforcement of law, for example by bounty hunters. See Becker and Stigler (1974), Landes and Posner (1975), and Friedman (2000, Chapter 18).

expected fine (0.25)× ($400) = $100, thus restoring efficient deterrence. This remedy for under-detection is referred to as ***probability scaling***, and it is a central prescription of the economic theory of law enforcement (Becker 1968).

The theory actually carries this policy to its logical extreme by recognizing that the probability of detection is itself a choice variable, which implies that overall welfare (including enforcement costs) can be increased by raising the fine to the highest possible level (e.g., the wealth of the offender) and correspondingly lowering the probability of detection. This is desirable because raising the fine is costless but lowering the probability of detection saves on enforcement costs. Thus, a given level of deterrence (i.e., a given expected fine) can be achieved at a lower cost by this sort of probability scaling. Although it is less obvious why, a similar argument also applies to non-monetary sanctions. Even though increasing a prison term is costly, it is still optimal to do this while correspondingly lowering the probability of apprehension.[26]

Were such a policy actually implemented, only a fraction of offenders (one in four in the above example) would be held responsible for the harm that they all committed. As a consequence, the one person who is actually punished would be paying for the harm that he caused, ***as well as for the harm caused by the three offenders who avoided detection***. This prescription therefore provides a significant shield of responsibility for wrongdoers in the furtherance of cost savings. The fact that actual criminal enforcement policy does not routinely implement this sort of scheme suggests that other factors are in opposition to it.

Undoubtedly the most important of these is the ***proportionality norm***, which is the deeply-held notion that punishment should fit the crime. As Adelstein (1981, p. 7) has observed, "Over hundreds of years, ours has

[26] Although it seems counter-intuitive, it is optimal in the Becker model (in a purely cost-minimizing sense) to set non-monetary sanctions at their maximum level. To see why, consider a prison term of 10 months and a probability of apprehension .5 such that the expected sanction is 5 months. If the cost per month of holding someone in prison is $1,000, then the expected cost of this sanction is $5,000. Now suppose that the prison term is raised to 20 months and the probability of apprehension is lowered to .25. The expected prison term remains 5 months, which will have the same deterrent effect on would-be offenders, and will have the same expected cost of $5,000. However, less money has to be spent on apprehension. Thus, overall costs—including harm from crime, punishment, and enforcement—must be lower. This logic shows that the sanction should be raised as much as possible, and the apprehension rate lowered proportionately.

been a legal order of retributive punishment tempered by the norm of proportionality, one that seeks an eye, but only that, for an eye." Early writers on crime such as Beccaria, Bentham, and Montesquieu, all of whom are seen as precursors to the modern economic approach to crime, echoed the importance of proportionality.[27] I will return to this issue in the next section.

A related objection to probability scaling is the aversion to wrongful punishment. Although the person who is punished actually committed an offense and so is not "innocent," he is punished for the acts of others in addition to his own. Finally, the extreme version of probability scaling, which would assess individualized fines equal to each offender's wealth, would necessarily entail differential treatment of offenders who committed the same crime. In addition, it would potentially subject low-wealth offenders to prison terms (so as to achieve additional deterrence) while allowing the rich to "buy" their way out of prison.[28] This would presumably violate the equal protection clause of the Constitution.

Another argument for why sanctions, whether in the form of fines or imprisonment, should not raised to the maximal level was pointed out by Stigler (1970). That is the idea of "marginal deterrence." If an offender faces a maximal penalty for some relatively minor offense, what is to deter him from committing a more serious offense instead of or in addition to it? As Stigler (p. 527) argues:

> If the offender is executed for a minor assault and for a murder, there is no marginal deterrence to murder. If a thief has his hand cut off for taking five dollars, he had just as well take $5,000.

The idea is that some additional punishment must be "held in reserve" for more serious offenses if offenders are expected to fully internalize the costs of their actions.[29] One might argue that marginal deterrence can always be achieved by expending more resources to detect and punish more serious crimes (thereby increasing the *expected* punishment for these

[27] See Beccaria (1764 [1986]), Bentham (1780 [1970]), and Montesquieu (1748 [1977]).

[28] See Polinsky and Shavell (1984) for a formal analysis of this point. Also see Lott (1987).

[29] See, for example, Shavell (1992) and Friehe and Miceli (2014) for formal analyses of marginal deterrence.

acts), but it is the severity of the resulting punishment that is the clearest signal of society's disapproval of an act. We will revisit the concept of marginal deterrence in Chap. 6 in connection with the idea of redemption.Finally, as noted above, critics of the economic model of crime argue that policies like probability scaling reflect a misguided effort by economists to sustain the fiction that criminal law is only about pricing crime, when in fact its actual purpose is to impose "sanctions for doing what is forbidden rather than prices for what is permitted." In reality, they argue, criminal law is about enforcing society's moral foundation (Lewin and Trumbull 1990, pp. 280–281). However, both of these ideas can be true—law can be about enforcing morality, but it can also be a way of signaling the harmfulness of acts so as to guide would-be offenders' decisions in a socially desirable direction. If certain behaviors are so harmful as never to be justified, then the price should simply be set sufficiently high so as to completely deter them, at least among those individuals who are responsive to incentives.

Proportionality of Punishment

The economic model's focus on deterrence, juxtaposed against the prevalence of proportionality as an enduring benchmark for punishment, warrants further comment. The preceding discussion of the underdetection problem has suggested that a fundamental tension exists between these two objectives—specifically, that deterrence must be sacrificed if proportionality is to serve as the basis for punishment policies. That conclusion, however, depends on what exactly is meant by "proportionality" in this context. Several possible interpretations are possible.[30]

The first interpretation, which is the most literal, is that punishments should be *equated* to harms. As Hart (1982, p. 161) notes, "In its crudest form [proportionality] is the notion that what the criminal has done should be done to him…." Obviously, this is objectionable on both moral and practical grounds. In fact, this understanding of proportionality most likely reflects an aversion to excessive punishment in relation to the perceived harmfulness of an act, as reflected by the Eighth Amendment's prohibition of "cruel and unusual punishment," as well as by recent calls for the repeal of "three-strikes" laws, which threaten harsh

[30] The following discussion is based on Hart (1982, pp. 160–170) and Miceli (2018).

punishments for petty crimes on repeat offenders. Clearly, such limits potentially conflict with a policy of probability scaling, and so are not consistent with an enforcement strategy whose sole aim is to minimize the costs of crime.

A second notion of proportionality is that punishments should *increase* with crimes. This approach is therefore concerned, not with the treatment of any particular crime, but with the relationship between crimes and punishments across the spectrum of offenses. Again, as Hart (1982, p. 162) describes it.

> what is required is not some ideally appropriate relationship between a single crime and its punishment, but that on a scale or tariff of punishments and offences, punishments for different crimes should be 'proportionate' to the relative wickedness or seriousness of the crime. For though we cannot say *how* wicked any given crime is, perhaps we can say that one is *more* wicked than another and we should express this ordinal relation in a corresponding scale of penalties.

This defines a "punishment schedule" that displays a monotonic relationship. In this sense, it embodies the idea of marginal deterrence as discussed above, while sidestepping the question of how any point on the schedule should be chosen.[31]

Proportionality can also be defined in terms of the *expected* punishment, which is the relevant measure from the perspective of a potential offender. It is, in other words, a forward-looking rather than a backward-looking concept of proportionality. This perspective is consistent with a certain form of probability scaling. Specifically, if the harm from an act is h and the probability of detection is p, the actual sanction should equal h/p, thereby giving an expected sanction of $p \times (h/p) = h$. Leaving aside the problem of measuring h, this obviously achieves proportionality of the expected sanction. Specifically, the expected sanction rises in proportion to harm across the spectrum of acts according to the scaling factor $1/p$. Of course, the usual understanding of proportional punishment is the backward-looking one that depends only on h because that is the point at which punishment is actually imposed on a particular offender.

[31] In other words, the proposed relation defines the slope of the punishment schedule but not its intercept.

This reflects the idea that justice is inherently a backward-looking concept, whereas deterrence is necessarily forward-looking.

Of course, the divergence between deterrence and proportionality is most dramatically revealed in the extreme version of probability scaling where the probability of apprehension is treated as a choice variable by the enforcer. Recall that the optimal (cost-minimizing) policy in that case is to lower the probability of apprehension and proportionally raise the sanction to the maximum extent possible—limited only by the offender's ability to pay a fine or the maximum prison term he could serve. In this case, there is *no* necessary relationship between actual punishments and harms.[32] Thus, there is no way to square this extreme version of probability scaling with the objective of proportionality.

Credibility of Law Enforcement

We have been focusing on the problem of under-detection of criminal acts and how that affects the efficacy of law enforcement. A different kind of enforcement problem concerns the *credibility* of threats to carry out the legally enacted punishment of wrongdoers. This issue represents a strategic decision on the part of enforcers of whether or not to carry out the threatened punishment.

The sequential nature of crime and punishment is the key element here. The specific sequence of decisions is as follows: (1) the government announces a prescribed punishment for a certain harmful act; (2) would-be offenders decide whether or not to commit the act; and (3) if the offender commits the act, the government decides whether or not to impose the threatened punishment. (For current purposes I will assume apprehension is certain.) The question of credibility concerns the relationship between the announced (threatened) punishment and the punishment that is actually imposed.

The potential problem here is that enforcers may have differing motivations at the announcement stage (before any crime has been committed) and the imposition stage (after a crime has been committed and the defendant apprehended). This can involve practical considerations regarding the cost of imposing punishment, but it can also reflect differing ex ante

[32] See Garoupa (1997) and Polinsky and Shavell (2007) for technical details.

versus ex post views on the purpose of punishment, such as the desire for proportionality (as discussed above) or mitigating circumstances.

For example, if the goal of threatening harsh punishments is to deter offenders from ever committing crimes and it is successful, no punishment ever has to be imposed. That is the ideal outcome. However, if some offenders choose to commit the crime anyway, for whatever reason, the enforcer faces a choice of whether to carry out the punishment as prescribed, or possibly to impose some lesser (or no) penalty, as dictated by the circumstances as they unfolded. For example, imposing a lesser punishment at this point would save enforcement costs, or might seem more appropriate given the circumstances of the crime at hand. However, if offenders correctly anticipate this deviation from the threatened punishment, they will be more likely to commit crimes in the first place.

The difficulty can be illustrated with a simple example depicting the strategic interaction between a rational offender and a law enforcer.[33] Table 3.2 displays the payoffs (measured in dollars) to the "enforcer" and the "offender" as a function of the various strategy combinations. The specific options for the offender are to "Commit" a crime, or "Not commit" a crime, while the options for the enforcer are to "Punish" or "Not punish" an offender who commits a crime, where "Punish" should be interpreted to mean "carry out the threatened punishment in the event of a crime." (Obviously, if no crime is committed, no punishment is actually imposed.) In each cell, the first number is the enforcer's payoff and the second is the offender's payoff.

Note that the payoff is zero for both parties if the offender does not commit a crime. If the offender does commit a crime, his payoff is −100 if he is punished, and 200 if he is not. For the enforcer, its payoff is −300

Table 3.2 The law enforcement game

		Offender	
		Commit	*Not commit*
Enforcer	Punish	– 300, −100	**0, 0**
	Not punish	– **200, 200**	0, 0

Note Boldfaced entries indicate optimal choices

[33] See Miceli (2019, Chapter 1) and Baker and Miceli (2021).

if it carries out the punishment, and −200 if it does not. Thus, −200 is the social cost of the crime, and −300 is the joint cost of the crime plus the cost of implementing the punishment.

Suppose initially that the two parties make their choices simultaneously (i.e., in ignorance of the other's choice). It turns out that there are two pure-strategy Nash equilibria of this game, as indicated by the bold-faced entries in the Table. They are (1) for the offender to commit the crime and the enforcer *not* to carry out the punishment (the lower-left cell); and (2) for the offender not to commit the crime (the upper right cell). Obviously, no punishment is actually imposed in the latter case, but the offender's belief is that it would have been imposed if the crime was committed.

To understand why these are equilibrium outcomes, it is important to define what "equilibrium" means in this type of setting. An outcome is an equilibrium if, once a particular outcome is reached, neither party would want to deviate from their chosen strategy. In other words, neither "regrets" their choice. In the first equilibrium (lower-left cell), if the offender switched from "Commit" to "Not commit," his payoff would drop from 200 to 0, given the enforcer's choice. Likewise, if the enforcer switched from "Not punish" to "Punish," its payoff would drop from −200 to −300, given the offender's choice. Thus, neither would want to make the change. At the other equilibrium (upper right cell), the offender would likewise lower his payoff from 0 to −100 if he switched from "Not commit" to "Commit" given the enforcer's decision to "Punish." Thus, his belief that the enforcer would carry out the threatened punishment successfully deters him from committing the offense. The situation is a little different from the enforcer. Its payoff remains at 0 if it deviates from "Punish" to "Not punish," and so it is indifferent between the choices. Thus, this no-crime equilibrium is only weakly sustained.

The existence of multiple equilibria in this game, though somewhat hard to interpret in practical terms, actually highlights the nature of the credibility problem facing the enforcer. When the threat to impose punishment is "believed," offenders are deterred (the second equilibrium), but when it is "not believed," they are not deterred (the first equilibrium). The resulting crime rate is thus very different, depending on which outcome emerges. In other words, it depends crucially on the credibility of the enforcer's punishment threat. Unfortunately, the current treatment of the problem offers no guidance on which equilibrium will actually arise. I would argue, however, that this exemplifies the tenuous nature of deterrence in the "crime and punishment game."

Some further insight into this issue can be gained, however, by explicitly taking account of the dynamic aspect of the interaction between the enforcer and the offender. It will be instructive to consider two scenarios that differ, depending on which of the parties moves first. Suppose initially that the offender moves first, which means that the enforcer *cannot* precommit to impose punishment if a crime is committed. Figure 3.1 depicts the game tree (extensive form) for this version of the game, which explicitly shows the sequential choices of the two parties. The resulting payoffs are shown at the terminal points, with the offender's payoff listed first. (The choices and the payoffs are the same as in Table 3.2, and the four terminal points correspond to the four cells in the table.)

To find the equilibrium (or equilibria) of this game, we proceed by backwards induction.[34] That is, we start with the choice of the second mover, in this version, the enforcer, given the prior choice by the first mover, the offender. If the offender commits the crime, the optimal choice of the enforcer is *not* to impose punishment since this saves the cost of implementation. Specifically, because the cost of the crime (−200) has already been incurred, it is sunk and so it has no effect on the enforcer's optimal choice *once we arrive at this stage of the game.* Conversely, if the offender does not commit the crime, the enforcer is indifferent between imposing and not imposing punishment (in actuality,

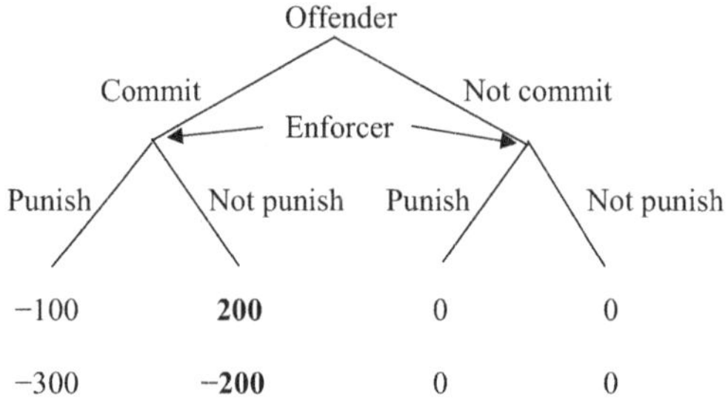

Fig. 3.1 Game tree for the law enforcement game when the offender moves first

[34] In the jargon of game theory, we are deriving the subgame perfect Nash equilibrium.

it has no decision to make). Either way, the offender's payoff from non-commission is zero, so the enforcer's indifference will have no effect on the determination of the overall equilibrium.

Now move back to the offender's prior decision. If he commits the crime, he anticipates that the enforcer will rationally refrain from imposing punishment, and so his payoff will be 200. On the other hand, if he does not commit the crime, his payoff is 0 regardless of the enforcer's choice. Given these two outcomes, he will clearly choose to commit the crime. This leads to a unique equilibrium of this sequential-move game; namely, (Commit, Not punish), as indicated by the boldfaced payoffs at that terminal point. This corresponds to the lower-left (high-crime) equilibrium in the above simultaneous-move game.

Let's now consider the scenario in which the enforcer moves first. This represents a situation in which the latter *can* pre-commit to impose a particular punishment. (I will comment later on what that means in practice.) The relevant game tree is shown in Fig. 3.2. Proceeding again in reverse sequence, if the enforcer adopts a credible policy to punish criminals, the offender will choose not to commit the crime, whereas if the enforcer does not commit to punish criminals, the offender will commit the crime. Anticipating these choices, the enforcer's optimal choice is obviously to commit to impose punishment as that yields a payoff of 0 rather than −200. Thus, the unique equilibrium of this version of the game is (Punish, Not commit), again as indicated by the boldfaced entries.

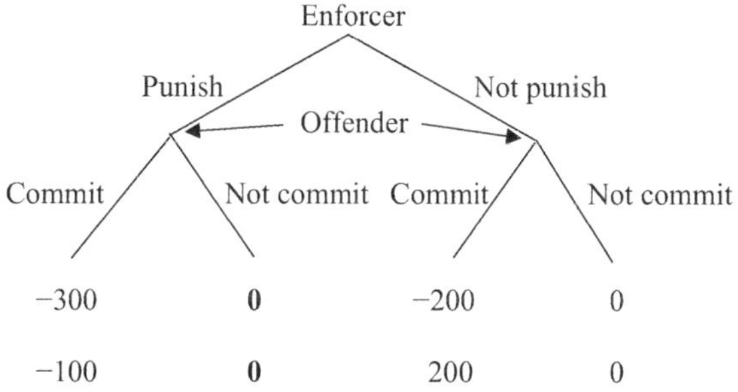

Fig. 3.2 Game tree for the law enforcement game when the enforcer moves first

Note that the enforcer does not actually have to impose the punishment in this equilibrium because its *credible* threat to punish criminals succeeds in deterring them. This represents what I will call the "paradox of punishment": when the threat to impose punishment serves its intended purpose, the punishment never has to be carried out. The problem, of course, is that complete deterrence is never possible in practice for various reasons: either some offenders are "irrational" (i.e., undeterrable), some miscalculate the benefits or costs of committing a crime, or some commit crimes inadvertently. That is when the threat to carry out a threatened punishment is tested.

As for the actual practice of criminal justice policy, the fact is that numerous decision-makers, with potentially conflicting motives, have a hand in the process. This includes legislatures, which initially set policies, and police, prosecutors, judges, and juries, who all play a role in carrying out those policies. As a result, the legal historian Lawrence Friedman (2004, pp. 91–92) noted that.

> it is misleading to talk about the criminal justice "system." The word "system" suggests a certain amount of order—hierarchy, clean lines of authority. ...The legislature passes laws, but has no responsibility for carrying them out. The police arrest, but the prosecutors decide whom to prosecute. ...Prosecutors can bring a defendant to trial, but the judge can let him go. So can the jury.

These potentially diverging motives reflect conflicting values regarding the appropriate way to assign responsibility for harmful acts. This ambivalence is particularly relevant with respect to criminal defendants because of the possibility of severe punishments, including deprivation of liberty (or worse), coupled with the stigma that comes with conviction for a crime. Thus, as we have noted, people are especially wary of wrongful or excessive punishment.Recent debates over legislatively-imposed sentencing guidelines versus judicial discretion in sentencing exemplify this conflict. Sentencing guidelines were first passed at the state and then the federal level in the 1980s as a way to rein in the perceived limitless discretion exercised by judges in the setting of criminal sentences—so-called indeterminate sentencing. This action was itself motivated by conflicting objectives—on one side were those concerned about unequal treatment of similarly situated defendants based on the luck of the judicial draw, while on the other were those who saw judicial discretion as undermining deterrence. The goal of the guidelines, then, was "to squeeze discretion out of the system, and to prevent judges from 'coddling' criminals" (Friedman 2004, p. 109).

Legislatively-set guidelines, to the extent that they are binding on judges, represent a way of committing to a punishment policy. They represent a clear statement of an intent to punish wrongdoers, with the hope of deterring them. One notable manifestation of that effort was the enactment by many states of "three-strikes" laws, which promised a harsh sentence to any offender committing a third offense, no matter how minor that offense was. The idea, of course, was to deter repeat crimes in the first place, thus obviating the need ever to invoke the third strike, but the key was the credibility of the threat. If a few undeterred lawbreakers had to suffer seemingly disproportionate punishments as a result, that was the price society was willing to pay to reduce crime. It is not a coincidence, therefore, that the sentencing guidelines and three-strikes laws were enacted during a time of rising crime rates in the United States.[35]

In 2005, however, the Supreme Court ruled that guidelines were not strictly binding on judges but only "advisory," thereby restoring at least some degree of judicial discretion.[36] Three-strikes laws have similarly been repealed or scaled back. These changes have obviously weakened the credibility of the punishment threat. Not coincidentally, they corresponded to a downward trend in crime rates beginning in the early to mid-1990s, when fear of crime was waning. It is dangerous to attribute a causal relationship here because of the multiplicity of factors that affect crime rates. Perhaps, however, one can discern a reverse causal effect in the sense that when crime rates were high, people tended to push for tough-on-crime laws to be enacted, whereas when crime rates were low or declining, they were more inclined to extend leniency to offenders. The problem with this oscillating approach to policy is that it clouds the ability of would-be offenders to anticipate the consequences of their actions, which is the key to maintaining a goal of deterrence.

[35] See Friedman (2004, pp. 106–111) and Miceli (2019, p. 208).

[36] See *United States v. Booker*, 543 U.S. 220 (2005).

Litigation Costs and the Social Versus Private Value of Lawsuits

We have noted that tort law is privately enforced in the sense that it is the victim of an accident rather than the government who must initiate a legal action for compensation. Under a rule that links responsibility to causation only—strict liability—the injurer has to pay the full amount of the victim's damages, and, according to the model of precaution, this provides incentives for injurers to invest in those measures that will most efficiently avoid accidents. In this sense, the victim's "private" incentive to seek compensation perfectly aligns with the "social" function of lawsuits aimed at mitigating accident costs. This is the theoretical linkage, anyway; in practical terms, the private and social value of lawsuits will not generally align.[37]

The primary reason for this divergence is litigation costs, which both sides must incur. These include both out-of-pocket legal fees and time costs. Because plaintiffs make the filing decision, these costs will discourage victims who have sustained small losses from filing suit, and this will work in the direction of there being too few suits. Also working in this direction is that plaintiffs will ignore the *social* benefits of bringing suit, which consists of the deterrent effect that the threat of a suit has on future defendants. An offsetting factor that works in the direction of too many suits is that plaintiffs will ignore the litigation costs that defendants must incur to defend themselves. The net effect of these various factors is ambiguous, and so it is not possible to say, as a general proposition, whether there are too many or too few lawsuits from a social point of view.[38]

Lawsuits are valuable assets, however, and so one way that plaintiffs could possibly offset the cost of bringing suit is use it as collateral for a loan to cover the up-front fees. A market for this sort of loan does not actually exist, but much the same outcome is effectively achieved

[37] See, for example, Shavell (1982).

[38] The misalignment may be less severe if the applicable liability rule is negligence. The reason is that, under negligence, a lawsuit would not be filed if the plaintiff believed that the defendant used reasonable precaution because the plaintiff would lose the case. Ideally, this would forestall excessive suits and simultaneously create efficient incentives to avoid accidents. In reality, of course, the system does not work perfectly, in which case the misalignment described in the text would continue to exist, though perhaps to a lesser degree.

by a contingency-fee contract, which many lawyers offer, particularly in personal injury cases. Under this arrangement, the lawyer pays the up-front cost of bringing the suit, and then retains a portion (usually a third) of any proceeds derived from the case, whether by settlement or trial. However, if no award is obtained, the plaintiff does not have to repay the initial filing cost. In effect, therefore, the lawyer lends the client the legal expenses and only requires repayment if and when the case produces a positive judgment.[39]

Such a contract has the dual advantage of overcoming the problem of plaintiffs' wealth constraints, and of giving lawyers an incentive to work hard for their clients because they have a stake in the case.[40] Some have argued, however, that contingency fees may promote excessive litigation, which is the reason that some countries have outlawed them. Countering this claim is that lawyers presumably would never take on a case that lacks merit, both for ethical reasons and because it would not yield a positive payoff. If anything, they might refuse some otherwise profitable cases because they have to foot the entire cost while only receiving a fraction of the payoff. The question here is again an empirical one.

A further problem with relying on private lawsuits to internalize the cost of accidents is that the harm from some hazardous activities is spread out over a large number of victims, and none of them may suffer a large enough loss to make it profitable to pursue a legal claim. When aggregated, however, the harm exceeds the costs of bringing a suit. The fundamental problem here is the existence of significant scale economies in pursuing such claims, given that the factual issues are common to the individual cases, and so there would be considerable cost savings by consolidating them into a single case. The class-action lawsuit is one way of doing this. This device is not without its own problems, however. One is the need to identify each of the victims and award the appropriate amount of compensation, tasks that will likely be most difficult in those very cases where the device is most needed—that is, when the harm is very dispersed (Posner 2003, p. 586). Social media eases this burden because

[39] Better than 95% of tort cases settle, which virtually assures some payoff. For economic analyses of contingency contracts, see Miceli and Segerson (1991), Miceli (1994), and Rubinfeld and Schotchmer (1998).

[40] In fact, agency theory has shown that the optimal (first-best) contract would involve plaintiffs "selling" their claims to the lawyer for an up-front payment equal to the expected value of the claim, and allowing the lawyer to retain the entire judgment.

it lowers communication costs, but it could also have the reverse effect of stirring up lawsuits with low merit that defendants would nevertheless be eager to settle to avoid the risk of ruinous judgments at trial.

This last possibility raises the issue of frivolous lawsuits, which are defined to be suits that have little or no legal merit, but which are filed solely in hopes of gaining a settlement.[41] This problem would seem to expand the scope of legal responsibility beyond those who actually caused harm, and so may actually lead to a risk of overdeterrence (i.e., excessive investments in safety). In assessing this problem, we first need to ask why such suits can ever succeed, even though they would not be profitable (by definition) for a plaintiff to take to trial.

The answer is that they can elicit settlement offers from defendants who wish to avoid the cost (and risk) of a trial. Consider, for example, a plaintiff who files a suit seeking \$2000, say, but which would result in zero recovery at trial based on legal merits and/or actual harm sustained. Suppose it would cost the defendant \$1500 to defend himself, in which case he would win and owe nothing. Alternatively, he can refuse to mount a defense, but then he would lose by summary judgment and have to pay the \$2000. Faced with these options, the defendant would be willing to settle out of court for any amount up to \$1500, the lesser of the two costs. Knowing this, plaintiffs would find it profitable to file such suits in the first place, assuming that the filing cost is less than the expected settlement amount.[42]

The risk of overdeterrence due to these sorts of suits lies behind the claim that many physicians practice "defensive medicine" (Danzon 1991). Our earlier discussion of litigation costs, however, concluded that there may be too many or too few "legitimate" suits from a social perspective. Thus, injurers may be over- or under-deterred by the threat of lawsuits. It follows that we cannot offer a general assessment regarding the impact of frivolous litigation on deterrence. If injurers expect to face too few genuine suits as a result of litigation costs, the possibility of suits filed by those who were not in fact injured will actually work in the direction of

[41] Some scholars distinguish between suits with zero merit, and suits with some merit but for which the expected value at trial is negative. I will not distinguish between them here.

[42] This example is based on Rosenberg and Shavell (1985). Other models in which frivolous suits succeed based on asymmetric information are examined in Bebchuk (1988, 1996) and Katz (1990).

correcting this problem (Miceli and Stone 2014). In this sense, the effect is similar to the way that probability scaling of criminal sanctions offset under-detection, and is also the economic rationale for punitive damages in certain tort cases, as we will discuss later. The difference is that these latter policies are (in theory) specifically calibrated to offset the degree of under-detection, whereas the number of frivolous suits is in no way systematically related to the extent of under-deterrence or overdeterrence of injurers.

Evidence: Proving Legal Responsibility

In both tort and criminal law, the assessment of responsibility involves a factual legal proceeding aimed at determining the guilt or innocence of the accused party. A trial is the method by which this is done. It is a procedure that combines factual evidence with the governing rule of law to arrive at a verdict. This determination invariably involves uncertainty, however, both because information is incomplete, and because the parties to the case have directly opposing interests and so will not generally have an incentive to reveal all they know to the court. In an adversarial system, each side produces evidence in support of its own position, with the hope that the truth will emerge. But the process is imperfect, and so errors are unavoidable. An economic perspective on trials is that the rules of legal procedure, civil and criminal, are designed to minimize the costs of these errors.

Consider first the *burden of proof*, which in both civil and criminal cases is on the plaintiff (prosecutor). This means that the plaintiff must persuade the court that its position is the one that should prevail. Assigning the burden of proof to the plaintiff means that, in cases lacking evidence, or where the evidence is inconclusive (i.e., the probability of guilt sits exactly at the decision threshold), the defendant will win, thereby increasing the likelihood that some guilty defendants will escape liability. If, on the other hand, the burden were shifted to the defendant to prove his "innocence," the bias would go in the other direction, and some truly innocent defendants would be held liable. Although these errors may be (roughly) symmetric in number, forcing defendants to prove their innocence will likely result in a substantially larger number of cases being filed, which will greatly increase litigation costs. This is the usual rationale for imposing the burden on the plaintiff. This conclusion assumes that the costs of evidence gathering are roughly the same for the two parties, which seems reasonable in most circumstances (Posner 2003, pp. 617–618). When the costs are not equal, the burden can be shifted to the party with easier access to evidence. An example of this is the doctrine of *res ipsa loquitur*, which shifts the burden to defendants in circumstances where they almost certainly have superior information about risk. (See the discussion of this doctrine in Chap. 5.)

The other part of the burden of proof is the application of the *standard of proof* to the evidence presented to the court. As noted, evidence will rarely be conclusive. It will, instead, generally result in a probability that the defendant was responsible for the alleged wrongdoing, and the court must then transform this probabilistic assessment into a specific ruling—either guilty or not guilty. The standard of proof is the means by which this is done; it is defined to be the minimum probability of defendant guilt that will result in a finding of legal culpability (guilt).

The standard of proof in a civil (tort) case is *preponderance of the evidence*, meaning that it is "more likely than not" that the defendant was responsible. The standard in a criminal case, by contrast, is *beyond a reasonable doubt*, which is a much stricter requirement; indeed, it requires near certainty that the defendant is guilty.[43] The economic approach to setting the standard of proof involves minimizing the costs arising from the two types of errors that can occur in any effort to arrive at the truth in the presence of uncertainty.[44] These are false positives (type I errors) and false negatives (type II errors).[45] A false positive in a trial context would mean finding a truly innocent defendant guilty (wrongful conviction), while a false negative would mean finding a truly guilty defendant not guilty (wrongful acquittal).

Some reflection should convince the reader that adjusting the standard of proof will necessarily have offsetting impacts on the probabilities of these two errors. If, for example, the standard were made stricter—that is, a higher probability of guilt were required to convict a defendant—then fewer convictions would occur. This would reduce the number of both correct and false convictions. As a result, the number of false positives would decrease, but the number of false negatives would increase.

[43] For example, some put the threshold at between 75 and 95% certainty (Posner, 2003, p. 620).

[44] See, for example, Miceli (1990), Posner (2003, p. 618)

[45] The type I and type II terminology is taken from hypothesis testing in statistics.

Conversely, relaxing the standard of proof would result in fewer acquittals, both correct and false. Thus, the number of false positives would fall, but the number of false negatives would rise. This trade-off is unavoidable given uncertainty. The only way that both types of errors could simultaneously be reduced is by gathering more or better evidence, or by developing better technologies for evaluating the evidence. The development of fingerprinting in an earlier era, and DNA analysis in modern times, are examples of this.

Why are the standards of proof different for civil and criminal cases? The setting of a preponderance-of-the-evidence standard for civil cases suggests that the two types of errors involve roughly equal costs. In a tort case, these costs consist of the dilution of incentives to take precaution by parties engaged in risky activities. As we will see below, an increase in either type of errors dilutes incentives, and so there is no obvious preference for reducing one or the other. By contrast, it is generally believed that the two types of errors do *not* have equal costs in criminal cases. Rather, the cost of false positives (false convictions) are taken to be much higher than false negatives (false acquittals).[46] The reason is that, although the dilution of deterrence is again present with both types of errors, the wrongful imposition of criminal punishment is particularly costly in terms of the social stigma attached to it, and it is only amplified if punishment takes the form of imprisonment. This view is epitomized by William Blackstone's observation that "it is better that ten guilty persons escape than one innocent suffer."[47] The tilting of the standard of proof strongly in the direction of acquittal reflects this cost difference.

The high standard of proof does not mean, however, that a large fraction of guilty defendants are acquitted. For one thing, the vast majority (better than 90%) of criminal cases end with a guilty plea (Miceli 2017, p. 319). It is of course possible that some of these defendants are innocent but have chosen to plead guilty rather than face a potentially harsher punishment at trial, given the available evidence. I will pursue the implications of this further in the next section.

I have asserted that both false acquittals and false convictions dilute the deterrent effect of trials. To see why this is true, suppose that the

[46] See, for example, Posner (2003, pp 618–619).

[47] Cited by Dillbary and Miceli (2023, p. 1299). We will return to this issue in the discussion of collective responsibility in Chap. 8.

gain to an injurer from engaging in a harmful act is g, the punishment for doing so is s, and the probability of wrongly escaping liability (a type II error) is ε_{II}. The expected benefit of engaging in the act is therefore $g - (1 - \varepsilon_{II})s$, where s is the magnitude of liability if convicted. If the injurer refrains from engaging in the act, on the other hand, he still faces expected liability of $\varepsilon_I s$, where ε_I is the probability of being wrongfully held liable (a type I error). Putting these factors together, we conclude that the individual will engage in the act if $g - (1 - \varepsilon_{II})s > -\varepsilon_I s$, or if

$$g > (1 - \varepsilon_I - \varepsilon_{II})s.$$

This clearly shows that an increase in either ε_I or ε_{II} reduces the deterrent effect of liability by lowering the right-hand side, which is the expected cost of committing the act. False acquittals obviously do this by lessening the expected amount of liability even when one actually causes harm, while false convictions create the possibility of incurring liability when one has done nothing wrong.[48] Thus, both types of errors weaken the ability of the legal system to accurately assign responsibility for harm to those who actually caused it.

Settlements and Plea Bargains: Negotiated Responsibility

Having reviewed the procedural elements of trials as the means by which legal responsibility is determined, we must acknowledge the reality that the vast majority of cases (better than ninety percent) in both tort and criminal law are resolved outside of the courtroom by negotiated settlements. To be sure, these settlements take place against the background of an impending trial, and so they must reflect the parties' beliefs (in consultation with their lawyers) about the likely outcome of a trial. It is nevertheless important to understand why settlement is so pervasive, and how it affects the determination of legal responsibility. This involves answering two questions; namely, which cases proceed to trial and which settle? And, how exactly do settlement outcomes compare to trial outcomes? The answer to the first question depends on the factors

[48] See Png (1986). It is usually assumed that $1 - \varepsilon_I - \varepsilon_{II} > 0$, for otherwise, there would be no cost of committing the act. In practice, this means that a truly guilty person is more likely to face punishment than an innocent person, or that $1 - \varepsilon_{II} > \varepsilon_I$.

that cause cases to settle rather than go to trial, and the second depends on the nature of bargaining between the parties in the shadow of a trial.

The first point to make is that, given the costliness of litigation, it is not surprising that most cases, both civil and criminal, settle. The reason is that a settlement can replicate the expected outcome of the impending trial while saving the trial costs. Suppose, for example, the expected liability of the defendant is $10,000 based on the best understanding of the facts and the evidence, and a trial will cost each side $1000. The defendant will therefore be willing to settle by paying the plaintiff any amount less than $11,000 (the expected liability of $10,000 plus trial costs of $1000), while the plaintiff will be willing to settle by accepting any amount greater than $9000 (an award of $10,000 minus trial costs of $1000). The $2000 "settlement range" corresponds to the joint savings in litigation costs.

This example reveals that the real question to be addressed is why *any* cases go to trial. Economic models of litigation attribute trials to one of two reasons. The first is *mutual optimism*.[49] Suppose in the above example that the two sides agree on the amount of money at stake in the case—say, $10,000—but the plaintiff predicts a 90 percent probability of winning based on the prevailing law, while the defendant puts that probability at only 50 percent. This could reflect different interpretations of either the governing law or the facts. The maximum offer the defendant will now make is $6000 (=0.5 ×$10,000 + $1000), while the minimum amount the plaintiff will now accept is $8000 (=0.9 ×$10,000 − $1000). Thus, a settlement range no longer exists, and so the case will necessarily proceed to trial.

The other reason trials may happen is if one of the parties has some relevant information that the other does not.[50] This situation involves *asymmetric information*, which can also lead to different predictions about the outcome of a trial and hence can also eliminate a settlement range. However, the reason is different—here it is due to a difference in knowledge rather than opinion. This difference is important for at least two reasons. First, rules requiring disclosure of information prior to trial

[49] See Landes (1971) and Cooter and Rubinfeld (1989).

[50] See Bebchuk (1984).

(e.g., mandatory discovery) are presumably aimed at offsetting information asymmetries—and thereby promoting settlement—but they may not offset differences in opinion.

Second, whether trials are due to differing information or differing opinions will affect our understanding of what types of cases end up going to trial versus settling. This *selection bias* is important because in the common law system, legal precedents are the product of appellate court cases, and only cases that make it to trial can ever reach that level. Thus, the lawmaking function of trials depends critically on what types of cases make it to trial.[51] This is true because legal disputes provide judges with the set of issues—the raw material—from which they can formulate new rules, or affirm old ones, and if these issues are not reflective of the overall population of cases, the body of law that emerges from the judicial process may not create the most efficient incentives for those engaged in potentially harmful activities. (Recall that an important function of trials is the deterrent effect they have on future defendants.)

It turns out that the optimism and asymmetric information models make very different predictions regarding what types of cases go to trial.[52] According to the optimism model, cases that fail to settle will be those where the plaintiff and defendant are both very optimistic, which means that they necessarily hold divergent opinions about the likely outcome of a trial. This presumably will be most likely when the case is a close one—that is, when each side assesses a probability of winning near 50 percent (Priest and Klein 1984). By contrast, the asymmetric information model predicts that cases in which the better-informed side holds very favorable information are more likely to go to trial. Thus, if plaintiffs are better informed, trials should have a high probability of plaintiff victory, whereas if defendants are better informed, trials should have a low probability of plaintiff victory. And since there is no systematic reason why one or the other side should be better informed, the asymmetric information model offers no specific prediction about plaintiff victory at trial—any probability is possible (Shavell 1996).

The second question posed above is how settlements compare to trial outcomes. This is important as it determines the amount of liability that defendants actually face in most cases, which is crucial for purposes of

[51] See, for example, Rubin (1977) and Priest (1977).

[52] See, for example, Baird et al. (1994, pp. 260–261).

deterrence.[53] As noted, settlements take place against the backdrop of a trial, and so the negotiated outcome must bear some resemblance to the expected trial outcome. The exact amount, however, will depend on bargaining between the parties, and so it cannot be pinned down with certainty. In the above example where the parties agreed on \$10,000 as the expected award at trial and each had litigation costs of \$1000, the settlement range was between \$9000 and \$11,000. Thus, if the parties evenly divided the difference, the settlement amount of \$10,000 would exactly coincide with the expected outcome at trial. However, if the bargaining strengths differed, the settlement would favor the better bargainer. Differences in the costs of litigation would also presumably impart a bias in favor of the party with the lower costs.[54]

In cases where the probability of plaintiff victory at trial is not certain, the settlement amount will be discounted in proportion to that probability. In the above example, if the parties agreed that the plaintiff had a seventy-five percent probability of winning, the settlement range would be between \$8500 (=0.75 ×\$10,000 + \$1000) and \$6,500 (=0.75 ×\$10,000 − \$1000), and if the parties evenly split the surplus, the settlement amount would be \$7500, which coincides with the *expected* judgment. The settlement thus discounts the defendant's responsibility in proportion to the extent to which the prevailing law and facts, as they are understood before the trial, supports the plaintiff's claim. In terms of economic incentives to avoid harm, this is the correct measure of liability because it reflects expected harm.

The discussion of settlement has so far not distinguished between civil and criminal cases because in many respects the processes are similar. Recall, however, is that in a criminal case, the plaintiff is not the victim but a prosecutor representing the state and backed by the resources of the state. Settlement of a criminal case, called a ***plea bargain***, is allowed, and indeed is the way that most such cases are resolved. The actual process

[53] See Polinsky and Rubinfeld (1988).

[54] See Cooter and Rubinfeld (1989, p. 1084). Formally, let J be the expected judgment at trial, C_p the plaintiff's cost of a trial, and C_d the defendant's cost of trial. The bargaining range would thus be between $J - C_p$ and $J + C_d$, which corresponds to the sum of the trial costs, $C_p + C_d$. If the parties evenly split this surplus, the settlement amount would be $S = J + (C_d - C_p)/2$, which reduces to J if $C_p = C_d$.

of settlement, and the reason that some cases end up at trial, however, mirrors the above discussion.[55]

From a policy perspective, however, there is an important difference between civil settlements and plea bargains, which, like procedural differences, reflects the different types of sanctions that are possible in the two areas. Obviously, a plea bargain can result in imprisonment, and in any case, it carries the stigma associated with any criminal conviction. For these reasons, courts have taken a much more cautious approach with respect to plea bargaining as compared to civil settlements as means of resolving cases.

In a series of cases the US Supreme Court has grudgingly permitted plea bargaining as a necessary evil given the heavy caseload facing budget-constrained prosecutors, but in so doing, it cautioned that there is a real concern about wrongful convictions (type I errors).[56] This is true because some innocent defendants, against whom the evidence is stacked, or who are very risk averse, might opt to plead guilty to a lesser charge rather than take their chances at trial. This concern obviously reflects the imperfection of a trial as a means of uncovering the truth. Thus, Easterbrook (1983, p. 320) has observed that there is "no reason to prevent [an innocent] defendant from striking a deal that seems advantageous. If there is injustice here, the source is not the plea bargain. It is, rather, that innocent people may be found guilty at trial." This, of course, is the fundamental problem facing law enforcement generally, whether its primary objective is to deter crime or to hold criminals responsible for their actions.

References

Adelstein, R. 1981. Institutional Function and Evolution in the Criminal Process. *Northwestern University Law Review* 76: 1–99.

Adelstein, R. 2017. *The Exchange Order: Property and Liability as an Exchange System*. New York: Oxford Univ. Press.

Baird, D., R. Gertner, and R. Picker. 1994. *Game Theory and the Law*. Cambridge, MA: Harvard Univ. Press.

[55] See, for example, Landes (1971), Grossman and Katz (1983), and Reinganum (1988).

[56] See the discussion in Adelstein (2017, Chapter 10). The key cases are *Brady v. United States*, 397 U.S. 742 (1970) and *Santobello v. New York*, 404 U.S. 257 (1971).

Baker, M. and T. Miceli. "Crime, Credible Enforcement, and Multiple Equilibria," *International Review of Law and Economics*, article 106030, 2021.
Bebchuk, L. 1984. Litigation and Settlement Under Imperfect Information. *Rand Journal of Economics* 15: 404–415.
Bebchuk, L. 1988. Suing Solely to Extract a Settlement Offer. *Journal of Legal Studies* 17: 437–450.
Bebchuk, L. 1996. A New Theory Concerning the Credibility and Success of Threats to Sue. *Journal of Legal Studies* 25: 1–25.
Beccaria, C. *On Crimes and Punishments*. Indianapolis, IN: Hackett Publishing Co., 1764 [1986].
Becker, G. 1968. Crime and punishment: an economic approach. *Journal of Political Economy* 76: 169–217.
Becker, G., and G. Stigler. 1974. Law Enforcement, Malfeasance, and Compensation of Enforcers. *Journal of Legal Studies* 3: 1–18.
Bentham, J. *An Introduction to the Principles of Morals and Legislation*, New York: Oxford Univ. Press, 1780 [1970].
Brague, R. 2005. *The Law of God: The Philosophical History of an Idea*. Chicago: Univ. of Chicago Press.
Brown, J. 1973. Toward an Economic Theory of Liability. *Journal of Legal Studies* 2: 323–349.
Easterbrook, F. 1983. Criminal Procedure as a Market System. *Journal of Legal Studies* 12: 289–332.
Coleman, J. 1992. *Risks and Wrongs*. Cambridge, UK: Cambridge Univ. Press.
Cooter, R., and D. Rubinfeld. 1989. An Economic Analysis of Legal Disputes and Their Resolution. *Journal of Economic Literature* 27: 1067–1097.
M., Cosgel, T., and Miceli. 2019. Toward a Theory of Religious Belief and the Emergence of Law. *Journal of Institutional and Theoretical Economics* 175: 692–713.
Dillbary, J., and T. Miceli. 2023. Of Sinners and Scapegoats: The Economics of Collective Responsibility. *Washington Univ. Law Review* 100: 1299–1351.
Doyle, A.C. 1930. *The Complete Sherlock Holmes, 2 volumes*. New York: Doubleday.
Frank, J. 1995. *Dostoevsky: The Miracle Years: 1865–1871*. Princeton: Princeton Univ. Press.
Frank, R. "A Theory of Moral Sentiments." In *Beyond Self Interest*, edited by J. Mansbridge. Chicago: Univ. of Chicago Press, 1990.
Friedman, D. 2000. *Law's Order: What Economics Has To Do with the Law and Why It Matters*. Princeton: Princeton Univ. Press.
Friedman, L. 2004. *Law in America: A Short History*. New York: The Modern Library.
Friehe, T., and T. Miceli. 2014. Marginal deterrence when offenders act sequentially. *Economics Letters* 124: 523–525.

Furlong, W. 1987. A General Equilibrium Model of Crime Commission and Prevention. *Journal of Public Economics* 34: 87–103.

Garoupa, N. 1997. The Theory of Optimal Law Enforcement. *Journal of Economic Surveys* 11: 267–295.

Grossman, G., and M. Katz. 1983. Plea Bargaining and Social Welfare. *American Economic Review* 73: 749–757.

Hart, H.L.A. 1961. *The Concept of Law*. Oxford: Oxford Univ. Press.

Hart, H.L.A. 1982. *Punishment and Responsibility*. London: Oxford Univ. Press.

Holmes, O.W. 1881[1963]. *The Common Law*. Boston: Little Brown.

Holmes, O.W. 1897. The Path of the Law. *Harvard Law Review* 10: 457–478.

Hylton, K. 2005. The Theory of Criminal Penalties and the Economics of Criminal Law. *Review of Law and Economics* 1: 175–201.

Iannaccone, L. 1998. Introduction to the Economics of Religion. *Journal of Economic Literature* 36: 1465–1495.

Iannaccone, L., R. Finke, and R. Stark. 1997. Deregulating Religion: The Economics of Church and State. *Economic Inquiry* 35: 350–364.

Norenzayan, A. 2009. *Big Gods: How Religion Transformed Cooperation and Conflict*. Princeton: Princeton Univ. Press.

Johnson, D. 2016. *God in Watching You: How the Fear of God Makes Us Human*. New York: Oxford Univ. Press.

Kahan, D. 1998. Social Meaning and the Economic Analysis of Crime. *Journal of Legal Studies* 27: 609–622.

Klevorick, A. "On the Economic Theory of Crime." In *NOMOS XXVII: Criminal Justice*, edited by J. Pennock and J. Chapman. New York: New York Univ. Press, 1985.

Landes, W. 1971. An Economic Analysis of Courts. *Journal of Legal Studies* 14: 61–107.

Lewin, J., and W. Trumbull. 1990. The Social Value of Crime? *International Review of Law and Economics* 10: 271–284.

Lott, J. 1987. Should the Wealthy Be Able to "Buy Justice"? *Journal of Political Economy* 95: 1307–1316.

Madison, J. 2008. The Federalist, 51. In *The Federalist Papers*, ed. L. Goldman. Oxford: Oxford Univ. Press.

Miceli, T. 1990. Optimal Prosecution of Defendants Whose Guilt is Uncertain. *Journal of Law, Economics, and Organization* 6: 189–201.

Miceli, T. 1994. Do Contingent Fees Promote Excessive Litigation? *Journal of Legal Studies* 23: 211–224.

Miceli, T. 2017. *The Economic Approach to Law*, 3rd ed. Stanford: Stanford University Press.

Miceli, T. 2018. On Proportionality of Punishments and the Economic Theory of Crime. *European Journal of Law and Economics* 46: 303–314.

Miceli, T. 2019. *The Paradox of Punishment: Reflections on the Economics of Criminal Justice*. Cham, Switzerland: Palgrave Macmillan.
Miceli, T. 2023. On economic theories of criminal punishment: pricing, prevention, or proportionality? *American Law and Economics Review* 25: 1–26.
Miceli, T. 2024. On the Impossibility of a Purely Objective Economic Theory of Crime. *Asian Journal of Law and Economics* 15: 209–219.
Miceli, T., and K. Segerson. 1991. Contingent Fees for Lawyers: The Impact on Litigation and Accident Prevention. *Journal of Legal Studies* 20: 381–399.
Miceli, T., and M. Stone. 2014. Piggyback Lawsuits and Deterrence: Can Frivolous Litigation Improve Welfare? *International Review of Law and Economics* 39: 49–57.
Montesquieu, C. *The Spirit of Laws*, Berkeley: Univ. of California Press, 1748 [1977].
Murdock, G., and D. White. 1969. Standard Cross-Cultural Sample. *Ethnology* 8: 329–369.
Nozick, R. 1974. *Anarchy, State, and Utopia*. New York: Basic Books.
Png, I. 1986. Optimal Subsidies and Damages in the Presence of Legal Error. *International Review of Law and Economics* 6: 101–105.
Polinsky, A. M. and S. Shavell. "The Theory of Public Law Enforcement." In *Handbook of Law and Economics*, edited by A. Polinsky and S. Shavell, Vol. 1, Amsterdam: Elsevier, North-Holland, 2007.
Polinsky, A.M., and D. Rubinfeld. 1988. The Deterrent Effects of Settlements and Trials. *International Review of Law and Economics* 8: 109–116.
Posner, R. 1985. An Economic Theory of the Criminal Law. *Columbia Law Review* 85: 1193–1231.
Posner, R. 2003. *Economic Analysis of Law*, 6th ed. New York: Aspen Publishers.
Priest, G. 1977. The Common Law Process and the Selection of Efficient Laws. *Journal of Legal Studies* 6: 65–82.
Priest, G., and B. Klein. 1984. The Selection of Disputes for Litigation. *Journal of Legal Studies* 13: 1–55.
Reinganum, J. 1988. Plea Bargaining and Prosecutorial Discretion. *American Economic Review* 78: 713–728.
Rosenberg, D., and S. Shavell. 1985. A Model in Which Suits are Brought for Their Nuisance Value. *International Review of Law and Economics* 5: 3–13.
Rubin, P. 1977. Why Is the Common Law Efficient? *Journal of Legal Studies* 6: 51–63.
Rubinfeld, D. and S. Schotchmer. "Contingent Fees." In *The New Palgrave Dictionary of Law and Economics*, P. Newman, ed., New York: Stockton Press, 1998.
Shavell, S. 1982. The Social Versus Private Incentive to Bring Suit in a Costly Legal System. *Journal of Legal Studies* 11: 333–339.

Shavell, S. 1992. A Note on Marginal Deterrence. *International Review of Law and Economics* 12: 345–355.
Shavell, S. 1996. Any Frequency of Plaintiff Victory is Possible. *Journal of Legal Studies* 25: 493–501.
Shavell, S. 2002. Law Versus Morality as Regulators of Conduct. *American Law and Economics Review* 4: 227–257.
Shavell, S. 2004. *Foundations of Economic Analysis of Law*. Cambridge, MA: Belknap Press.
Stigler, G. 1970. The Optimum Enforcement of Law. *Journal of Political Economy* 78: 345–355.
Wade, N. 2006. *The Faith Instinct: How Religion Evolved and Why It Endures*. New York: Penguin Press.

CHAPTER 4

Causation and Responsibility

The discussion to this point, focusing as it has on legal responsibility as a means of internalizing external harms, has relied on a casual basis for responsibility. In doing so, it has used the terms "responsibility" and "liability" (meaning the imposition of some legal sanction) more or less synonymously. This conflation, and more generally the meaning of both causation and responsibility, however, warrant further scrutiny.

First as to responsibility,Hart (1982) offers several possible definitions.[1] These include *role responsibility*, *causal responsibility*, and *liability responsibility*.[2] Role responsibility concerns a job or duty that a person is charged with carrying out, whether in an employment or a family setting, or as a member of society. The particular duty with which we are concerned here is to make all reasonable efforts to refrain from inflicting harm on one's fellow citizens, whether by accident or by intent.

Causal responsibility concerns a linkage between a person's act (or failure to act) and some outcome. This sense of responsibility is in fact virtually synonymous with causation as that concept is generally understood. As Hart (1982, p. 214) observes, "[i]n many contexts, … it is

[1] See particularly Chap. 9.

[2] He also discusses capacity responsibility, meaning the ability to comprehend the consequences of his actions. I will not consider this meaning as it lies outside of the scope of economic analysis.

T. J. Miceli, *Harm and Responsibility*,
https://doi.org/10.1007/978-3-031-74831-8_4

possible to substitute for the expression 'was responsible for' the words 'caused' or 'produced'...." To economists, this reflects a "technological" linkage between an input and an output, as reflected, for example, by the functional relationship between precaution and risk in the model of precaution.

Finally, liability responsibility concerns the attribution of some legal consequence for an act or failure to act, such as the imposition of a monetary fine or other form of punishment. Hart distinguishes this from moral responsibility, which can sometimes apply when legal consequences do not, and vice versa. This reflects the argument from Chap. 2 that, although law likely emerged from morality, the two realms of judgment are not perfectly coincident. In terms of incentives, the two concepts effectively serve the same purpose; namely, to impel some sort of action.

For current purposes, it is worth emphasizing that causal responsibility represents an inherent relationship that links actions and outcomes, or causes and effects, in a physical way. By contrast, the other two concepts of responsibility reflect conscious choices or policies made by society—either formally through law or informally through evolved moral judgments—regarding how it will respond to certain outcomes, particularly those that produce harm. Role responsibility defines those duties or obligations that direct one to avoid causing harm when engaged in potentially risky activities, while liability responsibility defines the consequences one will face if harm actually materializes. These two concepts therefore define the rules governing responsibility for harm—what those responsibilities are and the consequences for failing to carry them out. In this sense, they embody a constructed relationship between individual members of society and that society as a collective entity, which is manifested by the duty that individuals owe toward one another. It is this relationship that is the focus of the current study.

Having clarified the meaning of responsibility, I now turn to the idea of causation as the basis for legal responsibility. As we have repeatedly emphasized, causation underlies the standard economic approach to externalities, whether it takes the form of Pigovian taxes, tort liability, or criminal sanctions. As we have seen, this linkage promotes efficiency by giving the injurer—the "cause" of the harm—an incentive to avoid or mitigate that harm in the most efficient way, what we have called optimal deterrence. At the same time, the assessment of responsibility on the injurer fulfills a punitive impulse that most people inherently feel when a wrong has been committed, whether that urge is motivated by a primitive thirst for vengeance, or by its more civilized counterpart—the quest for retribution, or "just deserts."

The reliance on causation as the basis for legal responsibility for harm is epitomized by the rule of strict liability in tort law. According to this rule, once a causal connection between the action of some party A and the harm to some other party (or parties) B has been established, A is liable for the full amount of that harm.Posner (1972) notes that strict liability was the dominant rule during the formative years of tort law, but a decided trend toward negligence, or fault-based liability, developed in the nineteenth century. That trend, according to Epstein (1973), was motivated largely by moral rather than economic considerations based on the idea that liability also required fault.[3] Fault, or negligence, was therefore added on top of causation as the basis for assigning legal responsibility for most accidental harms. Epstein argues that this violated the principle of corrective justice, which is inherent in a casual basis for responsibility. Posner (1990, p. 322) cautions, however, that Epstein's approach to the assignment of liability borders on tautology in the sense that "the need for correction is built into the definition of the wrong."

A further problem with fault-based liability, according to Epstein, is that it fails to answer the question of who should be responsible when all parties involved in an accident acted reasonably, for in that case, fault does not uniquely attribute responsibility. Thus, some arbitrary "tie-breaker" has to be invoked. The same can be said, however, of causation. For example, we have noted that both the injurer and victim in an accident meet the but-for test for cause-in-fact in the sense that if either were removed, the accident would not have occurred. Thus, causation does not uniquely define a casual direction between them. We will return to this point below.

A further problem is that it is not clear whether causation as we have defined it is meant to be a *necessary* or a *sufficient* condition for assigning responsibility. By sufficiency we mean that, once a causal connection between A's action and B's harm has been established as a factual matter, A is responsible. Thus, no further inquiry is required, such as whether the harm was accidental or intentional, or whether A (or B) could have avoided the harm by taking some precautionary or evasive measures. In other words, A has no defense against the finding of responsibility. This is

[3] A different explanation for the move from strict liability to negligence is offered by Horwitz (1977); see the further discussion in Chap. 5.

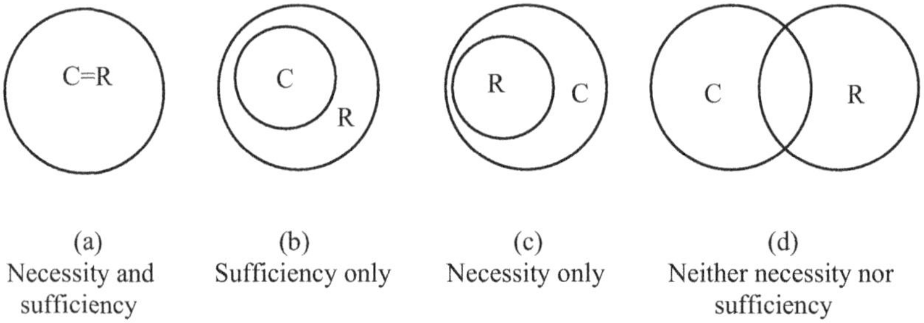

Fig. 4.1 Linkages between causation (C) and responsibility for harm (R). (**a**) Necessity and sufficiency. (**b**) Sufficiency only. (**c**) Necessity only. (**d**) Neither necessity nor sufficiency

the case with strict liability. By necessity we mean that no one *other than* A should be held responsible for the harm. Stated differently, anyone held responsible for B's harm must also have been a cause of that harm.

Figure 4.1 clarifies this distinction by means of a schematic depiction of the relationship between causation and responsibility for some accident. In each of the panels, the circle labeled C depicts the set of individuals who *caused* some harm in the physical (but-for) sense, while the circle labeled R depicts the set of people who are held *legally responsible* for that harm. Panel (a) depicts a strict causal basis for responsibility, as reflected by the fact that the two circles are exactly coincident. Thus, causation is both necessary and sufficient. In panel (b), causation is sufficient for establishing responsibility because circle C is strictly inside circle R. Thus, everyone who caused harm is responsible. However, causation is not necessary because some people who are held responsible did not cause harm—that is, circle C is strictly inside circle R. Conversely, panel (c) shows the case where causation is necessary but not sufficient in the sense that everyone who is held responsible caused harm, but some who caused harm are not held responsible. Thus, circle R is strictly inside circle C. Finally, panel (d) shows the case where causation is neither necessary nor sufficient for responsibility. Thus, only some people who caused harm are held responsible, and only some who are held responsible caused the harm. An extreme version of this case would be where the circles do not overlap at all, meaning no one who caused harm is held responsible, and no one who is held responsible caused harm.

In previous chapters we have seen various instances where responsibility departs from a purely casual basis in these ways, mostly as a consequence of imperfections in the mechanisms for assigning liability. For example, some injurers avoided liability because of litigation and detection costs, while some people who did not cause harm were held liable due to legal error. These are unavoidable problems that can in theory only be mitigated by a more accurate enforcement apparatus. However, in subsequent chapters we will see that such departures can also happen by design. Our purpose in exploring these departures will be to provide economic justifications for them; that is, to show that assigning responsibility for reasons other than strict causation can sometimes be a way of promoting efficiency or some other desired goal.

Our pursuit of this line of analysis will culminate in the conclusion, already noted above, that causation is not in fact a well-defined concept, and so cannot reliably serve as a basis for assigning responsibility. We have seen that the reason for this is the demonstration by Ronald Coase that causation is reciprocal in nature, meaning that both an injurer and a victim need to be present for harm to occur (Coase 1960). As a preview and illustration of the practical impact of this concept, I briefly consider here the use of Pigovian *subsidies* as an alternative Pigovian taxes as a response to externalities.

Let us return to the polluting-factory example depicted in Table 2.1, where we assumed that the operation of the factory "caused" harm to nearby residents. But now let us adopt the presumption that the factory has the legal right to produce at its profit-maximizing output level of four units, irrespective of the harm, perhaps because it was a pre-existing use. In a real sense, therefore, it is the movement of the residents into close proximity to the factory that causes the harm from pollution.

Once the residents are there, however, the factory's optimal output drops from four to three, as we saw above. In an effort to achieve this outcome, suppose that instead of taxing the factory, the government offers to pay it a subsidy of $2, the marginal harm, for each unit that it *reduces* its output. Starting from the initial output of four, the factory will find it profitable to reduce its output to three because the lost profit of $1 (=$16 − $15) from doing so is less than the subsidy. However, it will not reduce its output any further because the marginal reductions in profit thereafter exceed the subsidy of $2. Thus, the final output level will be three, which is the social optimum. The total cost of the subsidy is thus $2, which must be financed by taxes, either assessed on the residents benefitting from the reduced output, or somewhere else in the economy.

The important point is that under the subsidy, the factory faces an *opportunity cost* of $2 for each unit of output that it produces, which has the same incentive effect on its behavior as a tax of the same amount per unit of output would. Both policies therefore succeed in producing the efficient level of output. This reflects the fundamental equivalence in economic terms of an out-of-pocket expense and an opportunity cost (forgone payment) of the same amount. The lesson from this example is that paying the factory to reduce its output, or requiring it to pay taxes for the right to increase its output, will achieve the same outcome if the tax and subsidy amounts are both equated to the external harm. It follows that there is a degree of freedom in the assignment of responsibility for harm, at least as it relates to the goal of achieving efficient avoidance of harm.[4] It also illustrates the point that there is not a unique causal relationship here that can serve as a basis for assigning liability for harm.

The discussion of causation and responsibility in this chapter has set the stage for what follows. Part 2 will discuss various doctrines in both tort and criminal law that limit liability for individuals who cause harm. That is, it explores situations where causation is not a sufficient condition for responsibility. Part 3 then discusses tort and criminal doctrines that expand liability to individuals who did not cause harm; that is, situations where causation is not a necessary condition. Part 4 concludes by examining in more depth the consequences of the reciprocal nature of causation as described above. The most important insight that will emerge is that harm is itself a relative concept that is only meaningful in relation to a particular assignment of legal rights, a point that the preceding comparison of taxes and subsidies portrayed. This conclusion has obvious relevance for contemporary debates about such matters as cancel culture, freedom of speech, and identity expression. As to theory, it implies that the economic approach to law, depending as it does on the causal connection between harm and responsibility, cannot uniquely determine the assignment of legal rights. Although it can specify efficient prices and an

[4] There is an important qualification of this conclusion. The example demonstrated that taxes and subsidies in principle create equivalent incentives for avoidance of harm, but they do not create equivalent incentives regarding the location choices of either factories or residents. On this point, see Frech (1979) and Holderness (1989).

optimal structure for enforcing those rights, how they should be initially allocated is ultimately a moral or political question.

References

Coase, R. 1960. The Problem of Social Cost. *Journal of Law and Economics* 3: 1–44.

Epstein, R. 1973. A Theory of Strict Liability. *Journal of Legal Studies* 2: 151–204.

Frech, H. 1979. The Extended Coase Theorem and Long Run Equilibrium: The Non-equivalence of Liability Rules and Property Rights. *Economic Inquiry* 17: 254–268.

Hart, H.L.A. 1982. *Punishment and Responsibility*. London: Oxford Univ. Press.

Holderness, C. 1989. The Assignment of Rights, Entry Effects, and the Allocation of Resources. *Journal of Legal Studies* 18: 181–189.

Horwitz, M. 1977. *The Transformation of American Law: 1780–1860*. Cambridge, MA: Harvard Univ. Press.

Posner, R. 1972. A Theory of Negligence. *Journal of Legal Studies* 1: 29–96.

Posner, R. 1990. *The Problems of Jurisprudence*. Cambridge, MA: Harvard Univ. Press.

PART II

Reasons for Limiting Responsibility

"The admission of excusing conditions is a feature of the Distribution of punishment and it is required by distinct principles of Justice which restrict the extent to which general social aims may be pursued at the cost of individuals."

H.L.A. Hart (1982, p. 17)

CHAPTER 5

Limiting Responsibility: Tort Doctrines

This part turns to a discussion of factors that effectively shield from legal responsibility a party who caused harm. In other words, it offers reasons why causation is not a sufficient reason for imposing responsibility. This chapter considers doctrines in tort law that serve this purpose, and Chap. 6 discusses corresponding doctrines in criminal law. The goal will be to offer economic explanations for the various limitations of liability relative to a strict causal basis for responsibility.

Proximate Cause

The previous chapter discussed causation in the logical sense, what in tort law is called cause in fact. This also reflects the meaning that most people attach to causation. It specifically takes a backward-looking perspective that makes use of knowledge gained in hindsight as to how an accident actually unfolded by tracing exactly how the action or inaction of some individual contributed to the occurrence of the harmful event.

The law has another concept of causation, called *proximate cause*, which is forward-looking in the sense that it places the viewer at a point in time prior to the accident and asks what a reasonable person's expectations were or should have been, given the knowledge available at that moment. The usual test for proximate cause is the "reasonable foresight"

T. J. Miceli, *Harm and Responsibility*,
https://doi.org/10.1007/978-3-031-74831-8_5

test—that is, could the injurer have "reasonably foreseen" the consequences of his or her actions (or inactions) at that point in time? If the answer is yes, then that person's actions are considered proximate cause of the accident. If the answer is no, they are not, even if the situation satisfies the but-for test for cause in fact. The reason is that the connection to the accident is considered to be too remote to justify the assignment of liability.

The classic case of *Palsgraf v. Long Island RR* illustrates this concept.[1] The court stated the following facts:

> Plaintiff was standing on a platform of defendant's railroad after buying a ticket to go the Rockaway Beach. A train stopped at the station, bound for another place. Two men ran forward to catch it. One of the men reached the platform of the car without mishap, though the train was already moving. The other man, carrying a package, jumped aboard the car, but seemed unsteady as if about to fall. A guard on the car, who held the door open, reached forward to help him in, and another guard on the platform pushed him from behind. In this act, the package was dislodged, and fell upon the rails. It was a package of small size, about fifteen inches long, and was covered with newspaper. In fact, it contained fireworks, but there was nothing in its appearance to give notice of its contents. The fireworks when they fell exploded. The shock of the explosion threw down some scales at the other end of the platform many feet away. The scales struck the plaintiff, causing injuries for which she now sues.

In light of these facts, application of the but-for test clearly established that the railroad employees were cause in fact of the victim's harm. However, the court ruled that linkage was too remote to have been within the reasonable contemplation of the employees at the time they made their decision to assist the man onto the train. Thus, the railroad was not held legally responsible for the plaintiff's injuries because the actions of its employees were not the proximate cause.

This severing of legal responsibility from factual causation represents a conscious decision to limit the liability of the injurer. In law, this is sometimes described as the absence of a "duty" on the part of the injurer to protect the victim from certain harmful events (Keeton, et al. p. 274), but this explanation just begs the question of what circumstances give rise to a legal duty toward others in the first place. An economic explanation,

[1] 248 N.Y. 339, 162 N.E. 99 (1928).

by contrast, asks what benefit might be derived by limiting an injurer's liability in this way, and whether that benefit is cost-justified.

One benefit from a proximate-cause limitation is the savings in administrative costs because fewer lawsuits will be filed.[2] Offsetting this is that injurers will not fully internalize the costs that their actions impose and so may over-engage in harmful activities or underinvest in precaution. This mirrors the under-deterrence problem associated with litigation costs as discussed in the previous chapter. The logic here is that the excluded risks are so remote that rational injurers would not have accounted for them anyway, in which case the exclusion of liability is justified by the administrative cost savings.

In the *Palsgraf* case, for example, expanding the liability of the railroad for accidents of the sort described there would likely have no effect on the behavior of employees going forward because such outcomes are beyond the contemplation of most people. However, if allowed, they would open the gates to a flood of litigation with little or no offsetting benefit. Establishing the efficient scope of the proximate-cause limitation depends on specifying a threshold beyond which risks *are* perceptible and therefore should be accounted for by injurers. For example, if the actions of the workers in pushing the man on the moving train had caused *that man* to be injured, the railroad would certainly have been found liable because that risk was easily perceptible to the ordinary person. It turns out that the economic issues involved in the determination of the efficient threshold for proximate cause are the same as for setting a negligence standard, to which we now turn.

Negligence or Fault

We have previously noted that the predominant rule for assigning liability in tort law is negligence, which is the same thing as "fault." To say that someone is responsible for harm because it was their fault, however, is not the same thing as saying that they were the cause of the harm. From a legal perspective, one can cause harm but not be found at fault, whereas a finding of fault first requires that one be the cause. Thus, causation is necessary but not sufficient for a finding of fault.

[2] See Shavell 2004, p. 254; Shavell 1987a, b: Chapter 5; and Shavell (1980).

In legal terms, negligence is based on the existence of a duty "to conform to a standard of conduct, for the protection of others at risk" (Keeton, et al. 1984, p. 164). Failure to fulfill that duty—to meet the due standard—therefore results in liability for any harm that materializes, whereas meeting the duty absolves one of liability for any harm that occurs. The first question we need to address, therefore, is how the due standard is or should be determined.

For one thing, it should be objective in the sense that the same standard applies to everyone,[3] and to that end, courts have defined the so-called reasonable person, who embodies the qualities—knowledge, ability, cognition—of the average person. The due standard is then used to define the actions that a reasonable person is expected to take in the presence of a given risky situation.[4] What exactly constitutes reasonableness, however, leaves room for debate. Economic theory helps here by offering a rigorous test, called the Hand test, which was first proposed in *United States v. Carroll Towing Co.*[5]

The case concerned an accident caused by an unattended barge that broke free of its moorings and collided with another boat, causing it to sink. The owner of the sunken boat sued, claiming negligence on the part of the barge owner for failing to properly attend to it. In deciding the case, Judge Learned Hand offered the following procedure for determining negligence:

> [T]he owner's duty ... to provide against resulting injuries is a function of three variables: (1) the probability that she will break away; (2) the gravity of the resulting injury, if she does; (3) the burden of adequate precautions. Possibly it serves to bring this notion into relief to state it in algebraic terms: if the probability be called *P*; the injury, *L*; and the

[3] See Landes and Posner (1987, pp. 127–131), who discuss departures from the reasonable person standard for negligence. These are allowed, they argue, when the characteristics of a particular defendant depart in a significant and discernable way from the average person, both above and below average capabilities for recognizing and avoiding risk. As a result, their legal responsibility for harm is correspondingly scaled. This makes sense from an information cost perspective.

[4] Cooter and Ulen (1988, p. 11) distinguish the *reasonable* person in law from the *rational* person in economics. The latter is assumed to pursue his or her self-interest, whereas the former has a legal duty to take account of any risks his or her actions may impose on others.

[5] 159 F.2d 169, 173 (2d Cir. 1947). See the analysis of this case in Posner (1972).

burden, B; liability depends upon whether B is less that L multiplied by P; i.e., whether $B<PL$.

The application of this test is illustrated by the example in Table 5.1, which is based on the facts of the *Carroll Towing* case.[6] The table shows three actions that the barge owner could have taken in the face of a risk of the barge breaking away. These are: (1) post no attendant; (2) post an attendant only during working hours; and (3) post an attendant for 24 h. The owner's cost increases with each of these options, and the risk of an accident correspondingly declines. The final column, which computes the total expected cost (=cost of precaution + expected damages), shows that the cost-minimizing action is to post an attendant during the day only, which therefore constitutes the due standard. The key insight is that the objective is not to minimize the risk, but to minimize the overall cost.

Now consider how the Hand test would work in this example. It says that the barge owner (the injurer) would be negligent (liable) if he failed to take actions for which the court determined that $B < PL$. Suppose, for instance, that the owner had in fact posted no attendant, and the victim alleged that he should have posted one during working hours. In other words, the claim is that the owner's failure to post an attendant during working hours was a breach of his duty and hence constituted negligence. Using the data in the table, we would compute that $B = \$50$ (the cost of posting an attendant during the day); $P = 0.25 - 0.10 = 0.15$ (the increase in the probability of an accident from the owner's failure to post the attendant); and $L = \$400$ (the loss from the accident). It follows that $B = 50 < PL = 0.15 \times 400 = 60$, and so the barge owner would be found negligent according to the Hand test.

Table 5.1 Example of the Hand test for negligence

Owner's action	*Cost of*	*Probability of an accident*	*Damages from an accident*	*Total Costs*
No attendant	0	0.25	400	100
Attendant during working hours	50	0.10	400	90
Attendant for 24 h	95	0	400	95

[6] See Miceli (2017, pp. 27–28).

Alternatively, suppose that the owner ***had*** posted an attendant during working hours, but the barge broke away during the night. The victim might then allege that the owner's failure to post an attendant for 24 h was negligent. In this case, $B = \$95 - \$50 = \$45$ (the extra cost of posting an attendant for 24 h); $P = 0.10$ (the increase in probability from the owner's failure to post an attendant for 24 h); and $L = \$400$. In this case, $B = 45 > PL = 0.10 \times 400 = 40$. Thus, according to the Hand test the owner's failure to post an attendant for 24 h rather than only during working hours *would not constitute negligent*.

Application of the Hand test as just described therefore replicates the socially optimal outcome, which we had previously shown was to post an attendant during the day only. Thus, the due standard resulting from application of the rule coincides with the efficient level of injurer precaution. This correspondence will necessarily be true when the Hand test is applied in this marginal way; that is, by comparing the available options incrementally.

Consider next how injurers will respond to a negligence standard when defined in this manner. Specifically, will it induce them to meet the due standard (i.e., act efficiently)? Table 5.2 shows the court's ruling and the resulting costs for the injurer for each of the various care choices. Clearly the latter will minimize his costs by meeting, but not exceeding, the due standard—that is, by posting the attendant during the day only. The incentive to do so is enforced by the significant cost savings from complying with the standard. In particular, by complying the injurer incurs the \$50 cost of hiring the attendant for the day only, but avoids paying any damages in the event of an accident, thus saving \$40 in expected terms. Further, the injurer has no incentive to exceed the due standard (hire an attendant for 24 h) because that would involve a greater expenditure on care (\$95) with no further savings in liability.

Table 5.2 Injurer's behavior under a negligence rule

Action	*Ruling*	*Injurer's expected costs*
No attendant	Liable	\$100
Attendant during working hours	Not liable	50
Attendant for 24 h	Not liable	95

The conclusion that injurers will find it optimal to just meet the due standard under an efficiently-structured negligence rule is perfectly general.[7] The reason is the threshold feature of the rule, which allows injurers to *avoid liability* by complying with, but not exceeding, the standard. This is different from strict liability or Pigovian taxation, both of which also induce injurers to take efficient care, but they do this by imposing on them *the full cost* of any harm that they cause. The two approaches therefore create incentives for efficient accident avoidance, but in very different ways. This difference will turn out to be very important below.

The fact that both strict liability and negligence are efficient in terms of incentives for accident avoidance naturally raises the question of why negligence has become the predominant rule in tort law. Several explanations are possible. One is based on the Aristotelian notion of a "just law," which is one that is "capable of being complied with by those to whom it is addressed." The idea is that it is unjust to "impos[e] sanctions on people who lack a fair opportunity to avoid their imposition by complying with the law" (Posner 1990, p. 332). A negligence standard has this feature but strict liability does not, or so this argument goes. The problem with this argument is that it depends on what constitutes "avoidance" of liability. A negligence rule allows avoidance by taking due care, but strict liability also permits avoidance by refraining from engaging in the risky activity in the first place.

An objection to negligence on justice grounds is that it would seem unjust to leave *any* harm with "innocent" victims, given that the injurer is able to enjoy the benefits of the activity in question without having to pay any of the resulting external costs. In this sense, strict liability seems more just because injurers are required to pay the full costs associated with the activity in question. This is the view underlying Epstein's argument in favor of strict liability (Epstein 1973; Posner 1990, p. 341) .

An economic argument for negligence is that, like the proximate-cause limitation, it saves on administrative costs by reducing the volume of litigation. At the same time, however, it is likely that the cost *per suit* will be higher as compared to strict liability because of the greater need for fact-finding (such as the application of the Hand test). Further, the limitation of liability for injurers who comply with the due standard would

[7] See, for example, Shavell (1987a, b and Landes and Posner (1987).

likely result in excessive engagement in risky activities under negligence as compared to strict liability (Shavell 1980). This is true because due care is not generally based on how frequently an injurer engages in the activity (for example, how many miles one drives or how many units of a dangerous product a factory produces), but only on how carefully one conducts that activity on a per-unit basis.

This latter point relates to an influential explanation for the expansion of negligence during the first half of the nineteenth century when accidental injuries caused by industrial machinery, and especially railroads, exploded as a consequence of the Industrial Revolution (Keeton et al. 1984, p. 161). The argument is that negligence, along with other legal policies aimed at limiting the liability of injurers, were designed to subsidize business and economic development as a way to promote economic growth (Horwitz 1977; Posner 2003, p. 253).

There is, finally, a powerful economic justification for the superiority of negligence over strict liability which relates to the idea that victims as well as injurers can often affect accident risk. That this is true should be obvious—indeed, in many cases victims will have at least as much control over risk as injurers. For example, pedestrians should only cross busy streets at crosswalks, and consumers of dangerous products should only use them as directed and for the intended purpose. In the law-and-economics literature, settings in which both injurer and victim care affect risk are referred to as "bilateral care" accidents. (Recall our discussion of the model of precaution in Chap. 2.)

When both injurers and victims can take precautions, it turns out that strict liability is no longer an efficient rule because it fails to create incentives for victims to take optimal care. The reason is that victims expect to be fully compensated for their losses, and so have little or no incentive to take steps to reduce risk. Symmetrically, a rule of no injurer liability would eliminate any incentive for injurers to take precautions, but it *would* motivate victims to be careful because they expect to bear the full amount of their losses. It follows that in bilateral care problems, strict liability may not even be more efficient in terms of risk reduction than no liability. It depends on which party can more effectively reduce the accident risk.

Economists refer to a situation in which an individual has diminished incentives to avoid a risk because they do not expect to bear the full costs—whether to themselves or others—as a *moral hazard problem*. This is a term that comes from the insurance industry, and reflects the idea that when someone is insured against an adverse event, they have less incentive to avoid it. This presents a challenge for the design of an efficient liability rule in bilateral care accident settings because only one party can directly bear responsibility for the harm: either the injurer faces full responsibility (strict liability) or the victim does (no liability). Nor can shared liability resolve the problem because each party will then only have an incentive to be careful in proportion to the amount of harm that they expect to bear, and aggregate liability cannot exceed the total amount of harm.

Interestingly, a Pigovian tax approach to controlling harm offers one way out of this paradox because, as noted in Chap. 2, there is no requirement that the revenue from the tax has to be given to the victim. In the case where it is not, both parties have an incentive to take efficient precaution: injurers because they face full (out of pocket) responsibility for the harm, and victims because they do not expect to be compensated for their loss. By contrast, tort law doesn't have the freedom to "decouple" liability and compensation in this way.[8] As we will see, however, the negligence rule, when properly structured, *can* achieve efficient bilateral incentives by virtue of its threshold feature.

As an illustration, Table 5.3 describes a bilateral care problem in which the injurer and victim each have a choice between taking "care," costing \$10 for the injurer and \$12 for the victim, and "no care." Care by either party reduces accident risk by the same amount, from 0.50 to 0.35, while care by both reduces it to 0.20. The loss from an accident in all cases is fixed at \$100. As the table shows, the efficient outcome—the one that minimizes the sum of the costs of precaution plus expected losses—is when both parties take care (the fourth row).

The actual outcome in this situation will depend in part on the expectations that each party holds about the other's behavior (assuming for now

Table 5.3 Bilateral care accident example

Injurer cost	*Victim cost*	*Probability of loss*	*Loss*	*Total costs*
0	0	0.50	\$100	\$50
10	0	0.35	100	45
0	12	0.35	100	47
10	12	0.20	100	42

[8] For an analysis of "decoupled" liability rules, see Polinsky and Che (1991).

that neither observes the other's choice). This is a consequence of the interdependency of their decisions with respect to risk. Economists use game theory to determine the equilibrium outcome in such cases.[9] We now use the information in Table 5.3 to derive the equilibrium outcome under various liability rules.

Consider first equilibrium under a rule of strict injurer liability. The choices in this situation are depicted in Table 5.4, where the entries in each cell show the costs for the victim (left entry) and the injurer (right entry). First consider the injurer. Since he is liable for the victim's losses regardless of the latter's behavior, he will take care. This is verified by the lower cost for the injurer in the "care" column for both of the victim's choices, as indicated by the boldface entries.

As for the victim, because she expects to be fully compensated for her losses regardless of her care choice, she will have no incentive to take care.[10] This is verified by the lower cost for the victim in the "no care" row for both of the injurer's choices, again indicated by the boldface entries. The unique equilibrium is the lower-left cell, where only the injurer takes care (i.e., both entries are boldfaced). Total costs are therefore not minimized in this equilibrium.

The situation is symmetric under a rule of no injurer liability, though in this case it is the injurer who does not take care regardless of the victim's choice, and the victim who does take care regardless of the injurer's choice. Thus, the unique equilibrium is the upper right cell in Table 5.5. The equilibrium outcomes under strict and no liability are therefore symmetric in terms of incentives; that is, under each rule only

Table 5.4 Equilibrium under strict liability

		Injurer's choice:	
		Care	*No care*
Victim's choice:	Care	12, **30**	12, 35
	No care	**0**, **45**	**0**, 50

Note Boldfaced entries indicate optimal choices

[9] This is referred to as a Nash equilibrium. Brown (1973) was apparently the first to derive the equilibrium in bilateral care problems under different liability rules.

[10] In this example, both the injurer and the victim have *dominant strategies*—the injurer's is to take care and the victim's is not to take care.

Table 5.5 Equilibrium under no liability

		Injurer's choice: *Care*	*No care*
Victim's choice:	Care	**32**, 10	**47**, **0**
	No care	35, 10	50, **0**

Note Boldfaced entries indicate optimal choices

one party takes care. However, they are not equivalent in terms of total costs. Under strict liability, total costs are $45 whereas under no liability total costs are $47. This is because the injurer's cost of care is lower, and so strict liability is the more efficient rule in this example. This reflects the "least-cost avoider rule" for assigning liability, first proposed by Calabresi (1970), which prescribes that liability be assigned to the party that can avoid (or mitigate) the risk at lower cost. In this example, it is strict liability, but generally the efficient rule will be case specific.

The preceding result represents an important qualification to a purely causal basis for responsibility in bilateral-care accident settings. The reason is that both the injurer and victim can take steps to reduce the risk of an accident in such settings, and so both are causes of the harm in the Coasian sense. Thus, a rule that assigns liability based on "causation" is an empty concept; it is replaced here by one that assigns liability based on which party can avoid the harm at a lower cost.

This rule is not ideal, however, because it does not achieve the most efficient outcome—where both parties invest in precaution. We now show that a negligence rule *can* achieve that outcome, provided that the due standard is properly set. Specifically, in keeping with the above discussion that equated "due care" with "efficient care" according to the marginal Hand test, we assume here that the due standard is for the injurer to take care since that is cost-minimizing for either choice by the victim.[11] Thus, the injurer can avoid liability by taking care, but will he incur full liability if he does not take care. Table 5.6 shows the possible outcomes.

Begin again with the injurer. As under strict liability, his optimal choice is to take care regardless of the victim's choice. This is true

[11] Specifically, as shown in Table 5.3, care by the injurer lowers total costs whether or not the victim takes care. In a situation where multiple care choices are possible, the due care standard should be set at the one that minimizes costs. See Shavell (1987a, b) and Landes and Posner (1987) .

Table 5.6 Equilibrium under negligence

		Injurer's choice: *Care*	*No care*
Victim's choice:	Care	**32, 10**	12, 35
	No care	35, **10**	**0**, 50

Note Boldfaced entries indicate optimal choices

because the injurer's costs are lower in the "care" column for both choices by the victim. In contrast to strict liability, however, this choice is cost-minimizing for the injurer because it allows him to *avoid* liability.

The victim's optimal behavior under negligence turns out to be conditional on the expected behavior of the injurer. Specifically, if the victim expects the injurer to take care (the left-hand column), the victim minimizes her cost by also taking care (32 < 35). This is true because, with the injurer meeting the due standard, the victim must bear her own costs, and so she takes care, which is the efficient outcome. In effect, the victim behaves as if the rule were no liability. On the other hand, if the victim expects the injurer *not* to take care (the right-hand column), she will also refrain from care (0 < 12). In this case, the injurer will be found negligent and hence fully liable for the victim's damages, and so, as under strict liability, the victim has no incentive to be careful. The unique equilibrium in this case, however, is for both parties to take care (the upper left cell), given that the injurer will in fact take care regardless of his expectation of what the victim will do.[12] Thus, it is rational for victims to expect injurers to take care (i.e., to comply with the due standard), and so she will also take care.

It is worth emphasizing the role of expectations in this outcome, and particularly how the negligence rule acts to coordinate the beliefs of injurers and victims, who after all are "strangers" prior to an accident in the sense that they must make their decisions in ignorance of the other's behavior. One might expect this to result in unpredictable behavior, but in fact, the threshold feature of negligence acts as a powerful coordinating mechanism, and game theory provides the conceptual apparatus for thinking about how this coordination happens.

[12] In this situation, only the injurer has a dominant strategy—to take care.

According to the concept of Nash equilibrium, potential injurers and victims—by which we mean any parties engaging in risky activities—have to form expectations about how others with whom they might interact will behave. The preceding example shows that people will rationally expect would-be injurers to comply with the due standard under negligence because of the powerful incentive that the threshold feature of the rule creates for them to avoid liability. What's more, the law promotes this belief by generally compelling people to assume that others will not be negligent—that is, that they will comply with the law.[13] Thus, would-be victims rationally presume that any injurers with whom they might interact will meet the due standard, and so they had also better take care to minimize their losses.[14]

The ability of a negligence rule to achieve efficient incentives in bilateral care accident settings is one of the most important contributions economic theory has made to the understanding of legal doctrines.[15] The fact that this aspect of negligence is probably unrelated to the reason for its actual emergence as the predominant form of tort liability during the nineteenth century does not diminish this insight.[16]

Despite its efficiency, an important drawback of negligence is that it leaves victims uncompensated in the equilibrium outcome. That is, they bear any residual harm at the efficient equilibrium. Although this may seem unjust, one way to think about it is that, in a world where risk is unavoidable, people should reasonably expect to be able to avoid legal responsibility for residual harm as long as they abide by the law (i.e., exercise due care). This reflects the idea that negligence is a "just law" in the sense noted above.

That being said, there is clearly a "pro-injurer" bias built into negligence law as we have defined it so far. Perhaps in recognition of this,

[13] See, for example, *LeRoy Fibre Co. v. Chicago, Milwaukee & St. Paul Ry.*, 232 U.S. 340 (1914), in which Justice Holmes, in his concurring opinion, wrote that "as a general proposition people are entitled to assume that their neighbors will conform to the law…and therefore… are entitled to assume that their neighbors will not be negligent.".

[14] Accident settings in which the parties move in sequence create a potential problem, as will be discussed in section xx below.

[15] This is emphasized by Cooter (1985), who extends the insights from negligence law to other areas of the common law—particularly, contracts and property.

[16] For thoughts on this point, see Miceli (2012).

courts have also created a due standard of care for victims, called *contributory negligence*.[17] The availability of this standard creates a degree of freedom in assigning residual liability in cases where the injurer and victim have both taken, or both have failed to take, due care.[18] We will suggest a more specific explanation for contributory negligence below.

Causation Revisited

We next re-examine the role of causation, particularly as it relates to negligence law. We specifically reconsider both cause in fact and proximate cause with a particular focus on whether either concept interferes with the desirable incentive properties of the negligence rule as we have just described them.

Cause in fact. We saw above that the test for cause in fact is the but-for test, which forms the logical basis for causation as most people understand the concept. However, when paired with negligence, it actually limits the liability of injurers to those harms that are caused *by the injurer's negligence*. This interpretation of cause in fact is illustrated by Table 5.7, which adapts the example in Table 5.1 based on the *Carroll Towing* case. Recall that in that example, three different care choices by the barge owner affected the risk of the barge breaking free of its moorings and endangering other boats. We showed that the owner's optimal care choice, and hence the proper due standard according to the Hand test, was for the owner to post an attendant only during working hours.

Table 5.7 Injurer's costs under negligence

Owner's action	*Standard negligence rule*	*Negligence with cause in fact*
No attendant	100	60 = 100 − 40
Attendant during working hours	50	50
Attendant for 24 h	95	95

[17] See *Butterfield v. Forrester*, 11 East 60 (K.B. 1809).

[18] For a detailed analysis of the efficiency properties of the various forms of negligence, see Shavell (1987a, b) and Landes and Posner (1987).

Under the standard negligence rule as we have defined it so far, the barge owner would be liable for the victim's full expected damages of \$100 if he posted no attendant, but he would avoid any liability if he either posted an attendant during working hours or for 24 h. As column 2 of Table 5.7 (which replicates column three of Table 5.2) shows, the barge owner will minimize his costs by posting an attendant only during working hours, but no more. Grady (1983) has argued, however, that actual negligence law does not operate in this way. When augmented by the cause-in-fact requirement, he argues, injurers who fail to meet the due standard would only be held liable for the damages *that their negligence caused*. In the example, the barge owner would therefore only be held liable for the increment in damages that his failure to post an attendant during working hours, relative to posting no attendant, would cause. In the example, this amount is \$60, which is the difference between the expected damages of \$100 with no attendant posted, and the \$40 in expected damages when an attendant is posted during working hours.[19] The resulting adjustment in the injurer's costs are shown in column three of Table 5.7. Note, however, the injurer's costs are still minimized at the efficient level of care. Thus, the limit on liability created by the cause in fact requirement does not distort the injurer's incentive to meet the due standard of care. Its only effect is to lessen the injurer's savings in costs from meeting the due standard.[20]

Proximate cause. Proximate cause relates to negligence differently than cause in fact because of its forward-looking nature. Recall that, rather than looking back to determine the actual effect that a failure to take some precaution caused, it takes the point of view of the injurer prior to the occurrence of an accident and asks, what will be the likely effect of not taking that precaution? This coincides with the view taken by the economic model of accidents (the model of precaution). Thus, we can use the apparatus of that model to develop an analytical version of the reasonable foresight test for proximate cause. Although this test is applied retroactively, it constructs a counterfactual scenario that asks what the likely effect would be of some action that the victim (plaintiff) alleges the injurer (defendant) *should* have done. Specifically, it asks how much the "untaken precaution," if taken, would have reduced the likelihood of

[19] The \$60 liability is therefore computed as $(.25 - .10) \times 400 = 60$.

[20] This is a perfectly general result. See Kahan (1989).

an accident.[21] Note that this depends on the technological relationship between the set of actions that are available to the injurer prior to the accident and the resulting risk of harm to the victim.[22]

To examine this effect formally, let us define $p(x)$ to be the probability of an accident, which is a decreasing function of x, the amount the injurer spends on precaution. Now let x_0 be the level of precaution that the injurer actually took, and let $x^* > x_0$ be the level that the victim (plaintiff) alleges that the injurer *should* have taken. The difference $x^* - x_0$ is the untaken precaution, and $p(x_0) - p(x^*)$ is the amount that the injurer's failure to take precaution x^* increased the probability of an accident, as of the point in time the injurer made his care choice.[23] We can now formalize the reasonable foresight test in this context by asking whether this increased probability exceeds some hypothetical threshold level; that is, whether $p(x_0) - p(x^*) > T$ for some T.

The *Palsgraf* case provides an example of this reasoning. The court in that case found that the negligent actions of the railroad workers to push the man onto the train, although they were clearly a cause in fact of the injuries suffered by the plaintiff, were not a proximate cause because of the remoteness of the connection between the events. In fact, it is likely that $p(x_0) - p(x^*)$ was near zero in this case. As suggested above, however, had the injuries been suffered by the man that the employees actually pushed, the court may well have found that their actions *were* proximate cause because $p(x_0) - p(x^*)$ would have been substantially larger.

Even when proximate cause is found, however, the court would have to take the further step of determining whether the untaken precaution also constituted negligence. In other words, proximate cause is necessary but not sufficient for holding the injurer liable under negligence law. But notice that in applying the Hand test for negligence, the variable P, as we defined it, is equivalent to the increase in accident probability caused by the untaken precaution; that is, $P \equiv p(x_0) - p(x^*)$. Further, if we rewrite the Hand test as follows: $P > B/L$ (where, recall, B is the burden (cost) of the untaken precaution and L is the loss from the resulting accident), then it has the same form as the proposed reasonable foresight test, $P >$

[21] The concept of an untaken precaution is due to Grady (1989).

[22] See Cooter (1987).

[23] Note that $p(x_0) - p(x^*)$ is positive because $p(x)$ is a decreasing function.

T, where $T = B/L$. That is, it sets a threshold for the increase in the probability of an accident resulting from a failure to take some precaution. In this sense, the two tests are isomorphic, and therefore potentially redundant.[24]

Of course, there is no reason that the thresholds for the two tests need to coincide (i.e., no reason that T will in fact correspond to B/L). Thus, either can be the basis for absolving the injurer of liability, and both have to be satisfied for liability to be imposed. The lawyer for the defendant will therefore presumably pursue whichever is the more effective shield of liability, while the lawyer for the plaintiff will argue the opposite. As a practical matter, however, it would seem that an injurer's failure to take due care will usually raise the risk of an accident in a foreseeable way (i.e., $B/L > T$). Thus, cases in which proximate cause acts as a bar to recovery will nearly always fail the Hand test as well (as was true in the *Palsgraf* case).

A possible reason for the existence of apparently redundant tests is that the law has developed more than one way for courts to conceptualize the problem of allocating responsibility for risk in a variety of settings.[25] In some cases, it may be easier to use cost–benefit principles to decide a case, while in others it may be easier to rely on causal language. However, it is likely that these approaches will often converge on the same answer. And in any case, economic theory does not uniquely map onto legal rules. Whereas the former relies on mathematical tools to uncover fundamental concepts, the latter must be couched in ordinary language that can be described by judges and applied by juries.

Res Ipsa Loquitur

Negligence acts as a shield of liability for injurers provided that they have taken due care (i.e., have not acted negligently). The burden of proving the injurer's negligence, however, is on the victim (plaintiff), and that will often be a hard task, especially when the victim is not able to observe, or is not familiar with, the injurer's behavior leading up to the accident. This creates a potential incentive problem because it may allow injurers

[24] See Miceli (1996), who originally made this argument.

[25] See the discussion of this issue in Keeton et al. (1984, pp. 272–280).

to escape liability in some cases where they were in fact negligent. The situation is similar to the under-detection problem in criminal cases.

In situations like this, courts sometimes allow negligence to be inferred from the available evidence.[26] One vehicle for doing this is the doctrine of *res ipsa loquitur*, which means "the thing speaks for itself." Under this rule, the court interprets the occurrence of the accident itself as evidence of negligence. The idea is that the accident could not have happened, or at least would have been extremely unlikely, unless the defendant was negligent. In effect, the court shifts the burden of proof from the plaintiff to the defendant, who must prove that the accident was *not* due to his or her negligence.

An example is the case of *Escola v. Coca-Cola Bottling Co.*,[27] which involved a bottle of Coca Cola that spontaneously exploded in the hands of a waitress, causing her severe injuries. Obviously, the victim lacked the knowledge or expertise to prove that the manufacturing process was somehow defective. In holding the bottling company liable, the court therefore relied on *res ipsa loquitur* to argue that only a defective (i.e., negligently manufactured) bottle would have exploded in this way. It therefore inferred negligence from the circumstances of the accident and found for the plaintiff.

The question is whether this inference is justifiable from an economic perspective. Making use of the above notation, let us suppose that $p(x) > 0$ for any $x < x^*$ but $p(x^*) = 0$, where x^* is the due standard of care. In other words, an accident is only possible if the injurer took less than due care. In that case, the answer is clearly yes because negligence is a necessary condition for an accident (i.e., any accident necessarily involves negligence). But what about the more general situation in which $p(x) > p(x^*) > 0$; that is, where due care lowers the risk but does not completely eliminate it? In this circumstance, Hylton (2016, p. 139) argues that "*res ipsa loquitur* guides courts in a process similar to statistical inference."

To see how this works, consider the situation depicted in the game tree in Fig. 5.1. This shows the possible outcomes of a risky activity undertaken by two types of defendants: those who were negligent (chose $x < x^*$) and those who were not negligent (chose $x = x^*$). The probability of

[26] The discussion in this section is largely based on Hylton (2016, Chapter 8).

[27] 24 Cal.2d 453, 150 P.2d 436 (1944). This case is noteworthy as an important decision by which the governing rule in products liability cases transitioned from negligence to strict liability (Cooter and Ulen 1988, p. 431).

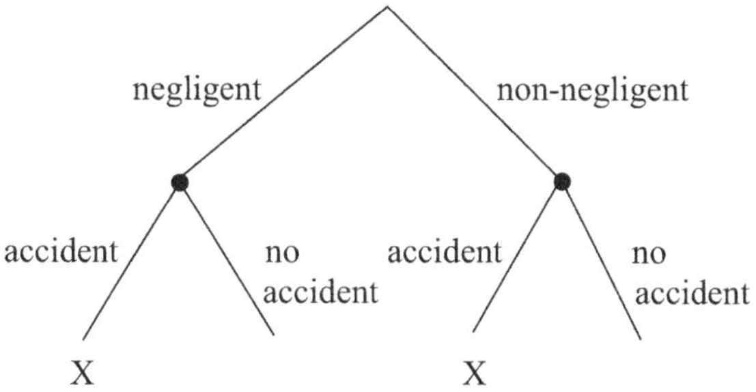

Fig. 5.1 Outcomes of a risky activity with a negligent and a non-negligent injurer

an accident is $p(x)$ for the former and $p(x^*)$ for the latter, where $p(x) > p(x^*) > 0$. Now consider the outcome in which an accident does in fact occur—that is, we end up at one of the terminal points labeled X in the figure. In one case, the defendant was negligent, and in one case it was not, but the plaintiff does not possess evidence to distinguish between the two cases.

The inference problem is whether it is reasonable for a court to interpret the occurrence of an accident as evidence of negligence, given that non-negligence lowers but does not completely eliminate the possibility of an accident. The formal problem involves computing the probability that the defendant was negligent, conditional on the observation that an accident occurred. This is done using Bayes' rule. To proceed, we need one additional bit of information—namely, the background fraction of negligent defendants among those engaged in the activity in question. Let's say that fraction is β. Then we would compute the conditional probability that the defendant was negligent, given that an accident has occurred, as follows:

$$P\left(\text{negligent}|\text{accident}\right) = \frac{\beta p(x)}{\beta p(x) + (1-\beta)p(x^*)}$$

The numerator is the fraction of negligent defendants among all defendants, multiplied by the probability of an accident in the presence of negligence, while the denominator is the overall (unconditional) probability of an accident. To illustrate, suppose $\beta = 0.5$, $p(x) = 0.3$ and $p(x^*) = 0.05$. Thus, negligence increases the chance of an accident by a factor of six. In this case, the above expression equals 0.87. Thus, given that half of all *potential* defendants are negligent, when an accident actually occurs, the court would have 87% confidence that *this particular* defendant was negligent.

Note that if $p(x^*) = 0$—that is, if due care completely eliminates the possibility of an accident—the above expression equals one. This is the special case we began with where negligence is a necessary condition for an accident. Further, as β, the fraction of negligent defendants, approaches one, this expression also approaches one, regardless of $p(x^*)$. On the other hand, as β approaches zero, the overall expression approaches zero. Generally speaking, therefore, the confidence the court can have in inferring negligence from the occurrence of an accident increases (that is, the expression gets larger) as $p(x^*)$ gets smaller (holding $p(x)$ fixed) and as β gets larger.

Note that this inference problem in effect replaces the standard Hand test for negligence with a different threshold test that sets a lower bound on the *probability* that the defendant was negligent. The minimum acceptable confidence level for actually finding negligence will depend on the court's standard of proof, which in a civil case is preponderance of the evidence, or more likely than not.

Hylton (2016, pp. 145–146) also discusses a different application of the *res ipsa loquitur* doctrine that he calls its "information-forcing" function. This reflects the idea that defendants will often have information regarding their behavior, and the shifting of the burden of proof under *res ipsa loquitur* will create an incentive for those defendants who were not negligent, and can verify that fact, to reveal this information to the court.[28] This may actually be the most important function of the doctrine. Obviously, production of this sort of information improves the ability of the court to correctly assign liability in accident cases by encouraging the disclosure of exculpatory evidence. In addition, such evidence improves the accuracy of the above inference problem by causing the value of β to rise (because non-negligent defendants reveal themselves), thereby increasing the magnitude of the conditional probability in the above expression. In other words, it incentivizes non-negligent defendants to "opt out" of the population of all defendants. This in turn makes the inference of negligence more reliable in those cases where information

[28] Chapter 8 discusses a similar information-forcing rationale for holding multiple possible injurers collectively responsible.

about the defendant's behavior cannot be easily conveyed to or verified by the court. As a result, occurrence of an accident is a clearer indication that the defendant was in fact negligent.

Contributory Negligence and Last Clear Chance

As previously noted, in many accident settings the contribution of victim behavior is as important, and in many cases more important, than injurer behavior in determining risk. In recognition of this, courts have created defenses for injurers that shift responsibility for accidental harms onto victims when the latter fail to take reasonable precautions themselves. We have already discussed one such defense, contributory negligence, which establishes a due standard of care for victims that bars recovery, even if the injurer was negligent, whenever the victim fails to meet the applicable standard of care.

When both parties are negligent, the victim's negligence is determinative, and so the injurer is absolved of liability. Some courts have framed this conclusion in terms of proximate cause, arguing that in such cases the victim's negligence was "an intervening, or insulating, cause between the defendant's negligence and the result" (Keeton et al. 1984, p. 452). Legalese aside, the assignment of full responsibility to the victim in such situations (i.e., when both parties are negligent) seems somewhat arbitrary, and indeed, dissatisfaction with that all-or-nothing feature of negligence rules has led to the adoption of comparative negligence in most states, as will be discussed below.

First, however, we discuss an interesting scenario in which contributory negligence potentially plays an important role in achieving the efficient outcome. This is when a victim observes prior negligence on the part of an injurer and chooses to engage in the risky activity anyway. Settings of this sort are referred to as sequential-care accidents, and they are worth studying in detail because they shed light on the possibility of strategic behavior by parties engaged in risky activities.

The case of *Butterfield v. Forrester*,[29] which first introduced the contributory negligence defense, is illustrative of the scenario in which the injurer acts first and does so negligently. The plaintiff in this case was riding his horse down a street when he collided with an obstruction that

[29] 11 East 60 (K. B., 1809).

had been negligently left there. A witness said that the plaintiff had the opportunity to see the obstruction, but was riding too fast to avoid it, and so fell from his horse and was injured. The court acknowledged the prior negligence of the person who left the obstruction in the street, and under ordinary negligence principles that would have made him liable for the victim's injuries. However, the court denied recovery based on the victim's contributory negligence because he failed to take reasonable steps to avoid the obstruction.

To fully grasp the relevant issues in this sort of case, consider the criteria we would like to apply for judging the actions of parties in this type of situation.[30] Obviously, the best outcome would have been for the injurer—the first mover—to be careful in the first place by not placing the obstruction in the street; and for the victim, moving second, to respond by also being careful. However, once the injurer has failed to meet the due standard of care—whether through inadvertence or accident—it next becomes desirable for the victim to take evasive actions to avoid the obstruction. In other words, once the first mover has been negligent, for whatever reason, it is efficient for subsequent parties to take "compensating precaution" to mitigate the risk that has been created. The ordinary negligence rule does not create such an obligation because the injurer's prior negligence would make him responsible for any accidents his negligence causes, regardless of any subsequent actions (or inactions) of the victim. The addition of a contributory negligence defense, however, creates a superseding obligation that requires victims who confront a dangerous situation, not of their own making, to take any reasonable steps to avoid harm. Failure to do so would therefore bar recovery for any resulting injuries.

It is worth noting that this issue did not arise in our previous discussions of bilateral accidents because we assumed there that injurers and victims were acting simultaneously, or at least in ignorance of each other's behavior. In that case, the best response of both parties was to act under the *assumption* that the other party was behaving efficiently. It is therefore the sequential nature of the decisions in the current setting that creates the problem because it enables the victim actually to observe, and possibly react to, the injurer's prior negligence. The introduction of contributory

[30] See Landes and Posner (1987, p. 76), on which this argument is based. Also see Wittman (1981).

negligence addresses this possibility by incentivizing precaution by any victim who happens upon prior negligence and has time to react.

Suppose, however, that it is the victim who moves first. Consider, for example, the case of *Davies v. Mann*,[31] which involved the owner of a donkey who tied it up by the side of the road. A wagon later drove by and collided with the donkey, killing it. The owner of the donkey therefore sought compensation for his loss based on the claim that the wagon driver was traveling at an excessive speed and so was unable to avoid the donkey. The court found both parties negligent—the donkey owner for having left the animal unattended in the street, and the wagon driver for traveling at an excessive speed. Under a contributory negligence standard, this should have barred the victim from recovering, but the court actually allowed the donkey owner to recover under the theory that the wagon driver had the "last clear chance" to avoid the accident. In the absence of such a duty, the court said, "a man might justify driving over goods left on a public highway, or even a man lying asleep there."[32] Thus, the court in effect created a catch-all duty requiring second movers—whether injurers or victims—to be careful. This represents a very sophisticated understanding by courts of the economic issues underlying this category of accidents.

There is a final point, however, which concerns the possibility of strategic behavior under a last-clear-chance standard. Grady (1988, p. 19) describes this possibility as follows:

> When someone has been negligent in the first place—one hopes, through inadvertence—the best thing left to do is to get the other party to make up for it. But there is a flip side to the coin. If the second party must compensate for errors, the first party may think about the payoff from being deliberately negligent.

This sort of strategic behavior may seem like a remote possibility—after all, why would someone knowingly put themselves in a risky situation?—but consider the following excerpt from F. Scott Fitzgerald's classic novel, *The Great Gatsby*. The narrator, Nick Carraway, is scolding Jordan Baker for her poor driving habits:

[31] 10 M&W 546, 152 Eng. Rep. 588 (1842).

[32] *Davies v. Mann*, 10 M&W 546, 152 Eng. Rep. 588 (1842).

> "You're a rotten driver," I protested. "Either you ought to be more careful or you oughtn't to drive at all."
> "I am careful."
> "No you're not."
> "Well, other people are careful," she said lightly.
> "What's that got to do with it?"
> "They'll keep out of my way," she insisted. "It takes two to make an accident."[33]

Jordan's reply represents an intuitive recognition that she can shift some of the costs of accident avoidance (i.e., of driving carefully) onto others in the knowledge (hope?) that other drivers will take evasive actions. The risk of such a presumption, of course, is that some drivers will either not have time or will otherwise fail to react, which may result in a serious accident. Still, is there any doubt that some people behave in this way?

The possibility of strategic behavior arises here from the conflict between the incentive of the first mover (whether injurer or victim) to be careful, and the incentive of the second mover to take extra care in the face of prior negligence. As we have prescribed, the latter is a desirable response to genuine mistakes or inadvertence, but the downside is the incentive it creates for intentional (strategic) negligence in the first place.

To fully grasp this, consider the sequence of events from the first mover's perspective. If the latter knows that a second mover has a legal duty to correct for prior negligence, he, the first mover, can in effect "offload" some of his costs onto others by being openly negligent, thereby eliciting a compensating reaction. In other words, a driver can be reckless knowing that the law compels other drivers to take evasive action whenever possible. Obviously, this is not a desirable transfer of costs, but the above exchange suggests that it is a real threat. Hylton (2016, p. 158) nevertheless argues that on balance, the benefit of encouraging compensating precaution outweighs the strategic risk. Ultimately, this is an empirical question. One might ask, however, if there is some way that courts could try to distinguish between cases of strategic behavior and inadvertence, and treat them differently.[34]

To that end, note that actual last-clear-chance cases can be grouped into two categories: those in which the victim is "helpless" and those in

[33] Fitzgerald (1995), p. 63.

[34] The following is based on Miceli (1997, pp. 64–65).

which the victim is merely "inattentive."[35] A helpless victim is one who is in a situation from which she cannot extricate herself, whereas a victim is inattentive if she merely fails to notice her peril. One supposes that strategic actors (like Jordan Baker) would never put themselves into a helpless situation, just in case an injurer fails to react. By contrast, inattentiveness would seem to be easier to feign while also allowing escape from a truly perilous situation.

Not surprisingly, virtually all courts allow recovery against a negligent injurer in helpless-victim cases based on the argument that failure to avoid harm here amounts to willful or wanton misconduct. An example is *New York Cent. R. Co. v. Thompson*,[36] which involved a woman who got her foot stuck in a railroad track and was hit by a train. The court allowed the woman to recover against the railroad because it found that the train spotted her predicament and had time to stop but did not.

Although most courts have also allowed recovery in inattentive-plaintiff cases, some have not.[37] Consider, for example, *Anderson v Payne*,[38] which involved a woman who was hit while walking along a road. In this case, the court denied recovery because it found that the victim "knowingly elected to walk on the forbidden side of the road and thus actively exposed herself to danger" (p. 86). This is Jordan Baker as a pedestrian, and the case for absolving her of responsibility for her negligent conduct is accordingly less compelling.

Comparative Negligence Versus All-Or-Nothing Rules

All of the liability rules we have examined so far impose the entire harm from an accident on either the injurer or the victim. We would therefore describe them as "all-or-nothing" rules. Dissatisfaction with the arbitrariness of this outcome, however, particularly when both parties failed to exercise reasonable care, has resulted in most states moving to a comparative negligence rule, which apportions liability for accidents according to "relative fault." The particular allocation of liability is computed in

[35] See Keeton et al. (1984, pp. 465–468).

[36] 21 N.E.2d 625 (1939).

[37] Keeton et al. (1984 p. 466).

[38] 54 S.E.2d 82 (1949).

different ways, depending on the "flavor" of comparative negligence that a jurisdiction adopts.[39]

While comparative negligence is appealing on fairness grounds, the question is whether it undermines the desirable incentive properties of negligence rules. To answer this question, we first consider a rule that allocates liability for accidents according to some arbitrary fractional division. Thus, the shares are determined independently of the parties' care choices. Let's call this rule "shared liability." Return to the example of a bilateral care accident in Table 5.3, where both the injurer and victim have dichotomous care choices—either care or no care. Under shared liability, they both will face one half of any damages, which in this example would be $50, regardless of their care choices.[40] Table 5.8 shows the resulting expected costs for the two parties for each of the four possible combinations of care. Using the same procedure as above, we find that the Nash equilibrium is for neither party to take care.[41] The outcome is therefore inefficient.The problem here is what Cooter (1985) has called the "paradox of compensation," which reflects the idea that in order for a party to have efficient incentives to take precaution, that party must bear the full amount of any damages from an accident. A shared-liability rule necessarily violates that requirement because neither party bears the full loss. (Any sharing rule where the shares sum to one will have the same effect.) Threshold rules avoid that problem by imposing the full damages on one of the parties while simultaneously setting a standard of behavior that the other party must meet to avoid liability. Further, when the due

Table 5.8 Equilibrium under shared liability

		Injurer's choice:	
		Care	*No care*
Victim's choice:	Care	22, 20	29.5, **17.5**
	No care	**17.5**, 27.5	**25, 25**

Note Boldfaced entries indicate optimal choices

[39] See Hylton (2016, pp. 170–172).

[40] If all of the damages are in fact incurred by the "victim," the rule would require the injurer to cover half of the victim's losses.

[41] In fact, "no care" is a dominant strategy for both parties.

standard is set at the efficient care level, the rule achieves an efficient equilibrium, regardless of whether the standard applies to the injurer or the victim. Based on this logic, it would appear that comparative negligence, in a quest for a fairer division of liability, necessarily sacrifices efficient incentives. It turns out, however, that this need not be the case. As long as liability is apportioned according to comparative *negligence* rather than some arbitrary division, efficient incentives can be restored.[42] This is true because, when the rule is specified in this way, it retains its threshold feature.

To illustrate, return to the example and note that in the case where one party takes care and the other doesn't, only the latter is negligent and so will bear all of the liability, as would be true under negligence or contributory negligence. It is only when both or neither of the parties takes care that liability is shared under comparative negligence. Let's continue to suppose liability is shared equally in either of these cases. (Recall that under the all-or-nothing rules, one party would "arbitrarily" bear all of the liability when both or neither are negligent.) The resulting costs under the various combinations are shown in Table 5.9. Using the usual procedure, we find that the unique equilibrium in this case is for both parties to take care.[43] Thus, the outcome is fully efficient. Further, in the efficient equilibrium the parties do in fact share the damages, and so the outcome is "fairer" than under ordinary negligence.

One objection to comparative negligence is that it is costlier to administer than the other rules because it requires courts to engage in a large amount of fact-finding. The reason is that most cases will not lend themselves to an easy computation of relative fault because the nature of the

Table 5.9 Equilibrium under comparative negligence

		Injurer's choice:	
		Care	*No care*
Victim's choice:	Care	**22, 20**	**12**, 35
	No care	35, **10**	25, 25

Note Boldfaced entries indicate optimal choices

42 For general proofs of this conclusion, see Shavell (1987a, b, Chapter 2) and Landes and Posner (1987, Chapter 3).

43 In this case, "care" is a dominant strategy for both parties.

care choices by the two parties will not generally be comparable. This obviously complicates the problem of determining a simple formula for sharing liability. Many critics of standard negligence rules will view these costs as worth bearing, however, in the interest of achieving a fairer (more just) apportionment of financial responsibility.

We have just seen that, as long as the computation of comparative negligence retains its threshold feature, it will create efficient bilateral incentives. The problems of compensating precaution and strategic negligence that we discussed in connection with the last-clear-chance doctrine can also be addressed under comparative negligence by suitably defining relative fault. For example, a greater degree of fault can be attributed to a negligent second mover. That party can also be seen as the "proximate cause" of the accident. This logic again reflects the idea that laws are expressed in words, while the theories are expressed in mathematical formulas, or at least mathematical concepts. The application of theory to practice therefore involves drawing a correspondence between the interpretation of the words in light of the economic problem the law in question is intended to solve.

Assumption of Risk

The assumption of risk defense is another potential shield of liability for injurers. It specifically bars recovery if the victim of an accident either explicitly or implicitly consented to the risk. In one sense, a victim can be said to have knowingly accepted the risk any time he or she engages in a potentially harmful activity. However, the assumption-of-risk defense contemplates both a greater opportunity, and a greater capacity, on the part of a potential victim for judging a risk before taking it on. Courts specifically require three conditions to be met in order to shift liability away from the injurer[44]: (i) the risk is an inherent and predictable element of the activity in question; (ii) the victim's participation in the activity is voluntary; and (iii) the victim had the opportunity to become aware of the risk. When these conditions are met, it is presumed that the victim was able to weigh the risk against the benefit of engaging in the activity and nevertheless chose to engage in it.

[44] See Hylton (2016, p. 159), who cites *Lamson v. American Axe & Tool Co.*, 58 N.E. 585 (Mass. 1900) as a case in which these conditions were met.

This situation is most often descriptive of an employment setting that involves some inherent risk,[45] though it can also arise in the context of the purchase of an inherently dangerous consumer product. In both of these contexts, the "injurer" effectively compensates victims via the market mechanism in the form of a wage or price premium. (The manner by which this occurs in the context of dangerous products is explicitly examined in the next section.)

How does this relate to an employment context in which a worker is injured as a result of negligence by a fellow worker rather than by the employer? This situation is covered by the *fellow servant rule*, which absolves the employer of liability unless the responsible worker had been negligently hired or if the workplace was itself unsafe.[46] From an economic perspective, this rule makes sense since assigning liability, in whole or in part, to the employer in such a case would dilute the incentives for workers to exercise precaution in their dealings with co-workers.

This conclusion, however, would appear to be in conflict with cases where an employer *is* held responsible for negligent behavior by its employees under the doctrine of *respondeat superior*.[47] The difference is that this extension of responsibility to the employer generally applies to cases in which the victim is someone other than an employee of the business. The rationale here is that the employer is in a position to monitor its employees' behavior, and/or discipline them after the fact for negligent actions with respect to people outside of the organization.

Existence of a Market Relationship

The analysis so far has focused on accidents between "strangers," by which we mean accidents involving parties with no prior economic relationship. This is to be distinguished from accidents in which the injurer and victim are engaged in a prior economic (market) relationship. The

[45] Keeton et al. (1984) acknowledge the overlap between contributory negligence and assumption of risk. They observe that the usual distinction is that "assumption of risk is a matter of knowledge of the danger and voluntary acquiescence in it, while contributory negligence is a matter of some fault or departure from the standard of conduct of the reasonable person…" (p. 482).

[46] See the discussion in Hylton (2016, pp. 160–163).

[47] See the further discussion of this doctrine in Chap. 8.

focus here will be on manufacturers of dangerous products which may cause harm to consumers, though it will be apparent that the analysis would apply to any market relationship (including employers and employees).[48]

Accidents caused by consumer products fall under the heading of products liability, which is a large and growing area of tort law.[49] The reason for treating these accidents separately from accidents between strangers is that they raise some important conceptual issues that bear on the question of assigning legal responsibility for harm. The key difference from the stranger scenario is not the voluntariness of the relationship per se, however, but that the market provides a mechanism by which the risk can be shifted prior to an accident.

The following analysis will be developed in the context of a competitive market setting so as to isolate the impact of the assignment of risk on product safety and consumer decision-making.[50] As a benchmark, we first consider the situation of a risk-free, or "safe" product, as depicted in panel (a) of Fig. 5.2. In the graph, demand is represented by the a downward-sloping demand curve labeled D_s, while supply, which in this case coincides with the marginal (=average) cost of production, is represented by the horizontal curve labeled *MC*. The negative slope of the demand curve can be interpreted as reflecting either a decreasing marginal valuation of the product by consumers (if people potentially buy multiple units), or as an arrangement of consumers from the highest to the lowest valuers (if people buy at most one unit). The equilibrium occurs at the point where the demand curve intersects the supply curve. The resulting price, P_s, equals the marginal cost, and the quantity purchased is Q_s, is the efficient level of production/consumption.

Now consider the situation of a risky product, which is identical to the safe product in all respects except that each unit purchased now subjects the buyer to the risk of some future harm. Let the probability of an accident per unit be p, and let the amount of harm in the event of an accident be h. Thus, the expected harm per unit is ph. The way this risk affects the market equilibrium depends on how the law assigns responsibility for any

[48] See Landes and Posner (1987, Chapter 10).

[49] However, this area of law was formerly governed by contract principles. See Epstein (1980) and Landes and Posner (1987, Chapter 10).

[50] See Landes and Posner (1987, Chapter 10). For an analysis of products liability in a non-competitive market setting, see Polinsky and Rogerson (1983).

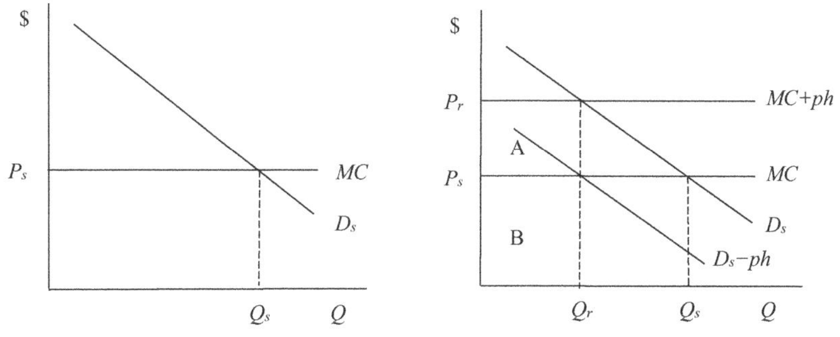

(a) Safe product

(b) Risky product

Fig. 5.2 Market equilibrium for a safe and risky product. (**a**) Safe product. (**b**) Risky product

harm that arises. In other words, it depends on the applicable liability rule. We will limit consideration (for now) to strict producer liability and no liability (also called *caveat emptor*, or buyer beware).

Consider first strict liability, under which the seller bears the full amount of harm any accident. This has the effect of shifting the supply curve up to $MC + ph$, as firms pass the expected liability costs onto consumers in the form of a higher price. The demand curve remains at D_s because consumers know that they will be fully compensated for any harms that they incur.[51] Thus, they behave as if the product were "safe." The resulting equilibrium involves a higher price (P_r), and a lower quantity (Q_r) as compared to the safe product, reflecting the impact of the risk as reflected by the price. This outcome is depicted in panel (b) of Fig. 5.2.

Although consumers do not directly bear any of the risk in this case, they consume less of the product because the higher price accurately signals the risk to them at the time of purchase. As a result, some consumers who would have purchased the product if it were safe are now discouraged from doing so by the higher price, while those who do purchase the product pay a premium that exactly reflects the per-unit risk. In this way, the market efficiently allocates output among potential

[51] This assumes, of course, that the legal system operates costlessly and that all losses are compensable.

consumers so that only those who value the product more than its total cost (production cost plus risk) purchase it.

Observe further that, although the firm is ultimately responsible for paying any damages in the event of realized harms, the "premium" that consumers pay at the time of purchase allows the firm to accumulate a pool of revenue that will exactly equal its expected future liability. This revenue is shown by area A in panel (b) of Fig. 5.2. In effect, firms are acting as insurance companies for consumers by collecting insurance premiums on top of their production costs, and then paying out claims (via the tort system) in the event of losses. In this way, strict producer liability effectively forces firms to bundle insurance with the sale of the product. The situation is identical to service contracts for durable consumer goods, except that here the coverage is mandatory (i.e., consumers cannot opt out of it).

Strict liability for product-related accidents is, however, a twentieth-century development. Prior to that, firms were not liable for harms caused by their products. It is therefore worth examining that situation in the above setting. When firms are not liable, they behave as if the product is safe. Thus, the supply curve remains at MC, reflecting only production costs. Consumers, on the other hand, reduce their demand for the product in proportion to expected risk. This causes the demand curve to shift down to $D_s - ph$, as shown in panel (b) of Fig. 5.2. The resulting equilibrium price is the same as for the safe product (P_s), but the *equilibrium output is the same as under strict liability* (Q_r). This is not a coincidence. In this case, the downward shift of the demand curve, reflecting future expected damages, deters some consumers from purchasing the product in the same way that the upward shift of the supply curve did under strict liability. And because the shifts are by the same amount (and equal to the expected harm), the reduction in output is the same. In fact, it can be shown that *any apportionment of liability* between the producer and the consumer will result in the efficient level of output, Q_r.[52]

The main difference between this scenario and that under strict producer liability is that here, firms do not act as insurers. Rather,

[52] To see this, let s be the share of producer liability and $1 - s$ the share of consumer liability. Thus, the supply curve will be given by $MC + sph$ and the demand curve will be given by $D_s - (1 - s)ph$. Equating these gives the condition for equilibrium output as $D_s = MC + ph$, which is both efficient and independent of s.

consumers have to "self-insure" by, in effect, setting aside some amount of money with each purchase to cover any future accident losses. The appropriate amount, aggregated across consumers, is again equal to area A in Fig. 5.2. For small losses, consumers will usually pay out of pocket at the time of a loss, but another option, especially for potentially large losses, is to purchase third-party insurance (if it is available) when buying a risky product. (Generic health insurance policies would presumably cover this cost.)

The discussion so far has assumed that risk is a fixed characteristic of the product, but in many cases the firm has the ability to reduce risk, for example by installing safety features. This corresponds to precaution, or care, as we have previously discussed. Because investments in safety are costly, however, there is an optimal level of safety that minimizes the sum of the cost plus the expected harm. The preceding logic can be used to show that firms will produce "optimally safe" products in this sense regardless of the assignment of liability, provided that consumers can accurately observe a product's safety level prior to purchase. The price will therefore adjust to reflect the lower risk, and consumers will willingly pay the premium.

The chief insight of the foregoing analysis is that, under the stated conditions (perfect competition and accurate perceptions of risk), the assignment of legal responsibility for product-related harms is irrelevant with respect to the extent of that risk. What's more, firms will produce optimally safe products, and consumers will make efficient purchases of those products, regardless of how liability for any harm is allocated. The stated requirements are, admittedly, rather stringent, but this is nevertheless a rather stunning conclusion. It is, in fact, a consequence of an important result in economic theory called the Coase Theorem, which will be discussed in greater length in Chap. 9. For now, it is sufficient to point out that it reflects the operation of the market mechanism which, when it functions properly, shifts risk between injurers and victims in such a way as to achieve an efficient allocation of resources regardless of how the law assigns liability. In this context, it implies that strict liability is not necessary to force injurers to internalize costs that they impose on victims. This is the key difference between accidents between market participants and accidents between strangers.

The preceding analysis also exemplifies the idea of reciprocal causation, which we have previously mentioned. For example, in the case of a risky product, is it the firm or the consumer that is the "cause" of a product-related accident? The firm offers a product for sale that it knows will cause some future harms, but consumers knowingly take on that risk when they purchase the product. Thus, both contribute to the occurrence of an accident in the but-for sense of causation. I will pursue the full implications of this reasoning in Chaps. 9 and 10.

We noted that the requirements for the preceding logic to apply are fairly restrictive. First, the injurer and victim have to be in a pre-existing market relationship, or at least have the ability to bargain before any accident occurs, and that mechanism must function well. One requirement for this is that the parties' perceptions of risk must be accurate. These conditions will often fail to hold. Consider just a few examples of how the mechanism may fail. First, as already suggested, optimal shifting of risk under a rule of no liability, or any rule that limits the producer's liability, requires the demand curve to shift by the correct amount.[53] If consumers underestimate risk, it will not shift down enough, and they will overconsume the product, while if they overestimate risk, it will shift down too much, and they will under-consume the product. Firms, on the other hand, will generally have accurate (or at least better) assessments of the riskiness of their products, and so a rule of strict liability will likely be more efficient because consumers can simply respond to the market price as a signal of risk.[54]

Working in the opposite direction is the fact that many product accidents are precipitated by misuse of the product by the consumer. This reflects the role of victim precaution, and we have seen that this works against strict producer liability because victims are not liable for their harms. One response to this problem is to couple strict producer liability with an assumption or risk or contributory negligence defense, either of which would allow firms to avoid liability if they can prove that consumers knew about the risk and consented to it, or that they misused the product (i.e., were contributorily negligent). This in turn would provide an incentive for victims to refrain from certain purchases or from misusing dangerous products.

[53] See Spence (1977), Shavell (1980), and Polinsky and Rogerson (1983).

[54] See Landes and Posner (1987, Chapter 10) for such an argument. A different bias on the part of consumers, referred to as "present bias," is due not to misperception of risk but to the placing of too little weight on future costs relative to present gains.

A final issue is that consumers may vary in their susceptibility to certain product risks. One example is food allergies, which make certain products perfectly safe for some consumers but risky for others. Another is when consumers vary in their capability for using certain risky products like chain saws, which require a certain level of strength, experience, or dexterity. These situations imply that it is optimal for firms to offer multiple varieties of the product, and for consumers to sort themselves based on their individual-specific risks or skills. For example, high-risk consumers might optimally be at the (P_r, Q_r) equilibrium in Fig. 5.2, while no-risk consumers would optimally be at the (P_s, Q_s) equilibrium. This bifurcated market outcome would not generally be possible under strict producer liability, however, because high-risk consumers, knowing they would be fully compensated for any product-related harm might choose to consume the cheaper (but unsafe) product. This might in turn induce firms to withdraw the unsafe product from the market altogether and instead sell a single variety based on the average risk across consumers. Consequently, the optimal outcome would not generally be attainable.

By contrast, the optimal outcome *would* be attainable under a rule of no liability because, with both varieties available, consumers would rationally sort themselves according to their actual risk, knowing they would have to bear any future losses. As noted, however, this outcome requires accurate perception of risk by consumers, the absence of which works in favor of strict liability. Thus, a trade-off potentially re-emerges.[55]

Capitalization and Entry: The Impact of the Land Market

Market shifting of responsibility does not always guarantee efficiency, even under ideal circumstances. To see why, return to the polluting-factory example from Chap. 2 (Table 2.1). In that example, the factory faced financial responsibility (strict liability) for its pollution, which caused it to cut its output back from the profit-maximizing level of four to the socially optimal level of three. Liability therefore internalized the externality. But suppose that the factory was in operation before any residents

[55] See Miceli and Segerson (2013) and Miceli et al. (2015). Another complication is the possibility of temptation bias, which may induce consumers to buy riskier but cheaper products because they are attracted by the lower price and underestimate the future risk. See Tsvetanov et al. (2021).

were present to experience the harm. We have seen that in this case, there is no externality because there is no victim, and so the profit-maximizing output of four coincides with the socially optimal output.

Starting from that point, imagine someone buys an adjoining parcel of land for residential use, thereby creating an external harm. If that individual has the right to sue the factory for the resulting harm under a rule of strict liability, the factory will cut its output back to three, as we have argued. Something we have not considered, however, is whether entry of the resident next to the pre-existing factory is socially desirable. When the resident has the ability to choose where to locate, this may not be true precisely because entry creates a harm that was not previously present. Thus, rather than taking the existence of both the factory and the resident as given, we need to ask whether or not entry of the latter is efficient.

To do that, we need to specify the gain to the entrant of moving to this location, not just the external harm that results. Suppose the gross value of entry to the new resident is \$5 This represents the value of this location relative to the entrant's next best option, and hence represents the most the resident would be willing to pay for the parcel in the absence of the harm from pollution. If this person is the highest bidder, entry would be efficient and would occur through the operation of the land market because the entrant would outbid any other buyers, again, absent the pollution.

When we take account of the pollution,[56] however, the net social benefit of entry is equal to the factory's profit, plus the resident's gain of \$5, minus the external cost at whatever level of output the factory chooses. Table 5.10 shows the relevant data. The final column shows that the optimal output after entry by the resident continues to be three, and this results in a net social gain of \$14, accounting for the entrants benefit and the harm. However, this is not necessarily the social optimum; we need to compare it to the net benefit *in the event that entry does not occur*. As noted, this is just the factory's profit, which is maximized at \$16. Thus, in this example it is *not* efficient for the resident to enter. The reason is that for output levels beyond 2, entry results in either no gain or a net loss, given by the difference between the entrant's benefit and the external harm.

[56] I am assuming the that value of the land to the current owner is normalized to zero.

Table 5.10 The effect of entry of a resident next to a polluting factory

Output	*Profit*	*Entrant's benefit*	*External harm*	*Net social benefit*
1	$7	$5	$2	$10
2	12	5	4	13
3	15	5	6	14
4	16	5	8	13
5	15	5	10	10

Let's now see if the market will yield this outcome. Suppose initially that the factory is strictly liable for the harm. Because the resident expects to be fully compensated for any damages, she will pay up to $5 for the land, and because we have assumed that this is the maximum anyone would offer, she will enter. The outcome is therefore inefficient. The situation is identical to a victim who fails to take care under a strict liability rule. In the current example, that manifests itself as inefficient entry.

Suppose instead that the factory is not liable for the harm. This rule reflects the common law doctrine of "coming to the nuisance," which absolves the factory of responsibility for any harm it causes to newcomers, given the factory's prior existence.[57]

In this case, because the entrant will have to bear any damages caused by pollution, she will discount her willingness to pay for the parcel by the amount of the harm; in other words, the price will "capitalize" the harm. The entrants are therefore effectively compensated for the harm up front in the form of the discounted price. As for the factory, because it is not liable for any damages, it will operate at the profit-maximizing output of four units. In this case, the resident will *not* enter because the value of this location is negative (=$5 − $8). Thus, the efficient outcome is achieved. Again, this conforms to the conclusion above that a rule of no liability induces efficient victim care, which in this case means non-entry.

It is worth noting that the irrelevance result from the previous section—the fact that the efficient outcome was achieved regardless of the liability rule—did not carry over to the current scenario, despite the shifting of liability via the price of land, because the transaction here is not between the injurer and the victim. Rather, it was between the victim and a third party—the current owner of the land. Any capitalization therefore

[57] See Wittman (1980) and Keeton et al. (1984, p. 634).

shifts liability to the seller, who must therefore sell at a discounted price. A desirable effect of this shifting is that the seller will have an incentive to seek out the buyer who is least susceptible to the factory's pollution, and hence is willing to pay the most for the land. In this way, the market will sort land users so as to minimize spillover effects between neighboring users.

What if the resident had been pre-existing and the factory sought to buy an adjoining parcel? Now the entry decision would have to be made by the factory, and so we would expect, based on the preceding logic, that strict liability would be preferred over no liability. Let us suppose that the factory is earning $10 in its current location. Absent the external harm, it would be efficient for it to enter as this would increase its profits to $16 at an output of four. Taking account of the harm, however, it would not be efficient for the factory to enter because, at the optimal output of three (given the pre-existing resident), its profit net of the harm would be $9 (=$15 − $6), which is less than its profit at its current location. In this case, a rule of strict liability induces the factory to make the efficient choice of not entering because it will expect to be held liable for the harm. Under no liability, by contrast, the factory will enter and produce four units of output. Thus, as expected, the conclusion from the previous scenario is reversed, reflecting the symmetry of the problem of internalizing harm.

The Judgment-Proof Problem and Limited Liability

The legal responsibility of individuals in financial terms is obviously limited by their ability to pay. This raises the possibility of a *judgment-proof problem*, which would dilute the incentives of wealth-constrained injurers to invest in reducing risk.[58] This will be true whenever the potential harm that an injurer can cause exceeds that party's resources for paying a liability judgment. Suppose, for example, that by taking an action costing $200 an injurer can reduce the expected harm to potential victims from $1000 to $500. This is efficient because spending $200 saves $500 in losses. If the injurer is held strictly liable for any losses, he will have an incentive to spend the $200 because it will reduce his total cost from $1000 to $700. But suppose that the injurer's available wealth is $400,

[58] See Shavell (1986) and Miceli and Segerson (2003).

which is the most he could pay in damages. Now he has no incentive to take the costly precaution because his total liability will be $400 whether he incurs the cost or not.

This example shows that the judgment-proof problem is a potentially important drawback of the tort system for internalizing harm. Several responses are possible.[59] One is to replace strict liability with a negligence standard which would allow the injurer to avoid liability altogether by incurring the $200 cost. In this case he *will* spend it because this is the maximum cost he will incur, and it is less than his ability to pay. This represents a further advantage of negligence over strict liability.

Another solution is some form of vicarious liability, which shifts responsibility to someone who does have the ability to pay a monetary judgment. For example, an employer can sometimes be held responsible for actions of its employees. In order to create incentives for care, however, the party being held responsible must have some ability to control the actions of the party actually making the care decision, for otherwise responsibility cannot be shifted to the actual decision-maker. For example, an employer can threaten to fire or otherwise discipline those workers who fail to act in careful ways. (See the further discussion of vicarious liability in the discussion of collective responsibility in Chap. 8.)

A third response to the judgment-proof problem is to require those engaged in risky activities to have liability insurance. Many states require drivers to have liability insurance as a pre-requisite for obtaining a driver's license, and mortgage lenders require borrowers to have homeowners' insurance. While insurance may protect victims from being inadequately compensated for their losses, however, it does not necessarily address the dilution of injurer incentives to avoid risk. Only if insurers are able to monitor injurers' behavior and condition premiums on that behavior will it have that effect. Modern technology has increased the ability of insurers to arrange that.

A final response is to subject injurers to the possibility of criminal punishment, on top of tort liability, for failing to meet a minimum safety standard. One of the key insights of the economic model of crime is that the use of imprisonment as a sanction should be limited to offenders

[59] See Shavell (2004, pp. 231–232).

whose wealth is inadequate to pay the optimally-deterring fine.[60] In this sense, the judgment-proof problem offers one explanation of the need for both tort and criminal liability as a response to external harms.

The judgment-proof problem also arises in the context of liability by business firms, where the liability of owners (shareholders) is limited to the value of their shares. In other words, the personal assets of shareholders generally cannot be pursued by victims. This limited liability provision of corporations represents an implicit subsidy to entrepreneurs by allowing them to externalize some of the risks associated with running a business, including liability risks. Our interest here is not in judging the merits of limited corporate liability from a policy perspective,[61] but only in assessing its impact on a firm's incentive to invest in safety.

One might expect that limited liability would impede investments in safety based on the above logic, but the situation turns out to be more complicated. In fact, it is possible to show that limited liability may actually cause firms to over-invest in safety.[62] The intuition is that, by increasing its spending on care up-front, a firm simultaneously lowers the risk of an accident and limits its future exposure to liability if one occurs. The following example illustrates the point.

Table 5.11 shows three possible levels of expenditure by a firm on care (or safety), where increases in spending reduce the risk of an accident that would cause harm of \$1000. The fourth column shows the expected damages (which equals the risk in column three multiplied by \$1000), and the final three columns show the firm's total expected cost under three different scenarios. The column labeled "No limit" is the case where the firm's assets are sufficient to pay the full damages of \$1000 plus the cost of care, no matter how much the firm spends, in the event of an accident. The boldfaced entry shows that the firm minimizes its costs by investing in a moderate level of safety. This is also the socially efficient investment because in this case, the firm internalizes the full social costs (i.e., there is no judgment-proof problem).

The next two columns show total costs when the firm's liability is limited to \$500 and \$1000, respectively. Consider first the scenario where

[60] See Becker (968) and Polinsky and Shavell (2007)

[61] See the discussion in Posner (2003, Chapter 14).

[62] See Beard (1990) and Miceli and Segerson (2003). This same possibility exists for individual injurers in those situations where care takes the form of dollar expenditures.

Table 5.11 The effect of an asset limit on firm safety decisions

Safety level	*Cost of care*	*Risk*	*Expected damages*	*Total expected cost*		
				No limit	A = *$500*	A = *$1000*
Low	$160	0.60	$600	$760	**$364**	$664
Moderate	250	0.50	500	**750**	375	625
High	360	0.40	400	760	416	**616**

Note Boldfaced entries indicate cost-minimizing choice

the firm's available assets equal $500. When it invests $160 in safety, that leaves $340 (=$500 – $160) to pay damages in the event of an accident. Thus, the firm's total expected costs are $160 + (0.60)($340) = $364. The other entries in this column are similarly computed. In this case, the firm minimizes its costs by investing in a low level of safety, which we have seen is too low from a social perspective. Thus, in this scenario, the firm's asset constraint causes it to underinvest, as conventional wisdom would predict.

Now consider the scenario where the firm's assets are limited to $1000. Following the same procedure to compute its expected costs for the various safety choices, we see that the cost-minimizing choice in this case is to invest in the highest level of safety. Thus, the firm's constraint causes it to *over-invest*. To reiterate, the reason for this paradoxical conclusion is that the firm reduces its exposure to liability in the event of an accident by spending more of its limited assets up front on safety. This lowers the risk, but in this case the firm spends too much from a social perspective because doing so provides a partial shield from liability if an accident occurs.

A final effect of limited liability on firm behavior is that it may affect organizational choices. For example, firms may strategically divest themselves of particularly risky phases of their production process by transferring them to subsidiary firms, which are themselves shielded by limited liability. To offset this incentive, a parent company may be held vicariously liable for the actions of a subsidiary or a sub-contractor.[63]

[63] See Ringleb and Wiggins (1990) and Brooks (2002).

Statutes of Limitations

A final way that tort liability is limited is by a statute of limitations for tort claims, which bars suits filed after a statutorily-set period of time for filing has elapsed. Although this dilutes incentives for by-now familiar reasons, there are two good economic arguments for imposing such a limitation. The first is that the quality of evidence deteriorates over time due to fading memories and other factors, thus resulting in a greater chance of legal error. This obviously impedes the attainment of justice, but more to the point, it mitigates the deterrent effect of legal responsibility as was shown in Chap. 3.

A second argument for a statute of limitations is that it saves on administrative costs. Even if the determination of liability is done without error, a finite statute of limitations will bar some lawsuits, thereby saving litigation costs. Further, the suits that are prevented are probably the weakest and hence more prone to error precisely because they are filed long after the accident. The optimal statute length balances these two benefits of barring suits against the dilution of incentives (Miceli 2000).

References

Beard, T. 1990. Bankruptcy and Care Choice. *Rand Journal of Economics* 21: 626–634.

Brooks, R. 2002. Liability and Organizational Choice. *Journal of Law and Economics* 45: 91–125.

Brown, J. 1973. Toward an Economic Theory of Liability. *Journal of Legal Studies* 2: 323–349.

Cooter, R. 1985. Unity in Torts, Contracts, and Property: The Model of Precaution. *California Law Review* 73: 1–51.

Cooter, R. 1987. Torts as the Union of Liberty and Efficiency: An Essay on Causation. *Chicago-Kent Law Review* 73: 1–51.

Cooter, R. and T. Ulen. *Law and Economics*. Glenview, Ill.: Scott Foresman and Co, 1988.

Epstein, R. 1973. A Theory of Strict Liability. *Journal of Legal Studies* 2: 151–204.

Epstein, R. 1980. *Modern Products Liability*. Westport, CT: Quorum Books.

Fitzgerald, F. 1995. *The Great Gatsby*. New York: Scribner Paperback Edition.

Grady, M. 1983. A New Positive Economic Theory of Negligence. *Yale Law Journal* 92: 799–829.

Grady, M. 1988. Common Law Control of Strategic Behavior: Railroad Sparks and the Farmer. *Journal of Legal Studies* 17: 15–42.

Horwitz, M. 1977. *The Transformation of American Law: 1780–1860*. Cambridge, MA: Harvard Univ. Press.

Hylton, K. 2016. *Tort Law: A Modern Perspective*. New York: Cambridge Univ. Press.

Keeton, W., D. Dobbs, R. Keeton, and D. Owen. 1984. *Prosser and Keeton on Torts*, 5th ed. St. Paul, MN: West Publishing.

Landes, W., and R. Posner. 1987. *The Economic Structure of Tort Law*. Cambridge, MA: Harvard Univ. Press.

Miceli, T. 1997. *Economics of the Law: Torts, Contracts, Property, Litigation*. New York: Oxford Univ. Press.

Miceli, T. 2012. Judicial Versus 'Natural' Selection of Legal Rules with an Application to Accident Law. *Journal of Institutional Economics* 8: 143–159.

Miceli, T. 2017. *The Economics Approach to Law*, 3rd ed. Stanford: Stanford Univ. Press.

Miceli, T., and K. Segerson. 2003. A Note on Optimal Care by Wealth-Constrained Injurers. *International Review of Law and Economics* 23: 273–284.

Miceli, T., and K. Segerson. 2013. Liability Versus Regulation for Dangerous Products When Consumers Vary in Their Susceptibility to Harm and May Misperceive Risk. *Review of Law and Economics* 9: 341–356.

Miceli, T., K. Segerson, and S. Wang. 2015. Products Liability When Consumers Vary in Their Susceptibility to Harm and May Misperceive Risk. *Contemporary Economic Policy* 33: 468–476.

Polinsky, A. M. and S. Shavell. "The Theory of Public Law Enforcement." In *Handbook of Law and Economics*, edited by A. Polinsky and S. Shavell, Vol. 1, Amsterdam: Elsevier, North-Holland, 2007.

Polinsky, A.M., and Y. Che. 1991. Decoupling Liability: Optimal Incentives for Care and Litigation. *Rand Journal of Economics* 22: 562–570.

Polinsky, A.M., and W. Rogerson. 1983. Products Liability, Consumer Misperceptions, and Market Power. *Bell Journal of Economics* 14: 581–589.

Posner, R. 1972. A Theory of Negligence. *Journal of Legal Studies* 1: 29–96.

Posner, R. 1990. *The Problems of Jurisprudence*. Cambridge, MA: Harvard Univ. Press.

Posner, R. 2003. *Economic Analysis of Law*, 6th ed. New York: Aspen Publishers.

Shavell, S. 1980. Strict Liability Versus Negligence. *Journal of Legal Studies* 9: 1–25.

Shavell, S. 1986. The Judgment Proof Problem. *International Review of Law and Economics* 6: 45–58.

Shavell, S. 1987a. A Model of Optimal Incapacitation. *American Economic Review* 77: 107–110.

Shavell, S. 1987b. *Economic Analysis of Accident Law*. Cambridge, MA: Harvard University Press.

Shavell, S. 2004. *Foundations of Economic Analysis of Law*. Cambridge, MA: Belknap Press.

Spence, A.M. 1977. Consumer Misperceptions, Product Failure, and Producer Liability. *Review of Economic Studies* 44: 561–572.

Tsvetanov, T., T. Miceli, and K. Segerson. 2021. Products Liability with Temptation Bias. *Journal of Economic Behavior and Organization* 186: 76–93.

Wittman, D. 1980. First Come, First Served: An Economic Analysis of 'Coming to the Nuisance.' *Journal of Legal Studies* 9: 557–568.

Wittman, D. 1981. Optimal Pricing Of Sequential Inputs: Last Clear Chance, Mitigation of Damages, and Related Doctrines in the Law. *Journal of Legal Studies* 10: 65–91.

CHAPTER 6

Limiting Responsibility: Criminal Doctrines

This chapter shifts gears by examining various criminal law doctrines that limit the responsibility of injurers who caused harm. The chapter also discusses some issues, like redemption, that outwardly reflect moral considerations but have criminal law implications. This continues the theme, first noted in Chapter 1, that criminal law shares a close affinity with morality in terms of their roles in controlling behavior. The discussion begins with the defining element of criminal law: intent.

Defining Intent

A criminal act consists of two parts: the act itself, called the *actus reus*, and a guilty mind, or criminal intent, called the *mens rea* (Katz 1987, p. 81). It is the latter requirement—the intent to cause harm—that distinguishes crimes from torts. There is a natural tendency to attach a higher degree of culpability for intentionally-imposed harm as compared to mere negligence, say, and a correspondingly greater inclination to hold the guilty party responsible in some way. This is reflected in most people's perception that criminal liability conveys a significant punitive element, coupled with some degree of moral judgment. The question is whether there is an economic basis for this distinction.

Although Posner (2003, p. 233) notes that the importance of intent is somewhat puzzling to economists, he goes on to propose several possible

T. J. Miceli, *Harm and Responsibility*,
https://doi.org/10.1007/978-3-031-74831-8_6

justifications for it, which ultimately turn, not on existence of intent itself (which is difficult to observe), but what it means or entails. As we saw, the Pigovian view of externalities only relies on causation; whether or not the injurer "intended" to cause harm was not relevant for purposes of internalizing it.

Like negligence or proximate cause in tort law, intent sets a threshold of behavior that divides those who are criminally responsible from those who are not. On a continuum of actions linked to the possibility of harm, intent clearly surpasses negligence and even recklessness, and hence it is seen as a basis for enhancing responsibility when the harm occurs.[1] The problem with relying on intent as the basis for assigning responsibility of any kind is that it necessitates an inquiry into the mental state of the injurer. This is in contrast to negligence, which we have seen can generally be established by observable elements of the accident. Oliver Wendell Holmes makes the case, however, that intent can often be inferred from the act itself, and so any inquiry into the offender's state of mind is unnecessary[2]:

> The test of criminality ... is the degree of danger shown by experience to attend [the act in question] ... In such cases the *mens rea*, or actual wickedness of the party, is wholly unnecessary, and all reference to the state of [the offender's] consciousness is misleading (Holmes 1881, p. 61).

In other cases, proving intent, however that is defined, will form the center of the criminal inquiry.

According to Shavell (2004, p. 552), intent means that a party desires some result and then acts in a way that increases the probability it will occur. Landes and Posner (1987, p. 150) offer the following more refined definitions:

> Undertaking an activity that the actor knows is almost certain to produce an injury within a short time but not desiring the injury to occur or benefitting from its occurrence;

[1] And even sometimes when it does not—see the discussion of failed attempts below.

[2] Posner (1988, p. 237) refers to this meaning of intent—specifically, using "the word 'intention' to describe particular actions irrespective of the actor's mental state"—as "quasi-behaviorist.".

Deliberately inflicting an injury, whether an injury that the injurer believes to be justified or one that he believes to be wrongful;
Deliberately inflicting an injury that the injurer knows is wrongful.

All three of these meet Shavell's definition. However, the first reflects "incidental" harm that arises as a possibly necessary by-product of some otherwise beneficial activity, and therefore may not meet the threshold for "criminal" intent. The second probably would meet the definition, and the third certainly would. In both of the latter two cases, the principal desire is to inflict an injury, whether or not there is some justification for doing so. Still, to say harm is caused deliberately is just another way to say it is caused intentionally and hence borders on tautology.

In an effort to develop a more objective understanding of these definitions, we can imagine a person contemplating engaging in an inherently risky activity like driving. The "baseline" is to choose not to engage in it at all, in which case there is no risk of harm. Any departure from that baseline creates a risk, the magnitude of which depends both on how often the injurer engages in the activity (e.g., how many miles he drives), and how carefully he engages in the activity (e.g., how fast he drives, or whether he drives while impaired). This is descriptive of the first definition above.

Note that the *probability* of harm is the relevant consideration here. Although that probability might be very small for each mile driven, if one drives a lot, the probability of *eventually* imposing harm can quickly become large. For example, if the probability of an accident per mile driven is 0.001, the probability that at least one accident will occur after driving 1000 miles is 0.63.[3] However, this presumably would not be a basis for imposing *criminal* responsibility. Nor would it trigger tort responsibility under a negligence standard provided that the driver satisfied the due standard of care—that is, drove carefully—during every mile. The probabilistic "inevitability" of harm in this case is the basis for intent according to definition 1, but it is almost certainly not what is meant by criminal intent.

[3] The probability of no accident per mile is $1 - .001 = .999$. Thus, the probability of no accident after 1,000 miles is $.999^{1,000} = .37$. Thus, the probability of at least one accident (assuming statistical independence of the risk of an accident for each mile driven) is $1 - .37 = .63$.

Definitions 2 and 3 are different because they involve the "deliberate" imposition of risk, which reflects the ordinary meaning of intent but does not independently define it. Landes and Posner attempt to place this on firmer ground by modeling it as a situation in which the injurer invests effort to *increase* the probability of harm in order to achieve some gain, whether that takes the form of the pleasure of actually inflicting pain, or will produce some monetary gain. This is the opposite precaution, or care, which constitutes an effort to reduce risk.

To formalize this, let us define $p(x,y)$ to be the probability of some harm occurring, which is decreasing in the injurer's efforts at precaution, x, and increasing in the injurer's effort to produce harm, y. The probability $p(0,0)$ is defined to be the risk from engaging in an activity while investing neither precaution nor any effort to increase the risk. The fact that $x = 0$ in this case might represent a failure to take due care and hence could constitute the basis for liability under negligence if an injury occurs. However, the fact that $y = 0$ implies no basis for assigning criminal responsibility because the individual did not actively seek to increase the risk. Thus, although both $x < x^*$ (the due standard of care) and $y > 0$ "increase" risk, and hence might subject the individual to tort liability under a negligence standard, only $y > 0$ would be considered "intentional" and hence a basis for criminal liability.

The distinction makes some sense from an economic perspective because investing in due care to avoid accidents ($x > 0$), and not investing in efforts to increase the risk of accidents ($y = 0$), are presumably both efficient if the goal is to minimize accident costs. Thus, the law assigns liability in ways that encourage these outcomes. Stated another way, it penalizes both $x = 0$ and $y > 0$. However, there is no obvious economic reason why this should be done by different areas of the law—i.e., tort law for $x < x^*$ and criminal law for $y > 0$.

The economic model of crime as first developed byBecker (1968) offers a different, but not incompatible, perspective on these issues. In that model, offenders can take actions aimed at yielding some benefit, but which will definitely cause some harm (as under definition 3). Thus, harm is not probabilistic. The model adopts a Pigovian approach by holding offenders strictly liable for the resulting harm (consistent with criminal law), but with the additional complication that detection of offenders is uncertain. This relates to the argument made in Chapter 3 that intent is linked to efforts to avoid detection, and so a more severe sanction is needed to deter harmful acts that are intentionally committed. In any case, however, the model *assumes* that the sanction is criminal in nature rather than explaining why it needs to be.

An early critique of the Becker model focused on the assumption that the benefits offenders receive from their harmful (criminal) acts are "counted" in social welfare. Although most of the subsequent literature has adopted this convention, the point continues to be debated.[4] The implication of counting those benefits is that some acts that deliberately increase risk are nevertheless potentially efficient in the sense of producing positive net benefits.[5] In other words, choosing $y > 0$ can sometimes be efficient. An example is exceeding the speed limit to get an injured person to the hospital or stealing food if one is starving. The economic model of crime therefore does not distinguish between "legitimate" and "illegitimate" harms, and in this sense is not really a theory of criminal law, or at least not a theory of the *content* of criminal law. (I will return to this point in Chap. 10.)

A Hand Test for Intent

The foregoing discussion concerning the ambiguity of the meaning of intent, combined with our earlier formulation of threshold tests for proximate cause and negligence, suggests that it might be useful to devise a kind of "Hand test" for criminal intent that does not necessarily rely on the offender's "state of mind." To that end, consider some conduct that a person is contemplating which promises a benefit of B, but which creates a risk of harm to someone else (i.e., involves choosing $y > 0$). Let P be the resulting probability of harm, and let L be the amount of the harm.[6] From a cost–benefit perspective, the conduct is beneficial if $B > PL$, or if the benefit exceeds the expected harm. Conversely, the conduct is not beneficial if $B < PL$. Now rewrite this condition as $P > B/L$; that is, as a threshold for the probability of harm. Note that this is an exact analog to the proposed "reasonable foresight" test for proximate cause, except that here, the purpose is to ascertain intent to impose harm.

[4] See Lewin and Trumbull (1990) and Friedman (2000, p. 230) for opposing views.

[5] Landes and Posner (1987, pp. 153–160).

[6] Based on our earlier notation, P is defined to be $p(y) - p(0)$ for some act $y > 0$, where it may not be true that $p(0) = 0$ because there may be some background risk. In any case, P is the *increase* in risk due to the injurer's conduct.

It is important to emphasize that, whether or not the threshold is met, *some harm has actually occurred*, and the purpose of the test is to determine, as a counterfactual exercise, whether the injurer should be criminally responsible for it. That involves asking what the injurer could have foreseen as the probable consequence of his decision to take an action that increased the risk of harm (setting $y > 0$). As our discussion above suggested, this is no different than failing to act reasonably to prevent a harm (choosing $x < x^*$). And, as has been emphasized, the optimal remedy would be the same in the two cases, assuming that the goal is to encourage only those acts that produce a net gain, and to deter those that would not.

The situations may not, however, be seen as morally equivalent. Specifically, many may see concerted efforts to cause harm ($y > 0$), regardless of any subsidiary benefits, as deserving of some greater degree of culpability, particularly if it entails $P = 1$. This brings us back to the distinction between intentional versus accidental harm, which divides tort law from criminal law in many people's minds.

The enhancement of punishment for "hate crimes" represents a further division within the category of intentional harms. It specifically suggests that acts motivated by hate, however that is defined, are more objectionable than "ordinary" crimes. Is that because they somehow involve a greater "intent" to cause harm to certain individuals? In terms of the above test, we might think about this in various ways.[7] One is to suggest that the offender derives more benefit from committing a hateful act and hence will devote more effort to carrying it out successfully. This implies a larger value of both B and P, which work in opposite directions regarding greater "intent" according to the above threshold test. In any case, the offender will be harder to deter, and this perhaps justifies imposing a harsher sanction, assuming that the goal is to deter the act in question.

Another perspective is that the gains obtained by certain acts are less worthy of being counted in welfare, according to the above critique of the economic model of crime. In other words, there is little or no offsetting legitimate justification for the act in question (i.e., $B = 0$), which clearly satisfies the above test for criminal responsibility. This, of course, involves a value judgment regarding what actions are and are not socially valuable,

[7] See Dharmapala and Garoupa (2004) for a formal analysis based on this logic.

a point that we have already touched on and will be expanded on in Chap. 10.

Working in the opposite direction to mitigate an injurer's legal responsibility is when some factor has combined with the injurer's conduct, either to worsen the risk or to justify the injurer's action. The defenses of necessity, duress, and self-defense fall into this category.[8] (We will discuss the defense of entrapment in a separate section below.) In all of these cases, the benefit of the act, *B*, may represent some other harm that the injurer is attempting to avoid, but which results in his having to cause a different harm for which he may be found liable. In this case, the proposed test can be interpreted as optimally balancing the competing harms, ideally by inducing the injurer, under threat of criminal responsibility, to avoid the greater harm.

A final point concerns the role of "victim precautions" in the context of intentional harms.[9] Potential victims of crime can often reduce the likelihood of their being victimized by taking preventive steps, like installing alarm systems or avoiding high crime areas. The situation is analytically identical to the bilateral-care model of precaution used above to describe accident settings, and is captured here by the fact that *P*, the risk of harm created by the injurer's conduct, is a decreasing function of actions taken by potential victims to mitigate the risk. (The amount of harm, *L*, may also be a decreasing function of victim precaution.) Recall from our analysis of optimal tort liability rules that one way to induce victims to invest in efficient precaution is to withhold compensation in the event of an accident.

As noted above, one of the chief differences between tort and criminal law is that any financial liability assessed against a criminal defendant is *not* handed over to the victim in the form of compensation. In this respect, criminal fines resemble Pigovian taxes, and so have the effect of creating efficient bilateral incentives—i.e., they both deter unreasonably harmful conduct by the injurer while simultaneously inducing efficient victim precaution by denying compensation.

Two caveats are worth noting here. First, some victim precautions may merely *divert* rather than *deter* crime.[10] That may happen, for example,

[8] See Shavell (2004, pp. 565–566).

[9] See the discussion in Hylton (1996).

[10] See Shavell (1991).

if some victims invest in precautions while others don't, and offenders, to the extent they can observe such precautions, opt for those potential victims who have not invested. In this case, victims will tend to overinvest in precaution because it simply results in one harm being substituted for another. In other words, there is no net reduction in crime, just displacement. The flip side of this is when precaution by one victim creates spillover benefits for other nearby victims. For example, a business that hires a private security firm will confer benefits on nearby owners. In this case, victims will underinvest because they ignore the full benefits of their investment. Optimal precaution in either of these cases would require coordinated efforts by victims; homeowners' associations and neighborhood watch groups represent such solutions.

Second, an objection to this line of argument is that victim precaution would not be necessary if injurers simply refrained from committing harmful acts in the first place (i.e., chose $y = 0$). Thus, victim precautions are only necessary because of imperfect law enforcement, and in effect represent a form of private enforcement.

Intentional Torts and Criminal Law

The boundary between torts and crimes most clearly resides in the category of harmful acts labeled "intentional torts." Indeed, many acts involving the intentional infliction of harm or the theft of property would qualify as both a tort and a crime and hence would be subject to sanctions available under both areas of law, though, as noted, the sanctions would be administered very differently. As we have emphasized, however, the economic approach to law, relying as it does primarily on the concept of optimal deterrence, would not recognize the need for these parallel forms of legal responsibility (except to the extent that one corrects for deficiencies in the other). For example, we have noted that criminal liability can be justified as correcting for inadequate private enforcement under tort law, or the inability of defendants to pay the requisite level of damages. And tort law provides for compensation of victims, which criminal law does not.

The hybrid nature of intentional torts is exemplified by the fact that punitive damages are often awarded in these cases. As the name suggests, punitive damages, in addition to compensating victims, are aimed at punishing a defendant for harmful conduct that exhibits "conscious and deliberate disregard of the interests of others," and is "willful or wanton"

(Keeton et al. 1984, p. 10). The objective, therefore, apparently is to express outrage at the conduct in question, which is further along the continuum than mere negligence but perhaps not as far along as criminal intent. The point is that there is clearly a moral dimension to the sanction, reflecting an objective beyond the mere "pricing" of harm.

Cooter has argued that preventing harmful acts rather than pricing them is economically justifiable when lawmakers can more easily determine the acceptable level of behavior than they can assess the costs of departing from it (Cooter 1984). This will be especially true when the acceptable level is zero—that is, when the act is definitely undesirable—but also when monetary valuation is difficult.[11] In these situations, sanctions are appropriately raised in order to punish violations.

The problem this approach to lawmaking creates for would-be violators, however, is that they have to learn what the acceptable level of behavior is. Parker (1993) argues that the requirement of *mens rea* for finding criminal behavior is actually a response to this informational problem facing offenders. He specifically argues that "…the *mens rea* doctrine, in its general form, performs the economic function of minimizing actors' investment in self-characterizing information," where, self-characterizing information means "awareness of the 'true' or objective nature of [an offender's] own conduct and the surrounding factual circumstances made relevant by the legal definition of the offense" (Parker 1993, pp. 745–746). The requirement of *mens rea* does this by absolving offenders of criminal responsibility for those violations about which they could not reasonably have known. In this sense, it is something like an "ignorance of the law" defense, which we will revisit below.

Note that this interpretation of the *mens rea* standard differs from the above "Hand test" for intent, which was based on the desirability of the act itself. Recall that under that approach, courts would conduct a counterfactual calculation to determine if the conduct in question satisfied a cost–benefit test. Under the current proposal, by contrast, courts would assume that the conduct is undesirable and would ask whether or not the offender should have known that fact. The tests are therefore aimed at ascertaining what an offender believed at the time of the violation, though they focus on different dimensions of the conduct. The purpose of both, however, is to remove the determination of intent from an assessment of

[11] I will return to this point in Chap. 10.

the offender's actual state of mind at the time and replace it with one that depends on what he should have known or believed.

Procedural Safeguards for Criminal Defendants

Criminal defendants are accorded the presumption of innocence, which the prosecutor must overcome in order to gain a conviction. This is the counterpart of placing the burden of proof on plaintiffs in tort (civil) cases, as discussed in Chap. 3. Criminal defendants, however, enjoy certain procedural safeguards that are not generally available to civil defendants. This reflects two fundamental differences between criminal and civil liability. The first is that the state, as the prosecutor in criminal cases, has disproportionate power in relation to most criminal defendants in terms of resources for pursuing a conviction. The second is that criminal conviction carries with it both the possibility of deprivation of freedom and a stigma that is not normally associated with civil liability, both of which make wrongful conviction costlier than wrongful acquittal in most people's eyes. Recall that we previously attributed the higher standard of proof in criminal cases to these same factors. Here, we discuss two additional safeguards for criminal defendants that are also unavailable to civil defendants.

The first is the Fifth Amendment right against self-incrimination, which means that a defendant cannot be compelled to testify at trial. In addition, the court is not allowed to draw an inference of guilt from a defendant's refusal to testify. On its face, this right would seem to be a shield mainly for guilty defendants. However, given that swearing an oath to tell the truth is "cheap talk," a truly guilty defendant who is compelled to testify would most likely lie, and this tendency would make testimony by any defendant, innocent or guilty, suspect. On the other hand, giving defendants the option of testifying or not may serve a sorting function that might actually make claims of innocence more believable.[12] It will be apparent that this logic resembles the "information-forcing" function that we attributed to the tort doctrine of *res ipsa loquitur*.

To see how this works, suppose θ is the fraction of truly guilty individuals among all defendants. Thus, $1 - \theta$ is the fraction of innocent

[12] This argument is based on Seidemann and Stein (2000).

defendants. Also, suppose that, given the option, i is the fraction of innocent defendants who would choose to testify, and g is the fraction of guilty defendants who would choose to testify, where it seems reasonable to assume that $i > g$. This situation is depicted schematically by the game tree in Fig. 6.1. The question of interest is whether the observation that a defendant chooses *not* to testify conveys some information about that defendant's guilt or innocence. In other words, what inference (if any) can be drawn about the defendant's type if a case ends up at one of the terminal points labeled by X?

We can answer that question by using Bayes' Rule to compute the following conditional probability:

$$P(\text{guilty}|\text{not testify}) = \frac{\theta(1-g)}{\theta(1-g) + (1-\theta)(1-i)}$$

At one extreme, $i = 1$ and $g = 0$; that is, only innocent defendants choose to testify. In that case, $P = 1$. Thus, the behavior of defendants is perfectly informative—choosing not to testify indicates certain guilt. At the other extreme, $i = g$; that is, both types testify with the same frequency. In that case, $P = \theta$, which is the underlying probability of guilt. Thus, nothing can be inferred from defendants' behavior. In the intermediate case where $i > g > 0$, as we have conjectured would be true under a rule that makes testifying optional, $P > \theta$. For example, if $\theta = 0.75$, $i = 0.6$ and $g = 0.3$, we would compute $P = 0.84$. Thus, some information is conveyed by a defendant's decision not to testify. It follows that the rule against self-incrimination actually works to the advantage of innocent defendants

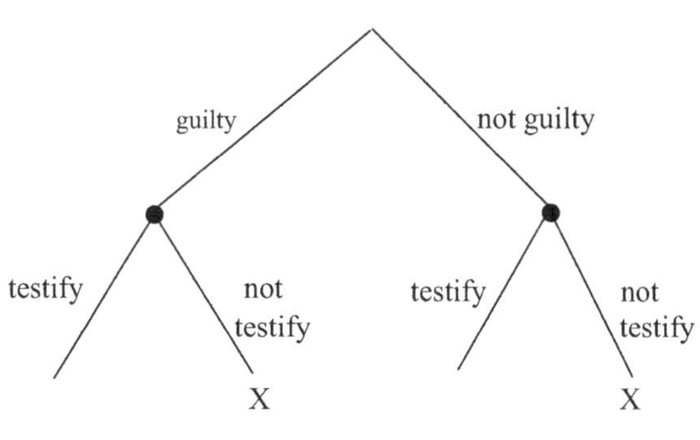

Fig. 6.1 Decision not to testify by innocent and guilty defendants

under the conditions we have assumed by making their protestations of innocence more believable.

The second safeguard of defendants in criminal cases is the Fourth Amendment prohibition of unreasonable searches and seizures in evidence gathering.[13] The use of a reasonableness standard here allows some but not all searches in recognition of the offsetting benefits and costs involved in efforts to solve a crime. To see this, we can again construct a "Hand test" for reasonable search.

The cost of search, call it C, represents the invasion of privacy, which would be especially high for truly innocent suspects given the cloud of suspicion that inevitably hangs over anyone who is the target of a criminal investigation. Offsetting this is the expected value of the search, which equals the probability that something of probative value is discovered (i.e., something which would be necessary for obtaining a conviction), P, multiplied by the value of obtaining a conviction, V. This latter value consists of the following benefits: the deterrent effect on future would-be offenders, the benefit of incapacitating dangerous offenders (in the case of imprisonment), and the benefit of justly punishing wrongdoers. According to the usual approach, the search is reasonable if $C < PV$. This condition suggests that more intrusive searches (those involving a higher C) are justified only when the crime is more serious (V is larger), or the evidence is more important (P is larger), or both. It is not clear, however, that courts actually take account of this trade-off. Consider, for example, the two ways this rule is typically enforced.

The first is the requirement of a warrant for conducting a search, which involves demonstrating to a judge that there is probable cause that the proposed target of the search committed a crime or is in the process of committing a crime. This requirement is pre-emptive and focuses primarily on ensuring that P is large enough to justify the search. The proposed test would therefore disallow those searches for which $P < C/V$. The other main enforcement mechanism is the exclusionary rule, which disallows the use of evidence that was "illegally" seized. This rule seems to center on C, the cost of the search, and would disallow evidence obtained by searches for which $C > PV$.

[13] This discussion is based on Posner (2003, Chapter 29).

In theory, therefore, the two approaches are equivalent ways of enforcing the threshold requirement for search.[14] In combination, they would deter searches in which either P is too low or C is too high on cost–benefit grounds. On the other hand, the tests may systematically prevent those searches for which the benefit of the evidence, captured by V, is the highest. For example, even if C is large and P is small, it may well be true that $C < PV$ if V is very large. Thus, focusing only on C and P will possibly disallow some valuable searches.

A different proposal for enforcing the exclusionary rule would allow victims of supposedly unreasonable searches to file a tort suit for damages.[15] Advocates of this approach argue that it would do a better job of balancing the benefits and costs because the police would face liability for the cost of the search (C), which they would presumably weigh against the expected benefit (PV). The problem with this approach, however, is that juries might be reluctant to award damages to "victims" after the fact, even if the search was unreasonable in an ex ante sense (i.e., if $C > PV$), if the search in fact turned up evidence that the individual had committed a crime. In other words, they might believe that the search must have been reasonable because it was productive. Anticipating this, the police might be emboldened to take "shots in the dark" because they would not expect to face the full cost of their actions.

Failed Attempts

Should attempts to impose harm that ultimately fail be punished as severely as those that succeed? (One might ask if they should be punished at all, given that the *actus reus* is technically absent.) From a deterrence perspective, Shavell (2004, pp. 556–559) argues that the answer depends on the reason for the failure. He distinguishes four categories[16]: (1) attempts that failed to produce the intended harm; (2) attempts that the offender chose to abandon before completion (i.e., before the harm occurred); (3) attempts that were interrupted before completion; and (4) impossible attempts.

[14] This is similar to our earlier demonstration that reasonable care can be enforced by a negligence standard or by a proximate-cause standard. For a different interpretation of the economic function of the exclusionary rule, see Friehe and Miceli (2018).

[15] Posner (2003, p. 713).

[16] Also see Shavell (1990).

To analyze these cases, we will employ the Hand test for intent proposed above. Recall that B is the offender's expected benefit from the contemplated act, P is the probability that it will cause harm, and L is the harm that would materialize if the attempt succeeds. It is therefore efficient for the offender to commit the act if $B > PL$.

Consider first acts that were completed but which failed to result in harm. Let s be the legal sanction for such acts (measured in dollars), which, because the harm did not materialize, represents liability for the *act* rather than for the harm per se. Also, assume that the offender's act is detected with certainty. The offender will therefore commit the act if $B > s$. This will coincide with the condition for efficiently undertaking the act if $s = PL$, which says that liability should be discounted by the probability of harm actually occurring. In other words, $s < L$ given $P < 1$. Thus, for the case of completed but failed attempts, liability should be positive but less than the actual harm that would have occurred. In other words, the sanction should be proportional to the (ex ante) probability of success.

Consider next abandoned attempts. This case involves offenders who have second thoughts and choose not the carry out the contemplated act, thereby avoiding the harm.[17] Suppose, however, the offender receives a fraction $q \geq 0$ of the gain B before suspending the act. This could reflect the "pleasure" of planning to impose the harm, even if the plan is not carried out. The focus here will be on the offender's decision to suspend the act once he has initiated it. For purposes of this case, we will assume that harm ensues with certainty if the act is completed (i.e., that $P = 1$). Thus, suspension is the only way the harm will be avoided once an act is initiated. It is therefore desirable to structure penalties so that offenders have an incentive to reconsider their actions after initiating them. Figure 6.2 depicts the situation schematically, beginning with the initiation of the act. The returns to the offender and society, respectively, are listed at the terminal points of the decision tree.

Once initiated, it is efficient for the offender to suspend the act if $qB > B - L$, or if $L > (1 - q)B$. In other words, suspension is efficient if the savings in expected harm exceed the forgone additional benefit. Note that this will always be true of acts that should never have been initiated in the first place (those for which $B < L$), and will be true for efficiently initiated acts (those for which $B > L$) if q is large enough. In both of

[17] In this sense, suspending the act is like mitigating the harm in sequential torts. See Shavell (1985).

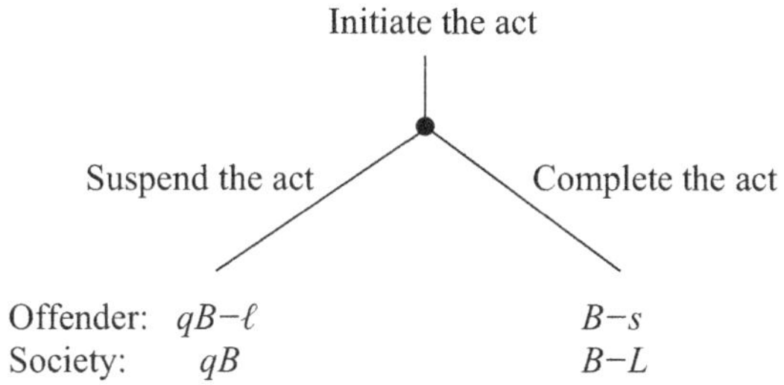

Fig. 6.2 Decision of whether or not to complete a criminal attempt

these cases, the saved harm at the point where suspension is possible exceeds any incremental benefits that would arise from completing the act. Crucially, at the point of suspension the already-realized portion of the benefit, qB, is sunk and so should have no effect on the decision of whether or not the offender should go forward with the act.

Consider now the offender's actual incentives, which depend on the legal sanctions. Let s be the sanction for a completed act and ℓ the sanction for an aborted act, where we assume both are discovered with certainty. If the offender initiates the act and carries it to completion, his expected return is $B - s$, whereas if he suspends the act, his return is $qB - \ell$. The offender will therefore suspend the act if $qB - \ell > B - s$, or if $s - \ell > (1 - q)B$. This will coincide with the above criterion for efficient suspension of the act if $s - \ell = L$. Thus, the *difference* in liability for acts that are completed and acts that are suspended should equal the avoided harm. Now, if offenders face full liability for completed acts—that is, $s = L$—it follows that $\ell = 0$. Thus, injurers who voluntarily abandon harmful acts before they cause any harm *should face no liability*. Again, the fact that the offender enjoyed some benefit from planning the act, but which resulted in no harm, is immaterial. Note that the preceding discussion captures the idea of marginal deterrence as was discussed in Chapter (and will be revisit in the discussion of redemption below.)

The third category of uncompleted attempts comprises interrupted offenses, which are attempts that are discovered before they have succeeded in causing harm, for example, if an offender is discovered "in the act." The situation is similar to failed attempts, for in both cases the harm was averted by events outside of the offender's control rather than by a conscious decision on the offender's part. Sanctioning such acts is therefore justifiable,[18] though its severity may be lessened relative to successful attempts in proportion to the probability that an interruption will occur. Thus, acts that are interrupted earlier, and hence would have a lower probability of ultimate success, would properly be punished less severely.[19]

The final category of failed attempts consists of those acts whose success is "impossible." Two notions of impossibility are distinguishable here.[20] The first concerns acts that could not possibly result in harm, such as the casting of a magic spell on the intended victim.[21] Note that this is in fact a special case of the first scenario above (failed attempts) in which the probability of harm equals zero, and so the appropriate sanction is zero. It is important to distinguish this from the case of "irrational" offenders—i.e., those who are mentally impaired—which is also a situation in which deterrence is not a relevant consideration. The difference is that irrational offenders may take actions that threaten actual harm. Thus, although an insanity defense may limit certain sanctions, some alternative approach that involves incapacitation, such as detention coupled with medical or psychiatric treatment, may be necessary to control the risk of actual harm in such cases.

The second type of impossibility is when the harm is possible but some contingency, unbeknownst to the offender, interferes with the latter's intended objective, rendering it harmless.[22] For example, in the Sherlock Holmes story *The Empty House*, Holmes's nemesis, Colonel Sebastian Moran, believes he has shot Holmes through an open window of his apartment when in fact he has shot a wax dummy that Holmes had placed there as a decoy. The act could therefore not have been harmful based on

[18] For example, Holmes (1881, p. 59) says that "An act which does not fully accomplish the prohibited result may be made wrongful by evidence that but for some interference it would have been followed by other acts coordinated with it to produce the result.".

[19] Shavell (2004, p. 558). In Chapter 8, we consider attempts that are interrupted as a result of preventive law enforcement efforts.

[20] See Shavell (2004, p.559) and Katz (1987, Chapter 6).

[21] I am assuming that the victim is unaware of the act. If he or she is aware, then some harm can in fact materialize if the victim believes in the efficacy of the act.

[22] The distinction between these two cases therefore depends on the common understanding of what is "possible." For example, the witch trials of the seventeenth century were based on the nearly universal belief that witchcraft *was* capable of inflicting harm on others. Thus, the practice of witchcraft, though it did not actually cause any harm, was treated as if it were harmful.

the facts *as they actually unfolded*, but it was nevertheless a criminal act in the sense that Moran intended harm and would have caused it but for the fact that Holmes anticipated the plan and took intervening steps to prevent it. Thus, there is an actual risk of harm because it cannot be anticipated that an intervening cause will arise to prevent the intended harm, and so offenders should not be able to rely on them as a defense when they do arise. In this respect, the situation is similar to interrupted attempts. Thus, some positive sanction, possibly discounted to reflect the probability of actual harm, will generally be necessary to achieve optimal deterrence.

Entrapment

Another justification for possibly mitigating a person's responsibility for committing a criminal act is entrapment. This defense reflects the idea that, although the offender actually committed the illegal act, he would not have done so, or would not have been able to do so, but for the enticement of enforcers. From a deterrence perspective, there is no benefit from punishing someone who had no intent to cause harm. Additionally, non-prosecution of offenders who were enticed into committing the act will deter enforcers from such wasteful spending of resources on entrapment activities that have no deterrence benefits (Shavell 2004, pp. 564–565).

But are these expenditures really wasteful? This hinges on the question of whether or not someone would have committed an offense but for the inducement of enforcers, which ultimately goes back to intent. Would the offender have committed the crime if a genuine (rather than a staged) opportunity had presented itself? If so, then the enticement may have served the useful purpose of diverting the offender into committing a harmless act rather than a harmful one—clearly a socially desirable outcome. In this sense, the situation is like an interrupted attempt, which we saw above does not generally excuse responsibility. But what if the staged opportunity were made so much more attractive than a genuine opportunity that the offender was induced to commit the act when he would not have done so otherwise? This seems like a more compelling justification for the defense.

In order to properly evaluate the entrapment defense as a basis for mitigating an offender's criminal responsibility, we must first examine criminal

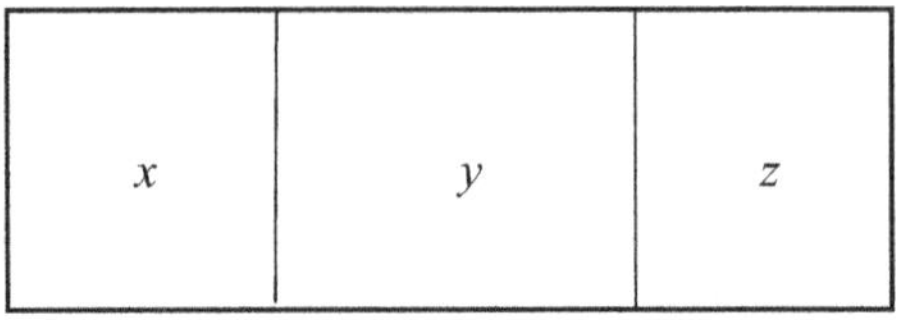

Fig. 6.3 Potential criminal opportunities ($x + y + z$), genuine opportunities (y), and stings (z)

solicitation as a law enforcement strategy.[23] Many crimes require would-be offenders to undertake a sequence of actions. They first search for a criminal opportunity, and if they find one, they decide whether or not to commit the act. For example, a potential purchaser of illegal drugs seeks a dealer, and having located one, decides whether or not to make a purchase. In this context, enforcers can create what appear to be opportunities by having undercover cops pose as dealers. This will do two things: it will increase the probability that a would-be buyer will locate an opportunity (because there are now more of them out there), but it will also increase the probability that the offender will be enticed into committing a harmless act. Figure 6.3 depicts the situation schematically.

In the figure, the area $x + y$ represents the set of potential criminal opportunities (e.g., locations where actual drug dealers might be found), and y is the set of actual opportunities (e.g., locations where a dealer is actually found at a given time). Thus, over a set time period, a would-be offender will locate an actual opportunity a fraction $y/(x + y)$ of the time. Now suppose that the police create z new opportunities ("stings"), making the total number of potential opportunities $x + y + z$. A person seeking an opportunity will now be successful a fraction $(y + z)/(x + y + z)$ of the time, which is higher than without the police stings. For example, if $x = 3$, $y = 5$, and $z = 2$, then without stings, the would-be offender will locate a "genuine" opportunity 62.5% percent of the time (5/8), but with the stings he will locate one 70% of the time (7/10). Thus, the offender's success rate rises.

The benefit of stings, however, is twofold: the first is the saved harm from diverting some offenders into harmless acts (the *diversion effect*), and the second is deterring some from committing any crimes at all (the

[23] This discussion is based on Miceli (2007). Also see Stevenson (2004) and Hay (2005).

deterrence effect). Consider first the diversion effect.[24] For sake of this discussion, let's suppose that an offender commits the criminal act whenever he locates an opportunity (either a genuine one or a sting). In the absence of stings, the would-be offender will therefore commit a harmful act 62.5% of the time that he searches (5/8), whereas in the presence of stings, he will commit a harmful act only 50% of the time that he searches (5/10). Thus, although the chances of an offender locating an opportunity rise with stings, the average level of harm declines, all else equal.

This conclusion assumes that offenders engage in the same amount of search for crimes with and without stings, but this might not be the case. Because stings make it more likely that an offender will be caught, the offender may be deterred from searching. Suppose, for example, that offenders who locate actual opportunities and commit them (the set y) are caught 50% of the time, whereas those who locate a sting (the set z) are caught with certainty. Thus, in the absence of stings, the probability of being caught conditional on searching for an opportunity is 0.31, which is the probability of locating an opportunity (=5/8 = 0.625) times the probability of being caught (0.50). However, in the presence of stings that probability of being caught is now 0.45, which equals the probability of locating a genuine opportunity (=5/10 = 0.50) times 0.50, plus the probability of locating a sting (=2/10 = 0.20) times one. Thus, the presence of stings raises the probability of getting caught for each search, which will deter some offenders.

This conclusion assumes that the sanction is the same for actual crimes and stings, which naturally raises the question of whether there is any justification for punishing those caught in a sting more leniently. Recall that the strict Pigovian approach to optimal deterrence prescribes that responsibility for harm should be imposed on those who caused it. The Becker model of crime adds the provision that the optimal sanction should be adjusted to account for the probability of avoiding detection—so-called probability scaling. Thus, suppose that genuine crimes impose harm of h, but because offenders are only caught half of the time, the sanction should be $h/0.5 = 2h$. Applying this same logic to stings,

[24] Note that this is different from the diversion of potential offenders to unprotected victims, as discussed above, which was substitution of one harm for another and hence was not an efficient form of investment. Here, by contrast, the diversion is to a harmless option and hence is socially desirable.

however, implies that the sanction should be zero because they impose no harm.

This simple approach, however, ignores two benefits of sting operations. The first is due to the practical impossibility of employing probability scaling because of the various limits on permissible sanctions. In that case, there *would be* a deterrence benefit from punishing those caught in a sting because the threat of this punishment would affect overall search behavior and therefore would help to correct for the under-deterrence of threatened sanctions for actual crimes. As already shown, stings raise the probability of detection of search, and so by adding some amount of punishment to those caught in a sting, the expected sanction from commencing search for criminal opportunities can theoretically be raised to a level that reflects the expected harm caused by actual crimes. In a sense, punishment for stings can serve a similar purpose as probability scaling. Although responsibility for the harm from those committing actual crimes is thereby partially shifted to those caught in stings, the fact that the latter had criminal intent would seem to justify this, even though they caused no actual harm. (In this sense, they are not innocent.)

The situation is similar (though not identical) to the case of impossible attempts that are interrupted by an intervening cause, as discussed above. A sting is an intervening cause in the sense that it renders the imposition of actual harm impossible. The current situation is a bit different because here, getting caught in a sting is only one possibility from commencing a search, and the *expected* sanction—reflecting the possible sanctions for genuine crimes and stings—induces would-be offenders to correctly internalize the actual harm across all possible criminal opportunities. In both cases, however, there is criminal intent.

A second economic benefit of stings is that enforcers can shift some resources from standard enforcement activities (i.e., actually searching for criminals) to stings, where apprehension is certain. In other words, the two activities are substitutes, and so ideally z should be raised and p lowered to the point where the marginal deterrence benefits of the two activities are equal.

We have assumed so far that all offenders who locate a criminal opportunity, whether in the form of a genuine one or a sting, actually commit the act, but this may not be true. If, for example, enforcers make a sting more attractive than an actual crime, they may entice an offender into committing an act that he would not have otherwise committed. This in fact appears to be the paradigmatic situation for which the entrapment defense was created, because the actions of the police are explicitly aimed at facilitating the commission of crimes rather than taking steps to divert or deter them. The defendant can therefore legitimately argue that he would not have committed the act but for the extra enticement offered by the enforcer.

Further, there does not seem to be good reason to engage in this type of enticement from a deterrence perspective. Still, it would be a difficult defense to mount because, although evidence of the "extra" benefit offered by the police may be available, the counterfactual claim that the offender would not have committed the act *but for this extra benefit* will generally be difficult to prove. In other words, was the enticement a decisive factor in triggering the act? Nevertheless, one suspects that courts would treat evidence of *any* enhanced benefits as a form of misconduct by the police, and that would be a sufficient basis for exonerating the defendant, or at least for mitigating his culpability.

Mistaken Beliefs

Another defense for criminal defendants is a claim that they held mistaken beliefs about some fact that contributed to their decisions to commit criminal acts. An interesting example of this is the famous English case of the Hammersmith Ghost (Clarke 2013, pp. 168–170). Beginning in 1803, residents of the Hammersmith section of London claimed to have been haunted by a roving spirit clad in a white shroud. One evening in early 1804, a police officer shot and killed what he thought was the ghost but in fact turned out to be a man wearing a white waistcoat and apron who was strolling home from work. The shooter was convicted of murder and sentenced to death, but the sentence was later commuted to 1 year of hard labor. Notably, the defendant's claim of self-defense, based on his mistaken belief, was denied because the victim had posed no actual threat to the defendant. The issue about mistake as a defense, however, continued to be debated in English law, and was only fully resolved in 1984 when a court ruled that if the defendant genuinely held a certain belief, even if the jury found it to be an unreasonable one, he was entitled to assert it as a basis for self-defense.[25]

As we have previously noted, the principal economic question is whether imposing criminal responsibility in a given case furthers the objective of deterrence, and that depends on what a defendant knows or believes at the time he or she commits the act in question. Thus, a person who commits a harmful act under a genuinely held but mistaken belief that it would not cause any harm, or in an effort to defend himself against an act that he believes would be harmful to him, should not face punishment on deterrence grounds (Shavell 2004, p. 563). As usual, however, the problem is that what a person actually knew or believed at the time of the harmful act is not observable and hence can be misrepresented to the defendant's advantage after the fact. This is why we have argued that the law generally substitutes "reasonable" beliefs—what a defendant *should have known*—for actual beliefs. For that reason, the court's eventual holding in mistaken-belief cases—that what the defendant *in fact* believed is the relevant factor, notwithstanding its unreasonableness—seems contrary to what economic theory would prescribe.

Katz (1987, p. 174) has argued that "[m]istakes wouldn't matter if there were no *mens rea* requirement" because it is the requirement to prove intent to harm that necessitates an inquiry into the defendant's state of mind in such cases. This observation is consistent with the perspective that deterrence does not require proof of intent, only causation. The threat of legal responsibility can equally discourage acts intended to inflict harm (called crimes), and to encourage efforts to avoid accidental harm (called torts).

It is true, however, that mistaken beliefs can frustrate the ability of the law to achieve deterrence in either context. For example, driving at an excessive speed in the mistaken belief that a road is not icy is no different than shooting at a person dressed in white in the mistaken belief that he is a ghost. In either case, a defendant can claim to have been mistaken about the actual circumstances, thus presenting the same legal challenge regarding assignment of responsibility. The question of whether

[25] See *R v Williams (Gladstone)*,78 Ct.App.R. 276 (1984). The court specifically said that "The reasonableness or unreasonableness of the defendant's belief is material to the question of whether the belief was held by the defendant... If the belief was in fact held, its unreasonableness, so far as guilt or innocence is concerned, ... is irrelevant".

the act was intended to cause harm is beside the point. For this reason, Holmes (1881, p. 48) argued for the principle that "[a] harmful act is only excused on the ground that the party neither did foresee, nor with proper care could have foreseen the harm." As we noted in our discussion of negligence law, the use of a reasonableness standard obviates the need to inquire into the defendant's actual understanding at the time he acted, while at the same time creating an incentive for potential injurers to take reasonable steps to learn about risks or consequences before acting. This logic applies equally to those acts labeled as torts and as crimes.

Ignorance of the Law

Closely related to a defense of mistaken beliefs is a claim of ignorance of the law. Although it is conventional wisdom that ignorance is not an excuse for committing a violation, that is not always true, nor is it necessarily a good rule. Laws are often complicated or obscure, and learning about all of the ways in which one can violate them would be a costly undertaking. Purely on cost grounds, therefore, it will sometimes be cheaper to allow violators to escape responsibility, at least for a first offense, because the harm from the illegal act is less than the cost of punishing the offender plus the effort that would have been required to learn about its illegality (Shavell 2004, pp. 562–563).

This excuse, however, is obviously not applicable to someone who continues to commit violations, for that person is on notice of the consequences of committing the act in question. And even for first-time offenders, claiming ignorance is like proving a negative—it is not generally a demonstrable fact. It is, consequently, a defense that is easily raised and difficult to refute, which is likely the reason for its general inapplicability. As Holmes (1881, p. 41) observed, "It is no doubt true that there are many cases in which the criminal could not have known that he was breaking the law, but to admit that excuse at all would be to encourage ignorance where the law-maker has determined to make men know and obey." And yet, the law routinely does grant leniency as a matter of course to first-time offenders, thereby embodying, if only implicitly, a kind of ignorance defense. This is reflected in the pervasiveness of penalty schemes that prescribe escalating punishments for repeat offenders.

The economic model of crime, however, has had a particularly difficult time in explaining these escalating structures. Indeed, according to the Pigovian view of punishment, penalties should be set equal to the harm from a forbidden act, reflecting the idea of "punishment as price." In this view, the characteristics of offenders, including their offense histories, are not a relevant consideration. The logic is no different from that which would apply to repeat purchasers of a consumer product (Posner 2003, p. 227). The fact that the offender (consumer) repeats the act should not cause the sanction (price) to increase, provided that the harm from the act (cost of the product) remains the same. Obviously, if repeat offenders commit more harmful acts, or are more likely to evade detection because they have become more experienced, that *would* justify enhanced penalties,[26] but absent such factors, the optimally deterring punishment should remain equal to the harm from the act.

Dana (2001) has argued, however, that this narrow view of punishment misses the role of the law in signaling the moral wrongfulness of harmful acts to potential offenders. This reflects the so-called "expressive," or educational function of law.[27] As Hart (1982, p. 6) has noted, "Why are certain kinds of actions forbidden by law and so made crimes or offences? The answer is: to announce to society that these actions are not to be done and to secure that fewer of them are done."

In principle, these two purposes—announcing that certain acts are illegal and setting a price on them—are not incompatible. Market prices are often characterized as serving this dual purpose. And like a price, an appropriately set legal sanction will only allow efficient crimes while deterring inefficient ones. This requires, however, that people are well-informed about the legal consequences of potentially harmful acts. This is where knowledge of the law (or lack of it) comes into play. If some people are unaware of the illegality of certain acts, they may commit them when they would have refrained from doing so if they had known they were illegal. For these individuals, knowledge of the illegality of an act is itself a sufficient deterrent, and once informed (or reminded) of that fact, they will never commit the act again. Actual punishment is not needed. Consequently, once such an individual is caught, there is no further social gain of imposing a costly sanction—the deterrence benefit has already been achieved. For these individuals, ignorance of the law is an excuse for imposing a lenient (or no) punishment for a first offense. The market

[26] The literature on repeat offenders is large; see, for example, Mungan (2010), Miceli (2013), and the references cited therein.

[27] See, for example, Hart (1982, p. 6), Cooter (1984, 1998), Sunstein (1996), Kahan (1998), McAdams (2017) and Miceli (2023b).

price analogy breaks down here because the price may not be known to the offender until after he or she has committed the act.

There is a downside to such a policy, however, which is that it invites violations from those individuals who *were* aware of the illegality of the act in question. Ideally, such persons would face punishment in proportion to the harmfulness of the act for a first offense, thereby deterring all but those who truly value the act more than the harm from committing it. In a world where people who were truly ignorant of the law could credibly prove that fact, leniency would be granted only for them.

The reality, of course, is that those who were ignorant of the law and those who were not cannot be reliably distinguished, and so all violators have to face the same punishment. An equal-treatment provision would also presumably compel this. It follows that some will be punished more harshly, and some less harshly, than would be necessary to achieve optimal deterrence. The result, according to Hart (1961, p. 88), is that

> At any given moment the life of any society which lives by rules ... is likely to consist in tension between those who, on the one hand, accept and voluntarily co-operate in maintaining the rules, ... and those who, on the other hand, reject the rules and attend to them only from the external point of view as a sign of possible punishment.

This distinction reflects the previously-noted difference between Madison's "angels" and Holmes's "bad men."

The trade-off regarding ignorance of the law, then, is this: harm-based punishments are needed to optimally deter knowledgeable offenders, but they result in unnecessary punishment costs for those who were truly ignorant of the law. The optimal policy ultimately depends on the proportions of these two "types" in the population of potential offenders. The following example illustrates the logical consequences of this trade-off.[28]

Consider an act that is definitely undesirable in the sense that the harm exceeds the benefit for everyone. (This is not an essential assumption.) For concreteness, let the harm from the act be \$200. Suppose further that the act is illegal, but a fraction α of those who might commit it are unaware of that fact. The remaining fraction, $1 - \alpha$, are aware of its illegality and also

[28] The example is based on Miceli (2023b).

of the sanction that would be imposed if they commit it. For simplicity, we will assume that offenders of either type are caught with certainty.[29]

We will consider two possible sanction levels—a "harsh" sanction, which will deter all would-be offenders (>$200), and a "lenient" sanction, which will deter the uninformed once they become aware of the illegality of the act (i.e., commit it and are caught). In fact, we can set the lenient sanction equal to zero—there is no benefit from setting it higher because, by construction, it will not deter the informed but would be costly to impose. Finally, let the social cost of imposing the harsh sanction be $100.

In a one-period setting, the comparison between the two sanctions is as follows. Under the harsh sanction, only the uninformed individuals will commit the act and will be punished. Thus, both the harm from the act and the costs of punishment will be incurred for these offenders. This results in total costs of $\alpha(\$200 + \$100) = \alpha(\$300)$. Under the lenient sanction, by contrast, all offenders will commit the act, but no punishment costs will be incurred. Thus, total costs are $200. The lenient sanction is therefore less costly if $\$200 < \alpha(\$300)$, or if $\alpha > 2/3$. In other words, the fraction of uninformed individuals among potential offenders must exceed some threshold. Of course, it is not possible to know this fraction, but in theory, it could be learned over time by experimenting with sanction levels, or, in a multi-jurisdictional setting with different policies, by observing variations in crime rates (controlling, of course, for any other inter-jurisdictional differences).

We can gain a more refined insight into the expressive function of law by taking a dynamic perspective. To that end, consider a two-period setting in which the same population of would-be offenders make decisions in each of the two periods. Uninformed offenders will commit a crime with certainty in the first period out of ignorance, but will be deterred thereafter regardless of the severity of the sanction. As noted, the mere fact of getting caught informs them of the illegality of the act and so they will refrain from repeating it. Informed individuals, by contrast, will respond to the sanction in both periods. Specifically, they will be deterred by the harsh sanction and will not be deterred by the lenient sanction.

[29] As we have noted previously, however, those who intentionally commit a crime will likely take steps to cover their tracks, which means they will probably be harder to detect that those who commit the act out of ignorance.

Table 6.1 Impact of penalty structure on crime decisions by initially uninformed offenders

Structure	*Outcomes*	*Total Costs*
Uniformly lenient	Uninformed commit in period 1 Informed commit in both periods	$200 + (1 - \alpha)200$ $= (2 - \alpha)200$
Uniformly harsh	Uninformed commit in period 1 Informed deterred in both periods	$\alpha(200 + 100)$ $= \alpha 300$
Escalating	Uninformed commit in period 1 Informed commit in period 1	200

In this context, we consider three penalty structures: (i) uniformly lenient; (ii) uniformly harsh; and (iii) escalating (i.e., lenient for a first-time offender and harsh for a repeat offender).[30] Table 6.1 summarizes the outcomes and the resulting costs under each structure.

Under the uniformly-lenient structure, uninformed individuals commit the act in period 1 but refrain in period 2, while informed individuals commit the act in both periods. Total costs over the two periods are therefore $(2 - \alpha)200$, consisting only of harm from the act since no punishment costs are incurred under this structure. Under the uniformly-harsh structure, uninformed individuals commit the act in period 1 only, while informed individuals are completely deterred. Total costs are therefore $\alpha 300$, consisting of harm plus punishment costs of the uninformed in period 1. Comparing these two structures, the uniformly-lenient structure involves lower costs when $\alpha > 4/5$. The range over which this structure is preferred has shrunk compared to the earlier example because informed individuals are now induced to commit crimes over two periods rather than just one. This illustrates the general point that the longer the time horizon, the less desirable will be the uniformly-lenient structure.

Now consider the escalating sanction, which punishes first offenses leniently but repeat offenses harshly. As the Table shows, all offenders commit period-one crimes, but neither type commits period-two crimes. The resulting social cost over the two periods is 200, reflecting the certainty of crime in period one, but complete deterrence in period two. It

[30] We do not consider a declining sanction, which, it can be shown, is dominated by the others.

should be immediately evident that this strictly dominates the uniformly-lenient structure—i.e., $200 < (2 - \alpha)200$ given $\alpha < 1$. Period-one costs are the same under the two structures, but the escalating structure deters all period-two crimes. Although it threatens a higher cost sanction in period two, this sanction is never actually imposed because all offenders are deterred.[31] (This reflects what I previously called the "paradox of punishment"—the fact that a harsh enough punishment is not necessarily costly because, if it is credibly threatened, it will never have to be imposed.) This is a crucial element underlying the argument in favor of escalating penalties.[32]

Finally, compare the uniformly-high and escalating structures. The latter is preferred if $200 < (300)\alpha$, or if $\alpha > 2/3$. Note that this replicates the threshold separating the uniformly-lenient and uniformly-harsh structures in the one-period model. Specifically, the escalating structure is preferred if the fraction of uniformed individuals in the relevant population exceeds 2/3. The reason is that the escalating structure induces the same period-one outcome here as the uniformly-lenient structure did in the one-period model—namely, both the informed and the uninformed commit crimes—but it completely deters crimes in period two. Likewise, the uniformly-harsh structure induces the same period-one behavior as it did in the one-period model—namely, only the uninformed commit crimes—while also completely deterring crime in period two. Thus, the same threshold separating two the penalty structures emerges here.

The preceding examples are only meant to be illustrative of the larger point that, while ignorance of the law is generally assumed to be an illegitimate reason to seek leniency for a prohibited act, the closely related idea that law is one of the ways that society signals wrongfulness of certain acts provides a countervailing argument in favor of leniency. It also comports with the belief (hope?) that most people are inclined to do the right thing, whether out of moral beliefs or public spirit, but they may not know what the right thing is in all circumstances, particularly unfamiliar ones. This argues for leniency for first-time offenses. It is also true that there will always be some individuals who will readily exploit such leniency to gain

[31] If some offenders are undeterrable, due to permanent or temporary mental impairment, they would be punished, but the resulting cost would be the same under the two structures.

[32] See Miceli (2019, Chapter 6) and the further discussion of this issue in the next section.

an advantage, and as this fraction grows or shrinks, the optimal policy will adjust accordingly.

Although the current explanation for escalating penalty schemes may be an appealing one, it undoubtedly misses some essential features of the issue. The next section will offer a very different explanation for imposing lenient sanctions on first-time offenders, even when they are fully informed.

Redemption

A widely-held rationale for granting leniency to first-time offenders is the possibility of redemption—the idea that everyone deserves a second chance. There is no pretense here that offenders were somehow ignorant of the law, and so that is not the basis for granting forgiveness. The rationale is instead based on the belief that there is some virtue in the granting of forgiveness, combined with the hope that the offender, in return, will reform his ways. Indeed, the concept of redemption implies a restoration to goodness of one who has strayed.

The idea is firmly grounded in Christian theology and is epitomized by the parable of the prodigal son from the New Testament (Luke 15:11–32). The story is of a man with two sons, the younger of whom asks for his inheritance and then proceeds to squander it in extravagant living. When he returns penniless, asking only to be taken on by his father as a hired servant, the father embraces him and celebrates his return. Although this naturally angers the faithful son who has remained devoted to the father, the lesson of the story is clearly one of redemption—that a sinner can be restored to righteousness merely by repenting his sins and seeking forgiveness. This ethic actually represented something of a departure from the Old Testament requirement of atonement for sins—that is, some form of "repayment"—as a pre-requisite for forgiveness. The story of the prodigal son, by contrast, suggests that redemption is available simply for the asking—that it could, in effect, be gotten for free.

In thinking about this story from a law enforcement perspective, the trade-off is as follows. On one hand, redemption encourages wrongdoers to mend their ways by allowing them to rejoin the community with little or no punishment. In this way, it creates marginal deterrence, a concept that we have previously discussed. The idea is that leniency lures offenders away from a continued life of crime. But on the other hand, leniency encourages crime by attaching little or no cost to the initial act of wrongdoing. This reflects the dual-edged nature of lenient punishment as discussed in the prior section.

Together, these ideas reflect the great debate over the nature of criminal punishment—the carrot versus the stick. Again, Hart (1982, p. 27) neatly summarizes the issue:

> Society is divisible at any moment into two classes (i) those who have actually broken a given law and (ii) those who have not yet broken it but may. To take Reform as the dominant objective would be to forgo the hope of influencing the second and … numerically much greater class. We should thus subordinate the prevention of first offenses to the prevention of recidivism.

The question is how to balance these competing objectives; specifically, how to attach some positive cost to initial crimes (the stick), while holding out the possibility of redemption for the undeterred as an inducement to refrain from committing future crimes (the carrot).

To examine this question more formally, consider a setting in which individuals can potentially commit crimes in each of two periods: when they are "young" and when they are "old."[33] We assume these individuals are motivated entirely by material gains, and so make their choices in response to expected benefits and costs. They are also foresighted in the sense that they can anticipate and respond to future consequences. Thus, they are fully knowledgeable of the law.

Suppose that committing a crime in either period yields a gain of G, but it is also subject to an immediate and certain sanction. However, the amount of the sanction depends on whether it is a first or a second offense. Let the sanction for a first offense be s_1 and for a second offense be s_2. (Note that a first offense can be committed by either a young or an old person, but a second offense can only be committed by an old person.) We will make no a priori assumptions about the relative magnitudes of these sanctions, except that they cannot exceed some total amount S, which is the limit of a person's ability to pay over a lifetime.

[33] The following discussion is based on Cosgel and Miceli (2018). Also see Miceli (2019, Chapter 6).

Thus, $s_1 + s_2 \leq S$. This could reflect a wealth constraint, a limit on the amount of time a person can serve in prison, or the value of their life.[34]

We will also assume (for now) that $S > 2G$. Thus, the maximum possible sanction exceeds the maximum gains obtainable from crime over the two-period time horizon. This implies that, in principle, the threat of criminal punishment should be able to completely deter crime. One way to do that would be to set both s_1 and s_2 just above G, which is feasible given the constraint on the sanctions. However, that is not the only policy that will achieve complete deterrence. In fact, it will be shown that any combination of s_1 and s_2 such that $s_1 \geq G$, up to and including $s_1 = S$, will completely deter crime. However, any scheme in which $s_1 < G$ will not deter an initial crime.

It should be clear why $s_1 < G$ will not deter someone, young or old, from committing an initial crime, but it is less obvious why setting $s_1 \geq G$ will deter *all* crime. To see why it does, consider the extreme case in which $s_1 = S$ and $s_2 = 0$; that is, punishment is fully "front loaded." Obviously, someone who did not commit a crime when young will not commit one when old because that would be an initial crime, and so s_1 will be the applicable sanction. However, if someone *did* commit a crime when young, he or she will definitely commit a second crime when old because $s_2 = 0$ would be the applicable sanction—i.e., the second crime is "free." The lifetime gains from this particular sequence of choices—that is, from committing crimes in both periods—is therefore $2G - s_1 - s_2 = 2G - S$. But this is negative by assumption. Thus, the individual will be deterred from such a strategy. The same logic would apply to any scheme with $s_1 > G$.

This conclusion reflects the attractiveness of the threat of a harsh initial punishment—the stick—for deterring crime. While this policy may sound good in principle, it is harder to justify in practice. One reason is the philosophical objection to excessive punishments, but the reason we will focus on here is marginal deterrence. Suppose that not all offenders are fully rational all of the time. Suppose, in particular, that some young people commit crimes inadvertently or due to temporary lapses in judgment. However, when they become old, they behave rationally, whether as a

[34] A more general interpretation of S might be that it represents the degree to which a person's internal moral beliefs can act as a restraint on his or her behavior. See Cosgel and Miceli (2018) for such an interpretation, which is based on the value of the "afterlife" to those who embrace that concept.

result of maturity or other influences. If such a person chooses to commit a second crime, the applicable sanction will be s_2. However, given the constraint on aggregate sanctions, that sanction is bounded such that $s_2 \leq S - s_1$. Thus, if s_1 was too large, s_2 will be insufficient to deter a second crime. It follows that s_1 also has to be bounded such that $s_2 = S - s_1 \geq G$. Combining this with the requirement that $s_1 \geq G$ to deter initial crimes, we have the following bounds: $S - G \geq s_1 \geq G$, which is feasible given that $S > 2G$.

This is exactly the logic of marginal deterrence, and it is accomplished in this case without the need to sacrifice deterrence of initial crimes. In other words, rational offenders are deterred from committing initial crimes, and those who irrationally committed an initial crime will, after re-embracing rationality, be deterred from committing a second crime. This is possible because the constraint on the aggregate sanction is sufficiently permissive. For example, a uniform sanction structure with $s_1 = s_2 = S/2$ will work.

The issue becomes more problematic, however, when the constraint on punishment is more restrictive. To illustrate, suppose now that $2G > S > G$. Thus, the maximal sanction can now deter at most one crime over an offender's lifetime. In this case, two penalty structures are worth considering: (i) $s_1 > G > s_2$, and (ii) $s_1 < G < s_2$. The first is a declining structure and the second is a rising structure. It would seem that the first is aimed at deterring first-time offenders, while second is aimed at deterring repeat offenders,[35] but that turns out not to be the case.

Under the declining scheme, a rational offender will in fact commit crimes in both periods. To see why, note that if a person refrains from committing a crime in period one, he will also refrain from doing so in period two because $s_1 > G$. However, if he *does* commit a crime in period one, he will commit one again in period two because $s_2 < G$. (At this point, the net loss from the period-one crime, $G - s_1$, is sunk.) The question, then, is which of these profiles yields the higher net benefit? The first yields zero, while the second yields $2G - s_1 - s_2$, which now is positive given our assumption that $s_i + s_2 \leq S < G$. Thus, the offender will commit crimes in both periods under this structure.

Consider next the rising penalty structure. Here, the offender will commit a single crime over his lifetime, either in period one or period

[35] It would never make sense to consider a flat structure with, say, $s_1 = s_2 = S/2$, because then there would be no deterrence.

two. If he commits a crime in period one, he will be deterred in period two because $s_2 > G$, whereas if he does not commit a crime in period one, he will commit one in period two because $s_1 < G$. The return from both of these profiles is $G - s_1$, which is positive. He is therefore indifferent between them. In either case, this structure deters at least one crime, which the declining structure did not do.

Focusing on the more likely case where the individual commits a crime in period one (i.e., when young) but is deterred in period two (i.e., when old) reveals the parallel between marginal deterrence and redemption. Redemption naturally connotes a change of heart on the part of the wrongdoer, as epitomized by the return of the prodigal son. This in turn induces the father to bestow leniency on him; in other words, remorse by the offender triggers leniency by the enforcer. Under marginal deterrence, the causal direction is reversed—it is the prospect of leniency that induces the wrongdoer to change his behavior. There is no change of heart per se, only a change in prices. Nevertheless, the two scenarios are observationally equivalent because motives are not observable, only behavior is, and laws administered by people can only be conditioned on things that are observable. Administration of punishments (or rewards) based on what is in one's heart is the exclusive province of an omniscient deity (as personified by the prodigal son's father) and one's own conscience.

The final issue to address in the current context is how differences in people's ability to pay legal sanctions (as captured by the constraint S) affect the ability of the law to prevent harmful acts by the threat of punishment. If, for example, S is very low for some people, they will be out of the reach of law. In our two-period example, if $S < G$ for some people, they would be completely undeterrable by the tools of criminal law. Their crimes would therefore be a background harm that society would either have to tolerate, or those individuals would have to be incapacitated after a first offense.

That leaves the two scenarios that we have already considered: where individuals can be completely deterred (those for whom $S > 2G$); and where individuals can only be partially deterred (those for whom $2G > S > G$). Presumably, both groups exist in a given society, but since they cannot be distinguished, a single penalty structure must apply to all. To illustrate the resulting trade-off in the most dramatic way, we will compare two penalty structures: (1) $s_1 = S$, $s_2 = 0$; and (2) $s_1 = 0$, $s_2 = S$. The first consists of a harsh (maximal) sanction for a first offense and a lenient (zero) sanction for a second offense, while the second consists of a lenient (zero) sanction for a first offense and a harsh (maximal) sanction for a second offense. The first epitomizes the idea of pre-emptive deterrence by the threat of harsh initial punishment, while the second reflects the idea of redemption.

We showed above that the first structure will deter all crimes among those individuals for whom $S > 2G$ (i.e., those who are "fully deterrable"), but it will not deter any crimes among those individuals for whom $S < 2G$ (i.e., those who are "partially deterrable"). In comparison, the second structure will result in first-period crimes by both types of individuals, but because it embodies marginal deterrence, it will also deter second-period crimes by both types.

In order to assess the relative desirability of these two structures, we need to employ a measure of social welfare. Following the standard approach, we will compute the net gain from a criminal act, given by $G - h$, where h is the external harm from the act (and which is greater than G), minus the cost of imposing the sanction, which we set equal to the level of the sanction, s. We also need to know the fraction of the two types we are considering. Let β be the fraction of fully deterrable types (those with $S > 2G$), and $1 - \beta$ the fraction of partially deterrable types (those with $S < 2G$). Table 6.2 summarizes the outcomes and resulting levels of welfare under the two punishment structures.

C = commit a crime; NC = not commit a crime.

Note that neither structure can fully deter crime over the two periods owing to the restrictive upper bound on the ability to pay by a fraction of the population. This limits the extent to which the threat of external sanctions can control overall behavior and therefore requires the enforcement

Table 6.2 Impact of penalty structure on fully and partially deterrable offenders

Structure	*Outcomes: (Period 1, Period 2)*	*Social Welfare*
1. $s_1 = S$, $s_2 = 0$	Partially deterrable types: (C, C) Fully deterrable types: (NC, NC)	$W_1 = (1 - \beta)[2(G - h) - S]$
2. $s_1 = 0$, $s_2 = S$	Partially deterrable types: (C, NC) Fully deterrable types: (C, NC)	$W_2 = G - h$

authority to choose between two scenarios: one that achieves full deterrence of a fraction of the population (structure 1), versus one that achieves partial deterrence of the entire population (structure 2). Comparison of the welfare expressions in the third column of the table shows that the latter is preferred to the former if the following inequality holds:

$$(1 - \beta)(h - G + S) > \beta(h - G).$$

The left-hand side of the above condition is the net savings in crime and punishment costs under structure 2, arising from the fact that marginal deterrence prevents partially deterrable types, who comprise a fraction $1 - \beta$ of the population, from committing period 2 crimes. This benefit is only attainable, however, at the expense of allowing fully deterrable types, comprising a fraction β of the population, to commit period-one crimes. That cost is the right-hand side.

Relating this back to the prodigal son story, the trade-off is between the prospect for redemption that leniency offers, which both entices prodigal sons to return and saves on the costs of punishing first-time offenders; versus the temptation that leniency creates for those who would otherwise be deterred by a harsh punishment to become prodigal in the first place. The choice therefore depends on the relative proportions of these two types in the population, as reflected by β. Specifically, as β approaches zero—that is, as the fraction of actual prodigal sons increases—the balance tilts in favor of offering leniency as an inducement for prodigals to refrain from further wrongdoing. Conversely, as β approaches one, the balance tilts toward harsh initial punishment.

It is tempting to relate the above analysis to the rise of Christianity during the early years of the first millennium.[36] It was the case that the Judaic (Old Testament) tradition out of which Christianity arose required atonement in the form of good works or restitution as a condition for redemption. Christianity broke with this requirement by effectively promising "free redemption" as long as the sinner professed faith in Jesus Christ, who had died to redeem the sins of all who accepted his divinity. Jesus thereby offered the ultimate form of vicarious responsibility for sin. This "innovation" of the Christian religion is consistent with the goal of the church to attract new members in its early stages, and although the reasons for the remarkable rise of Christianity are many and varied, the promise of free redemption was undoubtedly one of its attractions.

[36] See, for example, Stark (1996), Ehrman (2018), and Holland (2019).

Additionally, the above analysis showed that this is also the optimal policy when belief is moderate, as would have been true, say, during the early phases of a new religion.

As a final point, note that recent debates about three-strikes laws reflect a modern version of the above trade-off. As was discussed previously, the impetus for these laws was undoubtedly the rise in crime rates in some cities in the post-WW II period, which "put great pressure on the political system…toward toughness. … This led to such laws as the 'three strikes' law in California; under this law, a prisoner convicted of a third serious felony faced, in effect, life imprisonment" (Friedman 2004, pp. 108–109). The hope was that these laws would send a clear signal to would-be offenders that a continuing life of crime would ultimately lead to maximal punishment. For those undeterred by the threat, however, the strict application of the policy held out no hope for redemption while entailing high costs of detaining those convicted of a third strike. The perceived "shocking injustices" of the policy, however, soon resulted in efforts to scale it back (Friedman 2004, p. 108; Vitielo 2004).[37] The perpetual oscillation between these two viewpoints—the threat of harsh sanctions aimed at deterring offenders, versus the benefits of leniency for those who are undeterred, both for reasons of justice and the incentive for reform—reflect the continuing applicability of the trade-off embodied by the parable of the prodigal son.

The Impossibility of Redemption: Predestination

At the opposite extreme from free redemption is the impossibility of redemption. To continue the religious analogy, this was actually the message of the doctrine of Predestination, which was adopted by certain protestant sects (most notably, the Puritans) following the Reformation. The doctrine held that "from the beginning of time certain souls were 'predestined' to heaven and others sentenced to damnation" (Miller and Johnson 1963, p. 56). The hope of salvation was therefore unrelated to one's behavior on earth, thereby completely severing the link between responsibility and wrongdoing. In embracing this view, believers were rejecting the idea that redemption, or salvation, was a commodity that could be sold, which is what they perceived to be happening under the

[37] For a similar discussion, see Gladwell (2013, Chapter 8).

Catholic Church.[38] At the same time, however, the new doctrine apparently eliminated the role of divine surveillance and punishment as a means of controlling behavior.[39] Did this doctrine "throw the baby out with the bathwater"?

Glaeser and Glendon (1998, p. 430) have posited that people still engaged in good works out of "a desire to receive positive behavior from others by convincing them that [they were] a part of the spiritual elite." In other words, they behaved well in order to signal that they were among the select. The problem with such a system, however, is that it would have done little to restrain bad behavior outside of public view, which is precisely the realm where religion (or morality) has an advantage over secular law enforcement (as previously discussed—see Shavell (2002)).

Weber (1958, p. 115), by contrast, argued that this belief system was not just for show; rather, it was designed to convince *oneself* of one's select status:

> [H]owever useless good works might be as a means of attaining salvation, ... they are indispensable as a sign of election. They are the technical means, not of purchasing salvation, but of getting rid of the fear of damnation. ... Thus, the Calvinist, as it is sometimes put, himself creates his own salvation, or as would be more correct, the conviction of it. But this creation cannot, as in Catholicism, consist in a gradual accumulation of individual good works to one's credit, but rather in systematic self-control which at every moment stands before the inexorable alternative, chosen or damned.

Miller and Johnson (1963, p. 57) observed that such a theology "creates an eternal obligation upon men to be equitable, fair, and good, but who can say that any such morality is also binding on the universe?" This would seem to depict a grand form of self-delusion among believers that reverses the direction of causation—rather than good works leading to salvation, the expectation of salvation inspired good works.

In terms of day-to-day behavior, this belief, if truly internalized, has the virtue of dispensing with the need for people to continually reckon

[38] See, for example, Ekelund, et al. (1992) and Holland (2019, Chapter 13).

[39] According to Holland (2019, p. 318), Martin Luther came to believe that "God did not treat sinners according to their just deserts." In other words, "Salvation was not a reward. Salvation was a gift.".

the costs and benefits of individual actions, but instead inspires them to adopt an ethic of goodness that is emblematic of membership in the elect (Cosgel and Miceli 2018, pp. 216–217). At the same time, however, it also likely created a sense of resignation among many people that their fate was sealed regardless of their actions, thereby creating what Morgan (1968, p. 106) called the "Puritan dilemma," which was the question of how the church could survive in an environment where "the mass of men are excluded by [the church's strict] standards."

Contemporary Protestantism is, of course, a pale shadow of its Puritan roots in terms of acceptable behaviors and tolerance of diverse lifestyles. This is undoubtedly due to evolving social norms, but also to the substantially greater role of secular law enforcement in controlling people's behavior, thereby rendering much of the above debate an historical curiosity rather than a policy issue.

Non-Enforcement of the Law

We conclude this chapter on limits of criminal liability by considering the ultimate shield of legal responsibility; namely, intentional non-enforcement of the law. It is important to emphasize that this is different from lack of credibility of the threat to enforce the law, as discussed in Part 1. The issue here concerns a *conscious* decision not to enforce the law.

One reason for not enforcing a law is that its purpose is no longer relevant due to changing knowledge (or preferences) regarding what is harmful, coupled with the cost of repealing the law in question. Many such anachronistic laws remain on the books as relics of times past. What is relevant for current purposes, however, is when a law is enacted with *no intention of expending resources to enforce it*. What explains this seemingly irrational action?

One possible reason is the claim above that some, perhaps even most, people will refrain from committing an act once they are informed about its illegality. This again reflects the expressive function of the law—the role of the law in informing people about what acts are considered unacceptable. If enough people are dissuaded from committing an act simply by being told of its illegality, this can be a very cheap means of deterrence.

To illustrate the possible deterrent effect of mere enactment of a law, consider an act that would impose net harm of h dollars on society.[40] Suppose that in order to deter this act, the government would have to first enact a law notifying the public that the act is illegal, and then possibly to devote resources to enforcing the law. Let the "notice cost" be $50, and let the "enforcement cost" be $100. For simplicity, let us assume that if these costs are incurred, anyone contemplating the act would be deterred with certainty. In other words, harm of h dollars would be avoided by spending $150. (Think of enforcement costs in this case as assembling a police force or regulatory apparatus to apprehend violators.) This is obviously desirable on cost grounds if $h > \$150$[41]; that is, if the harm is large enough. The question of interest here is whether it is worthwhile to spend the $100 enforcement cost on top of the $50 notice cost.

Suppose that some fraction of those who would commit the act if it were legal will refrain from committing it if it were merely declared unlawful, even if there would be no intention of enforcing the law. This again reflects the idea that the mere declaration of the act as illegal will deter some people. Let's say this is true of one half of those who would potentially commit the act, whereas the other half can only be deterred by the threat of actual punishment (i.e., enforcement of the law). Now the government has three policies to choose from: (i) enact a law and actively enforce it, (ii) enact the law and not enforce it; and (iii) not enact a law.

Under the first option, everyone will be deterred and costs of $150 will be incurred (the costs of notice plus enforcement). Under the second option, only notice costs of $50 will be incurred, and half of potential offenders will be deterred while the other half will commit the act. Thus, total costs will be $50 + 0.5h$. Finally, under the third option, all potential offenders will commit the act, resulting in total costs of h.[42] Figure 6.4 graphs these various costs as a function of the harm, h.

As the graph shows, each of the three policies is optimal (cost minimizing) over some range of h. (This is indicated by the darkened

[40] This argument is based on Miceli and Mungan (2021).

[41] We are ignoring the question of whether the gain to the offender should be counted. Or we can just think of h as the net harm, where $h > 0$ means that the harm exceeds the offender's gain.

[42] We are assuming that people who are deterred by mere notice are not responding to the cost of the act per se, but to its illegality. In fact, most people will not know the costs of harmful acts, and thus they look to the law for guidance.

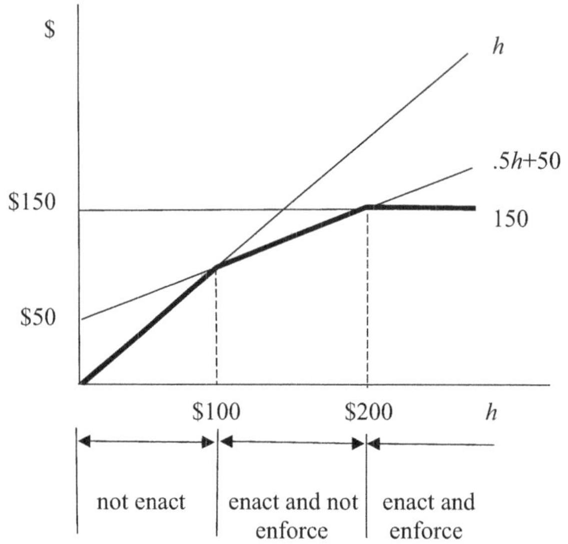

Fig. 6.4 Efficient enactment and enforcement decisions

segments.) As one would expect, the optimal policy for very harmful acts (those with h above \$200) is to enact a law prohibiting the act and enforce it, whereas at the other extreme, the optimal policy for acts that impose little harm (those with h between 0 and \$100) is not to enact a law at all. The optimal policy for acts that impose intermediate harms (those with h between \$100 and \$200) is to enact a law *but not enforce it*. For these acts, the mere enactment deters enough people to justify spending the notice cost, but the act does not impose sufficient harm to justify spending the enforcement cost. Further, as the fraction of offenders who are deterred by the mere enactment increases, the range of h over which that intermediate policy is optimal will expand at both ends. Specifically, the lower bound will fall below \$100 and the upper bound will rise above \$200.[43] Thus, the range for both of the other policies will contract.

[43] This is true because the curve labeled $.5\ h + 50$ will rotate downward. For example, if the fraction of offenders deterred by mere enactment rises to .6, the cost of the policy of enactment but non-enforcement is $.4\ h + 50$, and the bounds over which this policy is optimal become \$83.3 and \$200.

The advantage of enacting a law coupled with non-enforcement is that some deterrence can be achieved at no cost, which explains this seemingly anomalous policy. The degree to which this is optimal, however, obviously depends on the fraction of potential offenders who are amenable to this expressive function of law. This may be partially under the control of the government. For example, it will likely be influenced by how widely the enactment of a law is advertised and how convincingly its purpose is justified, for instance by public service announcements.

References

Becker, G. 1968. Crime and Punishment: An Economic Approach. *Journal of Political Economy* 76: 169–217.

Clarke, R. 2013. *A Natural History of Ghosts: 500 Years of Hunting for Proof*. New York: Penguin Books.

Cooter, R. 1984. Prices and Sanctions. *Columbia Law Review* 84: 1523–1560.

Cooter, R. 1998. Expressive Law and Economics. *Journal of Legal Studies* 27: 585–607.

Cosgel, M., and T. Miceli. 2018. The Price of Redemption: Sin, Penance, and Marginal Deterrence. *Journal of Economic Behavior and Organization* 156: 206–218.

Dana, D. 2001. Rethinking the Puzzle of Escalating Penalties for Repeat Offenders. *Yale Law Journal* 110: 733–783.

Keeton, W., D. Dobbs, R. Keeton, and D. Owen. 1984. *Prosser and Keeton on Torts*, 5th ed. St. Paul, MN: West Publishing.

Ehrman, B. 2018. *The Triumph of Christianity: How a Forbidden Religion Swept the World*. New York: Simon and Schuster.

Ekelund, R., R. Herbert, and R. Tollison. 1992. The Economics of Sin and Redemption: Purgatory as a Market-Pull Innovation? *Journal of Economic Behavior and Organization* 19: 1–15.

Friedman, D. 2000. *Law's Order: What Economics Has to Do with the Law and Why It Matters*. Princeton: Princeton Univ. Press.

Friedman, L. 2004. *Law in America: A Short History*. New York: The Modern Library.

Friehe, T., and T. Miceli. 2018. On the ROLE of the Exclusionary Rule for Optimal Law Enforcement. *Journal of Public Economic Theory* 20: 757–767.

Gladwell, M. 2013. *David and Goliath: Underdogs, Misfits, and the Art of Battling Giants*. New York: Little-Brown.

Glaeser, E., and S. Glendon. 1998. Incentives, Predestination, and Free Will. *Economic Inquiry* 36: 429–443.

Hart, H.L.A. 1961. *The Concept of Law*. Oxford: Oxford Univ. Press.

Hart, H.L.A. 1982. *Punishment and Responsibility*. London: Oxford Univ. Press.
Hay, B. 2005. Sting Operations, Undercover Agents, and Entrapment. *Missouri Law Review* 70: 387–431.
Holland, T. 2019. *Dominion: How the Christian Revolution Remade the World*. New York: Basic Books.
Holmes, O.W. 1881[1963]. *The Common Law*. Boston: Little Brown.
Hylton, K. 1996. Optimal Law Enforcement and Victim Precaution. *Rand Journal of Economics* 27: 197–206.
Kahan, D. 1998. Social Meaning and the Economic Analysis of Crime. *Journal of Legal Studies* 27: 609–622.
Katz, L. 1987. *Bad Acts and Guilty Minds: Conundrums of the Criminal Law*. Chicago: Univ. of Chicago Press.
Keeton, W., D. Dobbs, R. Keeton, and D. Owen. 1984. *Prosser and Keeton on Torts*, 5th ed. St. Paul, MN: West Publishing.
Landes, W., and R. Posner. 1987. *The Economic Structure of Tort Law*. Cambridge, MA: Harvard Univ. Press.
Lewin, J., and W. Trumbull. 1990. The Social Value of Crime? *International Review of Law and Economics* 10: 271–284.
McAdams, R. 2017. *The Expressive Powers of Law: Theories and Limits*. Cambridge, MA: Harvard Univ. Press.
Miceli, T. 2007. Criminal Solicitation, Entrapment, and the Enforcement of Law. *International Review of Law and Economics* 27: 258–268.
Miceli, T. 2013. Escalating Penalties for Repeat Offenders: Why Are They So Hard to Explain? *Journal of Institutional and Theoretical Economics* 169: 587–604.
Miceli, T. 2019. *The Paradox of Punishment: Reflections on the Economics of Criminal Justice*. Cham, Switzerland: Palgrave Macmillan.
Miceli, T. 2023. Expressive Law and Escalating Penalties: Accounting for the Educational Function of Punishment. *Review of Law and Economics* 19: 245–262.
Miceli, T., and M. Mungan. 2021. The Limit of Law: Factors Influencing the Decision to Make Harmful Acts Illegal. *Economics of Governance* 22: 293–307.
Miller, P., and T. Johnson, eds. 1963. *A Sourcebook of Their Writings*. New York: Harper and Row.
Mungan, M. 2010. Repeat Offenders: If They Learn We Punish Them More Severely. *International Review of Law and Economics* 30: 173–177.
Parker, J. 1993. The economics of mens rea. *Virginia Law Review* 79: 741–811.
Posner, R. 1988. *Law and Literature: A Misunderstood Relation*. Cambridge, MA: Harvard Univ. Press.
Posner, R. 2003. *Economic Analysis of Law*, 6th ed. New York: Aspen Publishers.

Shavell, S. 1985. Uncertainty Over Causation and the Determination of Civil Liability. *Journal of Law and Economics* 28: 587–609.

Shavell, S. 1990. Deterrence and Punishment of Attempts. *Journal of Legal Studies* 19: 435–466.

Shavell, S. 1991. Individual Precautions to Prevent Theft: Private Versus Socially Optimal Behavior. *International Review of Law and Economics* 11: 123–132.

Shavell, S. 2002. Law Versus Morality as Regulators of Conduct. *American Law and Economics Review* 4: 227–257.

Shavell, S. 2004. *Foundations of Economic Analysis of Law*. Cambridge, MA: Belknap Press.

Stark, R. *The Rise of Christianity: How an Obscure, Marginal Jesus Movement Became the Dominant Religious Force in the Western World in a Few Centuries*, San Francisco: Harper, 1996.

Stevenson, D. 2004. Entrapment and the Problem of Deterring Police Misconduct. *Connecticut Law Review* 37: 67–153.

Sunstein, C. 1996. On the Expressive Function of Law. *University of Pennsylvania Law Review* 144: 2021–2053.

Vitielo, M. 2004. Reforming Three-Strikes Excesses. *Washington University Law Quarterly* 82: 1–42.

Weber, M. *The Protestant Ethic and the Spirit of Capitalism*, translated by T. Parsons, New York: Dover Publications, 1958.

PART III

Reasons for Expanding Responsibility

"Responsibility is not a bucket in which less remains when some is apportioned out; there is not a fixed amount of punishment or responsibility which one uses up so that none is left for the other."

Robert Nozick (1974, p. 130)

CHAPTER 7

Expanding Responsibility: Tort Doctrines

The preceding chapters have focused on reasons why injurers—by which I mean those who *cause* harm—should sometimes be shielded from legal responsibility for some or all of that harm. In other words, it considered reasons why causation was not a sufficient condition for responsibility under both tort and criminal law. This part turns to the converse possibility by asking whether there are reasons for shifting responsibility, in part or whole, to "third parties"—those who did *not* actually cause harm. On its face, this seems more controversial than limiting liability because it extends responsibility to "innocent" individuals, and we have argued that wrongful punishment is particularly objectionable to most people. As in Part 2, the objective will be to offer economic explanations for departing in this way from a purely causal basis for responsibility. The focus of this chapter will be tort doctrines, and the next will be on criminal doctrines.

Uncertainty Over Causation: Existence of a Background Risk

One reason for expanding responsibility beyond the actual cause of harm is that causation is sometimes uncertain. This can be true for two reasons: either there exists a background risk of harm, as in the case of a certain illness that may be linked to exposure to some chemical; or the actual

T. J. Miceli, *Harm and Responsibility*,
https://doi.org/10.1007/978-3-031-74831-8_7

Table 7.1 Uncertainty over causation example

Action	*Cost of care*	*Background risk*	*Injurer's contribution*	*Harm*	*Expected harm*	*Total costs*
No care	$0	0.10	0.15	$100	$25	$25
Care	10	0.10	0.02	100	12	22

cause cannot be disentangled from multiple possible causes, as when multiple firms emit of toxic waste that seeps into the groundwater.[1]

Consider first the situation of a single possible injurer acting in the presence of a background risk. Table 7.1 provides an example that will allow us to address this question.

As in the discussion of tort liability above, the objective here continues to be to structure liability so as to induce the injurer to take optimal precaution against the risk.

In the example, there is a background risk of 0.10 that the victim will incur harm of $100. The behavior of the injurer contributes to this risk, but the extent to which it does so depends on whether or not the latter invests in some precaution (care). For example, a factory can filter its emissions of a toxic substance, thereby mitigating the risk of some illness to nearby residents. However, even in the absence of the emissions, there is a risk, and it is impossible to determine after the fact what the actual cause was. As the example illustrates, overall costs, including the factory's cost of care, are minimized when the factory invests in care. Investing in care is therefore socially desirable.

Importantly, note that the existence of the background risk contributes a fixed cost of $10 (=0.10 × $100) to the total cost regardless of the factory's choice, and therefore it has no effect on whether it is desirable for the injurer to invest in care. The reason care is desirable is that, by spending $10, the factory lowers *its* contribution of risk from 0.15 to 0.02, which results in an expected savings of $13 = (0.15 − 0.02)×$100. As a result, total expected costs fall from $25 to $12.

In terms of incentives for the factory, either a rule of strict liability for the full damages, or negligence, as studied in Chap. 5, can induce an efficient outcome. Under strict liability, the factory will face the full

[1] See, generally, Shavell (1985).

damages of \$100 whenever the victim suffers the harm, and so it will have an incentive to take care to minimize its costs, which in this case coincide with total costs. Under negligence, where the due standard is for the factory to invest in care, the latter will also invest because by spending \$10 it avoids expected liability of \$25. Under both of these rules, however, the injurer is potentially liable for harms that it did not cause; namely, those harms attributable to the background risk. It is obviously impossible to identify those particular harms after the fact, but some adjustments in the factory's liability can mitigate this possibility.

Consider first limits based on causation. As discussed above, cause in fact limits an injurer's liability to the damage caused by its negligence. In this example, care lowers the risk from 0.25 to 0.12, which we have seen results in expected savings of \$13. Thus, a negligent injurer would only be liable for this amount. However, this still exceeds the \$10 cost of care, so the injurer would continue to have an incentive to comply with the due standard. Note, however, that even under this limitation, the injurer's potential liability still includes the background risk.

Two other possible limits on the injurer's liability *do* explicitly account for the background risk. The first rule holds the injurer strictly liable in the event of an injury, but only for a fraction of the realized damages equal to the *conditional probability that the injurer was the cause of the injury*. The computation of that probability depends on whether or not the injurer took care. If the injurer did not take care, the probability equals $0.15/(0.15 + 0.10) = 0.60$, whereas if the injurer did take care, the probability equals $0.02/(0.02 + 0.10) = 0.17$. The injurer's total expected costs in these two cases, respectively, are

$$\text{No care}: (.15 + .10) \times \left(\frac{.15}{.15 + .10)}\right) \times \$100 = \$15,$$

$$\text{Care}: (.02 + .10) \times \left(\frac{.02}{.02 + .10)}\right) \times \$100 + \$10 = \$12,$$

The injurer therefore minimizes its costs by taking care, which is the efficient outcome. As for its scope of liability, although the injurer in fact caused the harm in some cases and did not cause it in others, it faces liability for some harm in *all* cases. The probabilistic limitation only limits it in expected terms.

A different causal limitation functions more like proximate cause in that it completely shields the injurer from liability for those injuries in which the conditional probability that the injurer caused the harm is less than some threshold denoted by t. If we set that threshold between the conditional probabilities when the injurer did and did not take care—that is, $0.17 < t < 0.60$—then the injurer will have an incentive to take care because by doing so it avoids liability. That is, by spending \$10 it avoids expected liability of \$25. The outcome under this rule is, in effect, identical to that under a negligence rule without the cause-in-fact limitation.

Uncertainty over causation can sometimes enable injurers to avoid liability, even when it is strict. For example, victims may find it difficult or impossible to prove any causation on the injurer's part, especially if the harm occurs after a long lapse of time. In this case, an injurer can effectively "hide" behind the background risk. One possible remedy for this is for a court to award punitive damages, which we have seen represent damages in excess of the amount of harm the victim(s) actually sustained. As we noted in the previous chapter, courts generally impose punitive damages when harms appear to have been intentionally imposed, or at least with some degree of recklessness. Economists, however, have focused on the role of punitive damages in possibly correcting for the underdeterrence problem (which, of course, may be linked to intent).[2]

Consider how this would work in the above example. Suppose the applicable rule is strict liability for the full damages (\$100), but victims only sue half of the time. The overall risk of harm if the injurer does not take care is 0.25 (including the background risk), resulting in expected harm of \$25, but even if injurers would be held liable for the full damages, they would only *expect* to face liability of $0.5 \times \$25 = \$12.50$. Conversely, if the injurer takes care, the risk falls to 0.12, and expected harm to \$12, but the injurer's expected liability is only \$6, making its total costs $\$10 + \$6 = \$16$. In this case, the injurer minimizes costs by not taking care. In order to fully correct for this, the injurer would have to pay double the damages, or \$200, in those cases where it is actually sued. The extra \$100 would be the punitive damage component.

The logic here, of course, is identical to that which justified probability scaling in the determination of optimal criminal sanctions, given less than certain detection. The difference is that in the criminal context,

[2] See, for example, Cooter (1989) and Hylton and Miceli (2005). Polinsky and Shavell (1998) argue, however, that the actual use of punitive damages does not seem to reflect the economic theory.

those who were caught and punished in effect paid for their own crimes and the crimes of those who got away with it. Here, by contrast, those subjected to punitive damages are often paying for past offenses of their own that went undetected, and so there is less of a sense of injustice from "over-penalization." Thus, while we noted that there are considerable impediments to scaled penalties in criminal law, civil courts have not hesitated to impose substantial punitive damage awards on tort defendants when the conditions warrant it (though the amounts are often reduced on appeal).

Multiple Injurers

The preceding discussion concerned uncertainty over causation resulting from a background risk that combines with the actions of an injurer to threaten harm to a victim (or victims). In other cases, the uncertainty concerns multiple injurers whose actions jointly threaten the victim with harm—so-called joint torts.[3] An example is when several firms dump toxic waste into a landfill that eventually contaminates the drinking water of nearby residents. Another is when two hunters fire at what they believe is a deer, but one of their bullets hits a third hunter.[4] In both of these situations, it is impossible to determine which injurer's action caused the victim's harm. In the groundwater example, it may truly be their combined actions—which raises the question of how to share the harm—whereas in the hunting example, it is definitely only one of the shooters.

The existence of multiple potential injurers presents a greater incentive problem than the background risk scenario because the total recovery that a victim can collect is limited by the amount of his or her damages. Under the rule of *joint and several liability*, the victim can seek compensation up to the full amount of the loss from either injurer individually, or from any combination of them, but total liability cannot exceed the amount of damage. As a practical matter, therefore, victims will pursue the defendant with the deepest pocket (greatest ability to pay), thereby shielding other injurers from responsibility. Further, the law does not generally allow the targeted defendant to seek reimbursement (or "contribution") from the

[3] See, for example, Chapter 7 in Landes and Posner (1987) .

[4] See *Summers v. Tice*, 33 Cal.2d 80, 199 P.2d 1 (1948).

other defendants, although there is some vagueness on this point.[5] Under these rules, the responsibility for harm is therefore not necessarily linked to an injurer's actual contribution.

To illustrate the incentive problem this creates, consider the case of two potential injurers whose actions combine to create a risk of harm. (The argument generalizes to more than two, and it will be evident that the problem only worsens as the number rises.) Let s_1 and s_2 be the shares of liability that each injurer expects to face in the event of an accident. Under joint and several liability, $s_1 + s_2 = 1$. Thus, although injurers cannot know with certainty what their shares will be in the event of an accident, they know that at least one of the shares will be strictly less than one. On average, therefore, both will rationally expect to face less than the full damages from any accident. Consequently, under a rule of strict liability, neither will have an incentive to take efficient care.

The situation is better if joint and several liability is combined with a negligence standard. In fact, the unique equilibrium outcome under this rule is for both injurers to choose efficient care regardless of the liability shares, provided that the due standard is set at efficient care. This is possible because, as we have seen, negligence allows injurers to avoid liability altogether by meeting the due standard. This conclusion is demonstrated by the example in Table 7.2.[6]

Here, two injurers contribute to the probability of harm, which each can individually reduce (from 0.30 to 0.15) by investing $50 in care. And

Table 7.2 Multiple injurer example

Actions	*Cost of care for injurer 1*	*Cost of care for injurer 2*	*Probability of harm*	*Harm*	*Total expected costs*
(NC, NC)	$ 0	$0	0.30	$1000	$300
(C, NC)	50	0	0.15	1000	200
(NC, C)	0	50	0.15	1000	200
(C,C)	50	50	0.05	1000	150

C = care, NC = no care

[5] A defendant who has been held liable can seek "indemnification" from other injurers, but the legal distinction between contribution and indemnification is somewhat vague. See Keeton et al. (1984, p. 341).

[6] See Landes and Posner (1987, Chapter 7) for a more formal proof.

if both invest, they reduce the risk to 0.05. As shown by the final column, the cost-minimizing outcome is for both to invest, and hence this represents the due standard for both under negligence. Thus, if both invest in care, neither is liable for damages. However, if either is unilaterally negligent, that injurer will be fully liable, while if both are negligent, they are jointly and severally liable, with s_i being injurer i's expected to share ($i =$ 1,2), where $s_i + s_2 = 1$. Because the injurers make their care choices in isolation, determination of the equilibrium depends on the expectations that each injurer holds with respect to the other's behavior. As in our analysis of negligence above, we derive the Nash equilibrium.[7] Table 7.3 shows the payoffs from the possible combinations of choices for arbitrary values of s_1 and s_2.

Consider first the behavior of injurer 1. If he expects injurer 2 to take care, he will also take care in order to avoid full liability (i.e., $50 < 150$). However, if he expects injurer 2 not to take care, he will only take care if $50 < s_1 300$, or if $s_1 > 1/6$. The situation is symmetric for injurer 2: if she expects injurer 1 to take care, she will also take care, but if she expects injurer 1 not to take care, she will only take care if $s_2 > 1/6$. Note first that if s_1 and s_2 are both greater than 1/6, joint care is the unique equilibrium. Suppose, however, that s_1, say, is less than 1/6 (which means that $s_2 > 5/6$). Thus, injurer 1 will be tempted to refrain from care. But since s_2 is necessarily *greater* than 1/6, injurer 2 will definitely take care, which would then leave injurer 1 to bear all of the damages—in effect, s_1 becomes one. Thus, injurer 1 will also take care to avoid liability, and so the unique equilibrium is for both to take care. The reason negligence works here, despite the possible sharing of liability, is that neither injurer

Table 7.3 Equilibrium under negligence with joint and several liability

		Injurer 2:	
		Care	*No care*
Injurer 1:	Care	**50, 50**	50, 150
	No care	150, 50	$s_1 300$, $s_2 300$

Note Boldfaced entries indicate optimal choices

[7] The analysis is identical to that for the bilateral care model above, except that here, the choices are by the two injurers rather than the injurer and the victim.

has an incentive to *unilaterally* refrain from care because that would subject that party to full liability regardless of their belief about s_i.

As an alternative to joint and several liability, consider a rule that assigns liability in proportion to the conditional risk, as examined in the background-risk case above. Here, each injurer would face liability in proportion to the probability that his or her actions caused the harm, conditional on an accident having occurred. Suppose in the above example that one of the injurers unilaterally chooses not to take care. The probability of an accident rises from 0.05 to 0.15. Using the above logic, the proportion of damages attributable to that injurer in the event of an accident is therefore equal to $(0.15 - 0.05)/0.15 = 2/3$, whereas the other injurer would face $1/3$ of the damages. If we assume that when both take care they share damages equally in the event of an accident (which occurs with probability 0.05), the comparison of the injurer's total expected costs with and without care (given that the other injurer is taking care) is as follows:

$$\text{Care by both}: (.05) \times (.5) \times \$1{,}000 + \$50 = \$75,$$

$$\text{No care by one}: (.15) \times \left(\frac{.10}{.15}\right) \times \$1{,}000 = \$100,$$

Thus, it is not advantageous for either injurer to unilaterally deviate from the joint-care outcome.

In an interesting case, a court applied a rule something like this to apportion liability among several firms that were known to have manufactured a certain drug that was later shown to be carcinogenic.[8] The case involved a woman who became ill long after having taken the drug, and so it could not be ascertained which manufacturer had sold it to her. The court therefore apportioned liability according to the market shares of the firms at the time of purchase, which in the current context can be interpreted as a proxy for their conditional probabilities of having been the seller. The preceding example shows that such a rule, if properly structured, creates efficient incentives for injurers to take precautions

[8] See *Sindell v. Abbott Laboratories*, 163 Cl. Rptr. 132, 607 P.2d 924 (1980). Also see Marino (1991).

against risk. As in all of these situations involving uncertainty over causation, however, the liability faced by injurers is not necessarily equal to the harm that they actually caused.

Liability for Risk

So far, we have focused on apportioning harm from accidents after they have occurred; that is, after some harm has materialized. As a general rule, this is a requirement for liability under tort law—that is, only victims of actual harm can sue for damages. In light of our discussion of the role of comparative risk in attributing responsibility for realized harm, however, it is not a large step to propose that liability could also be assigned prior to the imposition of harm based on the *risk of harm*.[9] This would seem to be especially attractive for those risks that have a long latency period, which, as noted, may present victims with great difficulty in ascertaining causation after the fact, and/or in identifying the injurer at all. For example, the manufacturer of a dangerous product may have gone out of business by the time harm materializes.[10]

The downside of allowing a "tort for risk," however, is that, by expanding the scope of liability, it could potentially lead to an avalanche of lawsuits, thus possibly crippling the ability of the legal system to enforce the rule. Further, it could actually trigger bankruptcy by firms engaged in the manufacture of risky products by creating a "race to file." Both of these possibilities would limit the ability of victims to seek compensation while also diluting incentives for injurers to take precaution.

To illustrate the issues, return to the example of a single injurer with a background risk. Suppose that the harm in question, if it actually materialized, would cost the victim $300,000. Suppose further that the injurer's liability under conventional tort law would be based on the conditional probability that the injurer caused the harm, once it materializes. Thus, with a background risk of 0.10 and an additional risk of 0.05 from the actions of the injurer, the relevant conditional probability would be $0.05/0.15 = 1/3$. If and when an illness occurs, the injurer's liability would therefore be $(1/3)(\$300{,}000) = \$100{,}000$. The resulting

[9] In other words, the sanction would be "act-based" rather than "harm-based." See Garoupa and Obidzinski (2011) for a model of this distinction.

[10] See, for example, Robinson (1985). For a formal analysis, see Miceli and Segerson (2005).

expected liability for the injurer *as of the time of exposure* would be equal to the probability of harm multiplied by the liability in the event of harm, or (0.15)($100,000) = $15,000.

By comparison, under a tort-for-risk rule, the injurer could be sued *at the time of exposure* for the expected harm attributable to that injurer's actions. This would also equal (0.15)(1/3)($300,000) = $15,000. The two rules—*ex post* probabilistic apportionment and *ex ante* tort for risk—would therefore expose the injurer to the same *expected* liability, and hence would have the same effects on the latter's incentives to prevent the harm before the fact. As we have suggested, however, the two rules would be very different in other respects.

The first difference is that the conventional (probabilistic causation) rule based on actual harm would result in far fewer lawsuits. Suppose, for example, that over some time period, the injurer sells 1,000 units of the potentially harmful product. On average, this will result in 150 injuries (0.15 × 1,000), and hence, 150 lawsuits under conventional tort law. If each lawsuit costs $1000, total expected litigation costs would therefore be 150 ×$1000 = $150,000. By comparison, under the tort-for-risk rule, the injurer would theoretically face a lawsuit by *every purchaser of the product* (because all are taking on some risk). Thus, total litigation costs over the set time period would 1,000 ×$1000 = $1 million. The tort-for-risk rule is therefore much costlier to administer. This would be partially offset by the fact that not all purchasers will file suit under the tort-for-risk rule because the discounted award of $15,000 may exceed the costs of filing for some. (A class action suit would possibly allow more victims to join in a consolidated case.) By contrast, the award of $100,000 in the event of an actual illness would likely induce all or most victims to file. Thus, the administrative costs under the tort-for-risk rule would almost certainly dwarf those under the conventional rule.

An offsetting disadvantage of the conventional rule is that a very large one-time judgment could bankrupt the injurer, thereby foreclosing any future victims from filing suit. (This would result in a judgment-proof problem as discussed in Chap. 5.) Although *expected* awards are the same under the two rules, actual payouts under the tort-for-risk rule are more predictable and limited in magnitude, and thus are perhaps more easily sustainable by a constant stream of revenue. Still, the sheer number of cases may overwhelm the firm's ability to pay claims.

Although tort law does not generally allow claims for mere risk, various forms of government regulation serve the same function by imposing

Table 7.4 Speed limit example

Speed	*B₁*	*B₂*	*Risk*	*SB₁*	*SB₂*
50	20	40	10	**10**	30
60	30	60	25	5	**35**
70	35	75	50	−15	25

Note Boldfaced entries indicate maximum benefits

sanctions for risky activities. For example, traffic laws threaten fines for driving at excessive speeds or otherwise engaging in reckless behaviors, and various regulations govern the safety of consumer products and the workplace.[11] Table 7.4 offers an example based on the imposition of a speed limit.

The net benefits for two drivers are shown by the columns labeled B_1 and B_2. These benefits include the gross value of driving at a certain speed less any risk the driver himself or herself incurs. Both drivers therefore receive increasing net benefits from driving faster, but driver two receives a greater benefit at every speed. The column labeled "Risk" shows the expected external harm at each speed, representing the harm to *other drivers or pedestrians*. This is not actual harm but the risk of harm as defined above. Note that it rises at an increasing rate with speed. The final two columns show the net social benefit for each driver, which equals the driver's private benefit minus the risk. The boldfaced entries show the maximized values for each driver, indicating that the optimal speed for driver one is 50 and the optimal speed for driver two is 60.

One approach for controlling this risk would be to impose a fine (Pigovian tax) on all driving, with the fine rising in proportion to the speed (risk).[12] Thus, the fine would coincide with the expected harm in column four. This regulation would work perfectly to induce both drivers to choose the socially optimal speed—50 for driver one and 60 for driver two. The cost of administering such a system, however, would be very high because both (all) drivers would be fined at all speeds. The ability to electronically monitor driving has substantially lowered this cost, but only at the expense of what many consider to be an excessive invasion of

[11] See Viscusi et al. (2005).

[12] The following discussion draws on Miceli and Mungan (2021).

privacy. In any case, fines would be assessed at every speed since driving is an inherently risky activity.

The advantage of a speed limit is to lower the need to sanction driving at speeds considered to be "legal," meaning speeds that impose "acceptable" risks. This would greatly reduce the need to impose sanctions, thereby lowering enforcement costs. The situation would be similar to a negligence standard, which we have seen lowers the number of lawsuits relative to a rule of strict liability. The main disadvantage of a speed limit is that it cannot be individualized, but rather would have to be applied uniformly to all drivers. In other words, it would have to be a "one size fits all" standard. In the above example, the optimal speed for the two drivers is different, and so, unlike the tax, a single speed limit would not necessarily achieve the most efficient outcome.

To illustrate, suppose that the speed limit is set at 50. Drivers who comply with the limit would therefore not be subject to a fine, but those who exceed it would be. Suppose the fine is set equal to the risk associated with the driver's actual speed. Thus, someone caught driving at 60 would incur a fine of $25, while someone caught driving at 70 would incur a fine of $50 (assuming in both cases that detection is certain). Given the limit of 50, both drivers would comply. For driver one, complying with the limit yields a benefit of $20 and no fine, whereas driving at 60 would yield a benefit of $5 (including a fine of $25), and driving at 70 would yield a net benefit of – $25 (including a fine of $50). For driver two, complying with the limit yields a benefit of $40 and no fine, whereas driving at 60 a net benefit $35 (=$60 – $25), and driving at 70 would yield a net benefit of $25 (=$75 – $50). If the limit were instead set at 60, both drivers would again comply.

Like a negligence rule, the desire to *avoid* a fine in this case is a powerful motivator. However, as the example illustrates, it achieves a less efficient outcome than a pure Pigovian tax because most drivers will "cluster" at the posted limit, resulting in some drivers driving too slowly and others driving too fast. There will also likely be some drivers who intentionally violate the limit and "willingly" pay the fine. This will be especially true if the limit is set fairly low. Suppose, for example, that driver two's benefit from driving at 60 is $66 rather than $60. If the speed limit remains at 50, she will exceed it and drive 60 because the net gain, including the fine, is now $41 (=$66 – $25), which is larger than the $40 gain from driving at the limit. This is actually socially desirable because driver two is acting efficiently—for her, the outcome is the same as it would be under the efficient Pigovian tax. This factor actually works in the direction of setting a lower limit, since some non-compliance promotes efficient behavior. However, it raises enforcement costs because more fines have to be imposed. Thus, choosing the optimal speed limit involves a balance between efficient behavior in the presence of risk and enforcement costs.

As a final point, note that compliance with a regulatory standard based on *risk* does not necessarily shield an individual from liability if an actual harm arises (i.e., if an accident occurs). For example, a driver who injures someone is not immune from a lawsuit for damages just because he or she was driving at the speed limit. It depends on the applicable liability rule. If the rule is strict liability, all that matters is that the driver caused the accident, and so whether or not he exceeded the speed limit would be immaterial for assigning liability. However, it would possibly be a relevant consideration under a negligence standard. As we have seen, the determination of negligence can depend on a number of factors, and failure to act reasonably with respect to any one of them would potentially be a basis for liability. For example, one could be found negligent for failing to signal when changing lanes even if complying with the speed limit.

Reparations for Slavery and Other Past Wrongs as Derivative Tort Claims

Tort claims for past harms brought by plaintiffs other than the direct victim(s) fall under the heading of "derivative claims." Claims for reparations for slavery provide the most prominent, and certainly, the most controversial, example of this legal theory of responsibility.[13] Note that this is not the same thing as collective responsibility (which we will discuss in the next chapter) in the sense that defendants are alleged to have benefitted from the past unlawful acts and plaintiffs to have correspondingly been deprived of benefits. Thus, while direct causation may be absent, the claim is that there exists a nexus between current plaintiffs and defendants, though this linkage becomes more tenuous as the amount of time that has passed since the original harmful act becomes larger. Still, the fundamental question is the same: is there any justification for holding

[13] This section is based on Hylton (2004).

someone responsible for harms that were caused by someone else in the past?

As a general proposition, courts have not looked favorably on derivative claims, even when they are contemporaneous with the harmful act. They have, for example, denied liability for harms because they were not judged foreseeable by the injurer, or were not proximately caused by the injurer's negligence. As an illustration, in the case of *Ryan v. New York Central Railroad Co.*,[14] the defendant railroad was held liable for burning down a house, but strangely, the court did not extend that liability to other houses to which the initial fire subsequently spread. This limitation seems to defy any common-sense interpretation of either foreseeability or proximate cause, at least as we have previously defined these terms.

As noted, the passage of time weakens the argument for such claims. Indeed, the traditional common law rule held that a tort claim "died" along with the original victim and/or the injurer. Thus, even a child whose parent was negligently killed had no cause of action, despite having been denied the sole means of support. This rule was changed by statutes passed at the state level, which allowed causes of action for wrongful death by surviving family members.[15] This reflected a sensible change both in terms of compensating victims, who suffered real and immediate harm, and for creating the obviously desirable incentive for injurers to refrain from killing rather than merely injuring their victims.

Extending this logic to reparations claims, however, introduces a much longer time lag between the harmful act and the claim for liability. Specifically, reparations would both award compensation to parties who were not the direct victims, and extend responsibility to parties that did not directly cause the harm. And while there may be a moral or corrective-justice argument for doing this,[16] the question of interest here is whether there is any economic basis for it.

Hylton (2004) discusses two legal theories on which such a damage claim could possibly be based: that for unpaid wages, and that for restitution. The first would be based on some measure of the wage that a slave would have been paid under ordinary market conditions at the time (i.e., as part of a consensual labor contract), while the second would be based

[14] 35 N.Y. 210 (1866).

[15] Keeton, et al. (1984, pp. 940–961).

[16] See the sources cited in Hylton (2004, pp. 1241–1243).

on the surplus value (profit) that the slave owner received from the slave's labor. Both would be computed net of the in-kind compensation that a slave actually received (food and housing). Suppose, for example, that a slave's daily labor produced gross value of $20, the cost of feeding and housing the slave was $5, and the market wage for the work in question was $10. Liability for unpaid wages would equal $5 (=$10 – $5), which is the market wage less the in-kind compensation, while a restitution award would be $15 (=$20 – $5), which is the owner's gain net of costs.[17]

In examining these alternatives, let us initially set aside the time (and moral) dimensions and focus on how the measure of damages would affect the incentives of injurers (slave owners). The key question is whether the goal of liability is to internalize the harm suffered by victims or to eliminate the gain received by injurers. The first reflects the objective of requiring injurers to fully account for the impact of their conduct on victims. In the current context, this involves retroactive payment of market-level wages net of in-kind compensation so as to reflect the actual contribution of the slave's labor input to the owner's productive activity. Note, however, that this approach reserves all of the surplus from the exchange for the employer, which is what motivates the latter to engage in the activity in the first place.

While this theory makes sense in settings where market exchange is not possible or practical (i.e., in the presence of true externalities), that clearly was not the case with slave labor, where a market either existed or could easily have been brought into existence. Engaging in forced labor in such a setting therefore involves what Posner (1985) has called "market bypass," by which he means forcing an exchange when a market alternative was available or would have been feasible.[18] Awarding unpaid wages after the fact does nothing to discourage this sort of activity, whereas depriving the employer of any benefits from the activity (disgorgement) presumably would discourage it. In this sense, restitution effectively labels the act as socially undesirable. As Hylton (2004, p. 1246) observes, "...slavery would appear appropriate for a restitution-based damage claim because the slaveholder has stolen the labor of his victim, a classic case of bypassing the market."

[17] Compare this to a consensual employment relationship at a wage of $10, where the worker's net return is $10 – $5 = $5 and the employer's net gain is $20 – $10 = $10.

[18] I will return to the market-bypass theory as an alternative to the conventional Pigovian-based theory of crime due to Becker (1968). (See Chap. 9.).

As noted above, however, both theories of compensation are weakened by the time lag between the harmful act and the claim. The case for compensation (unpaid wages) is weakened by the fact that the passage of time creates so many possible ways that the wages, if they had been paid, would have been diverted or dissipated over time, and hence not ultimately passed down to subsequent generations. The claim for restitution is weakened by the dilution of the message which liability is meant to send—namely, that the activity in question is not a socially acceptable one when conducted non-consensually, and any realized gains will eventually have to be disgorged.

It follows that the greater the length of time between the harmful conduct and the assignment of responsibility, the lesser will be its intended impact. Amplifying this point is the argument that the law needs to be settled at some point in order for people to form stable expectations. Recall that this was an important rationale for statutes of limitations as discussed in Chap. 5. For these reasons, Hylton (2004) ultimately reaches the conclusion that the above tort theories fail to offer a convincing *economic* case for reparations. The moral case for reparations is obviously beyond the scope of the current study.

References

Becker, G. 1968. Crime and Punishment: An Economic Approach. *Journal of Political Economy* 76: 169–217.

Cooter, R. 1989. Punitive Damages for Deterrence: When and How Much? *Alabama Law Review* 40: 1143–1196.

Garoupa, N., and M. Obidzinski. 2011. The scope of punishment: an economic theory. *European Journal of Law and Economics* 31: 237–247.

Hylton, K. 2004. Slavery and Tort Law. *Boston University Law Review* 84: 1209–1255.

Hylton, K., and T. Miceli. 2005. Should Tort Damages be Multiplied? *Journal of Law, Economics, and Organization* 21: 388–416.

Keeton, W., D. Dobbs, R. Keeton, and D. Owen. 1984. *Prosser and Keeton on Torts*, 5th ed. St. Paul, MN: West Publishing.

Landes, W., and R. Posner. 1987. *The Economic Structure of Tort Law*. Cambridge, MA: Harvard Univ. Press.

Marino, A. 1991. Market Share Liability and Economic Efficiency. *Southern Economic Journal* 57: 667–675.

Miceli, T., and M. Mungan. 2021. The Limit of Law: Factors Influencing the Decision to Make Harmful Acts Illegal. *Economics of Governance* 22: 293–307.

Miceli, T., and K. Segerson. 2005. Do Exposure Suits Produce a Race to File? An Economic Analysis of a Tort for Risk. *Rand Journal of Economics* 36: 613–627.

Posner, R. 1985. An Economic Theory of the Criminal Law. *Columbia Law Review* 85: 1193–1231.

Robinson, G. 1985. Probabilistic Causation and Compensation for Tortious Risk. *Journal of Legal Studies* 14: 779–798.

Shavell, S. 1985. Uncertainty Over Causation and the Determination of Civil Liability. *Journal of Law and Economics* 28: 587–609.

Viscusi, W., J. Harrington, and J. Vernon. 2005. *Economics of Regulation and Antitrust*, 4th ed. Cambridge, MA: MIT Press.

CHAPTER 8

Expanding Responsibility: Criminal Doctrines

This chapter turns to criminal doctrines that have the effect of shifting responsibility, in whole or in part, from individuals who actually caused harm to others who did not. Again, the emphasis will be on offering explanations for these doctrines from an economic perspective.

The Felony Murder Rule

The felony murder rule is a provision of criminal law in some jurisdictions that allows a criminal defendant to be charged with first-degree murder if a person is killed while that defendant is in the process of committing a felony, even if someone else actually committed the killing.[1] It is not required to prove intent on the part of the defendant, as is ordinarily required under criminal law, or even that the defendant's actions were directly responsible for the death. What is required is that the causal link between the offense and the death not be too remote in the sense that the actions of the defendant created a reasonably foreseeable danger

[1] See Adelstein (2017, pp. 200–205). As an example, see *McGautha v. California*, 402 U.S. 183 (1971), which concerned an armed robbery carried out by two gunmen, one of whom shot and killed the store owner. However, both were charged with first-degree murder.

T. J. Miceli, *Harm and Responsibility*,
https://doi.org/10.1007/978-3-031-74831-8_8

to the victim's life. In other words, the defendant's participation in the underlying offense was a proximate cause of the victim's death.

Interestingly, recall that our discussion of proximate cause in the context of tort law was that it served as a *limit* on an injurer's liability for accidental harm. Here, by contrast, it is a basis for *expanding* a defendant's criminal liability. This can be reconciled as follows. In both contexts, cause-in-fact (actual causation) is a pre-requisite for responsibility. In tort law, the additional requirement of proximate cause (reasonable foreseeability) is also needed (possibly combined with negligence). In criminal law, the usual requirement beyond causation is intent, which, as we have seen, requires some amount of deliberation or planning, and hence goes beyond mere foreseeability. The effect of the felony murder rule is to dispose of the need to prove intent per se and replace it with the weaker foreseeability standard. The basis for liability therefore expands to look more like that in tort law.

One explanation for this expansion of criminal liability is simply that an offender is morally culpable for all of the consequences of his acts, including those that he did not intend but could have foreseen. Because intent to commit the underlying crime is present, liability should extend to any subsidiary consequences of it. This also makes sense from an economic (deterrence) perspective, because those contemplating potentially harmful acts should take full account of any harms that a reasonable person could anticipate will arise as a consequence of those acts.

Another perspective on this doctrine is that it represents a move in the direction of "collective responsibility" in the sense that responsibility for some offense falls on a group of individuals, even if only some members of that group are actually "guilty" of the offense. Most people find this concept objectionable both because of its departure from individual responsibility and their general aversion to wrongful punishment. And yet, collective responsibility has been an important law enforcement strategy throughout history, and it remains pervasive in modern law. We will return to this in more detail below.

Preventive Enforcement

Law enforcement generally involves the assessment of responsibility only after someone has been accused and convicted of an unlawful act. We have previously discussed instances of wrongful or excessive punishment, but these have been treated as "errors" to be avoided or minimized to the extent possible. The principal economic purpose of punishment is to deter crime, and we have seen that errors dilute that function. But even error-free enforcement cannot deter all crimes. This raises the prospect of pre-emptive deterrence—that is, seeking to prevent crimes before they happen. I will consider two forms of this: preventive enforcement and incapacitation.

Preventive enforcement is the counterpart in criminal law to a tort for risk. An example is the so-called Terry stop, which is a brief detention of a person based on a reasonable suspicion that he or she is involved in criminal activity.[2] Examples include stopping and frisking a pedestrian, and pulling over an automobile for a minor infraction in order to investigate the possible commission of a more serious crime.

Law enforcement policy generally involves a combination of prevention and detection. The advantage of prevention is that, when successful, it avoids harm; the disadvantage is that it imposes costs on some innocent individuals given that suspicion is not certainty. The question is, how much "inconvenience cost" is society willing to tolerate in order to avoid the harm from actual crimes? This is a balancing question of the sort that we have frequently encountered throughout this study, and as we have seen, it is generally resolved by the application of a threshold (reasonableness) test.

Suppose that commission of a particular crime requires a preliminary act x which is not, by itself, criminal. Indeed, innocent people sometimes engage in this act. The question is whether observation of x by the police should result in some intrusive enforcement action that will thwart a crime if one is intended, but which imposes a cost on some innocent people. Let the harm from a crime be h, let the cost of intrusion to an innocent person be c, and let q be the probability that x in fact signals a crime. Now consider two policies: ***never intervene*** when x is observed, and ***always intervene***. The first results in expected costs of qh,[3] while the second results in expected costs of $(1 - q)c$. Intervention is therefore preferred if $(1 - q)c < qh$, or if

$$q > \frac{c}{h + c}$$

[2] Such actions are permitted by the Supreme Court in *Terry v. Ohio*, 392 U.S. 1 (1968). The discussion of this strategy here is based on Mungan (2018).

[3] Note that the harm from crime in this case, h, includes the cost to the victim plus cost that will have to be expended to apprehend and punish the offender.

This establishes a threshold rule that would authorize preventive intervention if the belief that the observed behavior is associated with criminal behavior is high enough. Like the Hand test for negligence, this can be interpreted as a reasonable-suspicion standard, which is what the Supreme Court has in fact authorized. Note that this condition is more likely to be met for more severe crimes (larger h) and for less intrusive interventions (smaller c). Thus, as was true of negligence, the meaning of reasonableness will necessarily be case-specific.

A more extreme form of preventive enforcement involves actually detaining individuals who are thought to impose a risk of future harm on society, thereby making it physically impossible for them to do the harm. This reflects the incapacitation function of imprisonment or other forms of detention. One approach to pre-emptive detention is to detain a subject before he has committed any harmful acts. The analysis of this option is in principle identical to that for preventive enforcement above—if one is observed engaging in acts that indicate a sufficiently high propensity to commit an actual crime, it is optimal to detain him on cost–benefit grounds. This is a very severe form of prevention, however, because it involves deprivation of liberty, and so even if it is cost-justified in a narrow sense, it is not generally permitted in American law. Only a person who actually commits a harmful act is sometimes incapacitated so as to prevent him or her from committing future harmful acts. In this case, detention serves the dual purpose of punishing the previous act and preventing future acts.

When someone is detained, the optimal duration of that detention will depend on the trade-off between the cost to society of holding him compared to the prevented harm during the term of imprisonment. Specifically, if the cost of incapacitation per unit of time is d, and the prevented harm per unit of time is h, then the individual should be detained as long as $d < h$ (Shavell 1987). However, if and when h falls below d, the individual should be released. Although it seems likely that a person's propensity to commit crimes will decline with age, the opposite tendency—that an offender will harden into an inveterate criminal with more time in prison—is also possible. Thus, the optimal duration of incapacitation will be individual-specific.

Finally, we note that the deterrence and incapacitation functions of imprisonment are not incompatible—offenders can be deterred by the threat of prison and incapacitated by actual imprisonment. Ideally, the optimal prison term should balance these two functions.[4] This involves the following trade-off. Raising the prison term for a convicted offender will increase deterrence by making offenses costlier to future offenders (general deterrence), while at the same time preventing the current offender from committing harmful acts during the term of his imprisonment (specific deterrence). Offsetting these benefits is the cost of detaining an offender longer than would be justified on the grounds of incapacitation. The individualization of punishments on ex post fairness grounds complicates this balancing act because it makes it difficult for potential offenders to predict the costs that they will face, thereby clouding the deterrence function.

Collective Responsibility

Both the felony murder rule and the various forms of preventive enforcement just discussed have raised the concept of "collective responsibility," by which we mean the spreading of responsibility to some individuals who may not have actually caused any harm. On its face, this conflicts with the notion of individual responsibility, which for many embodies a fundamental element of justice and is the only morally defensible basis for punishment. It is nevertheless true that the assignment of guilt to an entire community of which the wrongdoer is known (or thought) to be a member has been pervasive throughout history. More surprisingly, perhaps, is that some forms of this sort of group punishment persist in modern society. The question is whether these actions are economically justified, irrespective of whether they are morally acceptable.

The conventional view associates collective responsibility as a law enforcement strategy with ancient societies.[5] The Trojan War, in which a Greek army besieged the City of Troy in an effort to avenge Paris's kidnapping of Helen, epitomizes this idea.[6] Modern wars waged against nations known to harbor terrorists represent a modern version of this same strategy. The ancient concept of "pollution," the belief that a wrongdoer conferred guilt on his community or family, reflects a similar

[4] See, for example, Miceli (2010) and Shavell (2015).

[5] See, for example, Posner (1983), Parisi and Dari-Mattiacci (2004), Miceli and Segerson (2007), Dillbary (2021), and Miceli (2019, Chapter 7).

[6] See Wood (1998) for a survey of the historical evidence for this war.

idea. The most famous example of this in ancient history was the pollution of Thebes, brought about by Oedipus's murder of his father (albeit unknowingly).

Other ancient examples of collective responsibility are found in the Hammurabi Code (a provision of which allowed a victim of robbery or murder to seek retribution from the city where the crime took place), the Old Testament (e.g., the stories of Noah (Genesis: 7) and Sodom and Gomorrah (Genesis: 18–19)), the New Testament (King Herod's decree requiring the killing of all newborn babies in the vicinity of Bethlehem in response to the reported birth of a messiah in that town (Matthew 2: 1–16)), and Roman law (which contained various examples of collective responsibility (Harries 2013)).

Scholars attribute the pervasiveness of collective responsibility in ancient times to two characteristics of pre-modern society. The first is the absence of a centralized government capable of enforcing laws, which meant that it usually fell to a victim's family, kinship group, or community, to retaliate against an injurer (Posner 1983). Friedman (2000, Chapter 17), for example, describes the legal system in Iceland during the time of the sagas as one in which laws were privately enforced, and anyone who defended or shielded a lawbreaker could himself be held responsible for the damages. Old English law as described by Blackstone's *Commentaries* similarly described a provision that instructed residents of a village in which a robbery took place "to make hue and cry after the felon," and held the entire village responsible if they could not locate the offender.

The second characteristic of ancient society that supposedly justified the practice of group responsibility is that punishment was based on a desire for retaliation or revenge.[7] Parisi and Dari-Mattiacci (2004, p. 497) note, for example, that "several ancient rules of talionic justice require that the penalty be imposed with uncompromising symmetry, replicating the harm suffered by the victim and his or her family." And if the actual offender could not be located, the vengeance could be exacted vicariously from the latter's family. These same authors argue, however, that the transition from group to individual responsibility, as depicted in the Bible, reflected the emergence of the notion that it was unjust to punish

[7] See, for example, Holmes (1881, p 6), who contends that much of modern law is grounded in the impulse for revenge.

the innocent for the crimes of the guilty (Parisi and Dari-Mattiacci 2004, pp. 502–503).[8]

Nevertheless, and somewhat surprisingly, various forms of group punishment, or something very much like it, persist in modern law and society.[9] Two examples from classic literature are found in Samuel Taylor Coleridge's poem, "The Rime of the Ancient Mariner," which attributes guilt to a crew of sailors for the killing of an albatross by one of them; and the writings of Nathaniel Hawthorne, which embodies the idea of guilt being inherited by an offender's ancestors.[10] Two more recent examples are the cases of *People v. Cowart*[11] and *Brown v. City of Oneanta*.[12] The first case concerned a shooting at an outdoor party in Chicago that resulted in the death of one of the attendees. At least twenty-eight shots were fired by multiple shooters, and although it was impossible to identify the person who fired the fatal shot, one man, Charles Cowart, was charged and convicted of murder, although the verdict was later overturned on appeal. The second case concerned the rape of an elderly women who could only identify the assailant as a young black man with a cut on his hand. The police responded by investigating 250 black males in the surrounding community. None of them was ultimately charged, but the court found the sweep legal, despite the obvious cloud of suspicion that it created for the suspects.

A persuasive defense of this approach to law enforcement is that the "innocent" members of the punishment group may actually deserve to share in the true offender's culpability. The above example of a nation that goes to war with another that is known to harbor terrorists or otherwise condone their actions epitomizes the argument. As Levmore (1995b, p. 99) observes, "we are accustomed to the fact that war claims the lives of innocent people," but "one nation may be justified in warring against another nation when the other nation is unable to control the actions of some of its inhabitants."

[8] The Aeschylus (1953) trilogy *Oresteia* embodies a similar theme of transitioning from a society where justice is vengeance-based to one where it is law-based.

[9] See, for example, Levmore (1995a, b) Levinson (2003), and Dillbary and Miceli (2023, 2024).

[10] Hawthorne's ancestor was a judge at the Salem Witch Trials. See Buell (1986, p. 360).

[11] 81 N.E.3d 1023 Ill. App., 2017).

[12] 221 F.3d 329 (2nd Cir. 2000).

Similar logic underlies the tort doctrine of *respondeat superior*, which holds an employer vicariously liable for the harmful actions of one of its employees. The idea is that the employer should have taken steps to monitor or control the former's actions. This assumes the ability of the former to monitor the latter's behavior, coupled with the existence of some contractual levers (e.g., the ability to penalize or terminate an employee) that can be used to control the latter's actions. The doctrine in effect enlists the employer as a surrogate law enforcer under the threat that failure to act as such will result in the employer himself being subject to a sanction. A more mundane but familiar example of this same principle is when an entire class is punished for the actions of one schoolyard prankster. The justification is that this serves the double purpose of motivating the class to turn over the actual offender, and enlisting the powerful effect of peer pressure to deter future infractions.[13]

A common thread linking these examples is the savings in enforcement costs owing to the superior ability of certain groups to discipline their own members. And if they fail to carry out that task, whether out of loyalty or group solidarity, it is justifiable to punish the entire group, which by its inaction implicitly shares in the offender's guilt. This reflects the information-forcing rationale for holding a group of defendants liable even when there is no evidence of their actual complicity (other than concealing the true offender's identity).[14] An offsetting factor is that such a strategy may backfire if members of the target group develop an "us-versus-them" mentality that ultimately breeds resistance to law enforcement generally. This would particularly seem to apply to close-knit groups, like fraternities, religious cults, and nations that harbor terrorists (Kahan 1998).

There is a very different economic rationale for group punishment that has nothing to do with peer monitoring or information extraction, but relates instead to the idea of probability scaling in the economic theory of criminal law.[15] Recall from Chap. 3 that this practice also involves a kind of conscious "error"—namely, punishing someone more harshly than their crime warrants; in essence, punishing one person for those

[13] This resembles peer monitoring in employment settings. See, for example, Kandel and Lazear (1992).

[14] See the discussion of this same concept in connection with the doctrine of *res ipsa loquitur* in Chap. 5. Also see Levmore (1995a).

[15] As discussed in Chap. 3.

offenders who avoided detection. We will see that group punishment, like probability scaling, can also serve as a response to the problem of costly detection of criminal offenders, and as such may be part of an efficient (cost-minimizing) enforcement strategy.

To that end, consider the following characterization of the detection problem.[16] Suppose an offense has been committed and the actual offender is a member of a known group, which could be very large. Gathering of evidence and interviews with witnesses can reduce the group of suspects to an ever-smaller number until eventually, the most likely suspect is identified. If the probability of that suspect's guilt is large enough, he or she is prosecuted. This characterization is consistent with the approach taken in the economic model of crime, which defines p to be the probability that the actual offender is apprehended and punished. If the cost of the sanction to the offender is s, then the expected sanction from the offender's perspective is ps. This represents the offender's expected cost of committing the crime and hence establishes the level of deterrence as signaled by the threat of punishment.[17]

The idea of probability scaling, as we previously discussed, is that the same level of deterrence can be achieved by any combination of p and s that maintains the desired product, ps. Thus, if s is a fine that can be raised costlessly, then a given level of deterrence can always be achieved at a lower enforcement cost by simply raising s as much as possible and proportionately lowering p. In other words, catch fewer offenders but punish those who are caught as harshly as is feasible or permissible. Fairness considerations aside, this represents an efficient policy.

The possibility of group punishment extends this logic to a different margin by relaxing the constraint that at most one person can be punished for the crime.[18] Suppose that it is determined that n suspects will be punished, where $1 \leq n \leq N$, and N is defined to be the size of the *smallest group of which the offender is known with certainty to be a member*. (Think, for example, of any Agatha Christie story.) The process of detection involves winnowing N down to n.

[16] See James (2011, Chapter XIII) for a popular account of this process.

[17] The question of how or whether offenders learn p and s is another matter. See, for example, Miceli, Segerson, and Earnhart (2022).

[18] We are assuming throughout that there is in fact a single offender.

As a first pass at this, imagine that the n members of the "punishment group" are chosen at random. The probability that the true offender is among this subgroup is $p = n/N$. For example, if there are 1000 members of the overall group (N) and 100 are chosen at random to be punished, the probability that the true offender will be among those punished is $100/1000 = 0.10$. Leaving aside for now the question of whether this would ever be an acceptable strategy, note that its impact on deterrence would be no different than a more concerted, but still imperfect, effort to identify the actual offender that only succeeds ten percent of the time. In both cases, would-be offenders would perceive that $p = 0.10$. However, the enforcement cost of the group punishment strategy would be substantially lower because it involves no effort to identify the true offender. Carrying this argument to its logical extreme, the group punishment approach can theoretically achieve certain punishment simply by setting $n = N$; that is, by punishing the entire group known to contain the offender. By contrast, achieving certainty under individual punishment with costly detection would probably not be possible for any reasonable expenditure of resources (i.e., $p = 1$ could never be achieved).

The following example illustrates the optimal enforcement policy that emerges from this line of reasoning.[19] Consider a crime that imposes social costs of \$500 and continue to assume that the offender is known to be a member of a group containing 1000 people. Thus, if n people are chosen at random to incur a sanction s, the probability that the actual offender will be punished is $n/1000$. Suppose the sanction takes the form of a fine in an amount s (yet to be determined). The expected sanction is therefore $ns/1000$. Optimal deterrence is achieved if this is equated to the social cost of the crime, or if

$$\frac{ns}{1000} = 500$$

Multiplying by 1000 gives

$$ns = 500{,}000$$

Any combination of n and s that satisfies this equation therefore achieves optimal deterrence while entailing zero enforcement costs (because selection of the punishment group is random). Table 8.1 shows the

[19] See Dillbary and Miceli (2023, 2024).

possibilities for different values of n between 1 and 1000. Figure 8.1 illustrates this graphically, where the downward-sloping line, called the iso-deterrence line, shows those combinations of n and s such that $ps =$ \$500.

The top line in the table, corresponding to point A in the graph, represents random individual punishment—that is, one randomly selected person is fined. In order to achieve optimal deterrence under such a policy, however, the fine would have to be set at \$500,000. To understand this, think of the calculation of a member of this group who is contemplating committing a crime. Optimal deterrence requires that he anticipate an expected sanction equal to \$500, which is the harm that his act will impose on society. Knowing that the person to be punished will

Table 8.1 Group punishment example, where $ns = 500{,}000$

n	s
1	\$500,000
25	20,000
50	10,000
100	5000
500	1000
1000	500

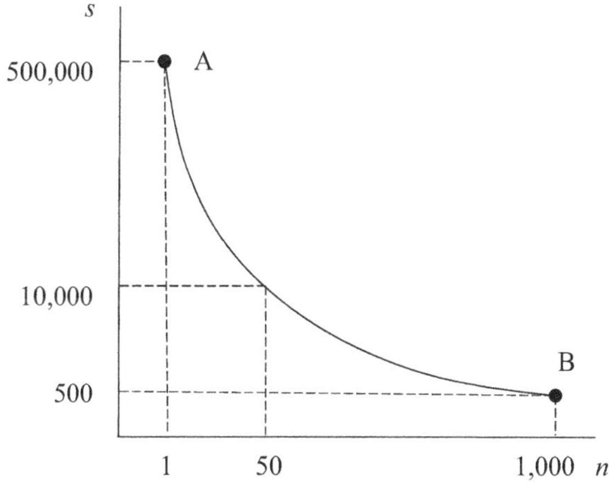

Fig. 8.1 Optimality of group punishment

be chosen at random, he computes the probability that he will be the one fined to be $1/1000 = 0.001$. In order for this to result in an expected fine of \$500, the actual fine must therefore be \$500,000. This, of course, is an extreme version of probability scaling as discussed above.

At the other extreme—corresponding to the bottom line in the table and point B in the graph—everyone in the group is punished when a crime is committed. In this case, a would-be offender faces certain punishment if he commits the act, and so the expected fine equals the actual fine, which would be set at \$500. This policy represents pure group punishment and therefore entails wrongfully punishing 999 people.

More generally, *any* point between A and B along the iso-deterrence line in Fig. 2 (corresponding to the rows of Table 8.1) achieves optimal deterrence with zero enforcement cost. Thus, there is a degree of freedom in choosing the size of the punishment group (n) and the size of the fine (s). As was true of probability scaling, however, the fine will be limited by the ability of offenders to pay a high fine. This constrains how low n can be set—that is, how small the punishment group can be. Suppose, for example, that the offender's maximum ability to pay is \$10,000. Then only those points on the iso-deterrence line between $n = 50$ and 1000 are possible. It follows that as the ability of offenders to pay a fine becomes more constrained, the minimum punishment group capable of achieving optimal deterrence grows.

The preceding enforcement scheme was not intended to be a practical policy proposal, though, as the catalog of examples above suggested, some version of it has been, and continues to be, used in various contexts. The purpose of the analysis was instead to demonstrate that the optimality of group punishment—as objectionable as it may seem—is just a logical extension of probability scaling in the standard economic model of crime. We have seen that scaling up fines saves on detection costs by effectively punishing one individual for the crimes of many; group punishment saves on detection costs by punishing many individuals for the crime of one. Both strategies therefore expand legal responsibility for harm, though along different margins: probability scaling increases the severity of punishment beyond the harm caused by an individual offender, whereas group punishment increases the scope of punishment to include non-offenders.

In both cases, the resulting savings come at the cost of some form of wrongful punishment—either excessive punishment or punishment of the wrong person—and for that reason, both practices are morally objectionable to most people. It is for this reason that actual law enforcement policies strive to identify the actual offender and to impose a punishment on that individual in proportion to the crime that he actually committed. As we have seen, these values are embodied in the substantial protections of criminal defendants, who are presumed innocent, along with the various impediments to punishments deemed to be excessive in relation to the harm inflicted. The higher costs of detection, and the costs of the procedural safeguards of those accused of crimes, are the price society is willing to pay to advance those values. That has not always and everywhere been the case, however, as the above examples illustrated.

Insurance as Collective Responsibility

Despite moral objections to collective responsibility, I will conclude this chapter by demonstrating that there is a close correspondence between collective responsibility and insurance. Insurance is a response to *risk aversion*, by which economists mean a dislike of fluctuations in income resulting from purely probabilistic events.[20] Suppose, for example, that a person will suffer a loss of $500,000 if a fire burns down that person's house. Let's say that the probability of a fire in any given year is 1/1000, or 0.001. The expected loss per year is therefore 0.001 ×$500,000 = $500, which represents the actuarially fair cost. A risk-averse person would, by definition, be willing to pay something more than $500 to avoid that loss. This extra amount is what permits an insurance company to offer policies which will cover the loss in return for a yearly premium above $500, say $525, thereby allowing them to earn a profit from the sale of such policies.

The reason the company is willing to take on the risk is that, by selling a very large number of policies, it can make the number of claims it has to pay very predictable. This is a consequence of the Law of Large Numbers, which says that when a random event is repeated a large number of times, the outcome approaches the expected value.[21] In this example, across the set of all policies sold, on average one in a thousand will result in a claim.

[20] See, for example, Hirshleifer and Riley (1992, Chapter 2).

[21] Insurance companies also reduce their risk by diversification, which means selling to customers whose risks are uncorrelated.

And since the revenue generated from those 1000 policies will amount to \$525,000 = 1000 ×\$525, the company will expect to make profit of \$25,000. Of course, its actual profit will not be perfectly predictable—in some years it will make less than \$25,000, and in some years more—but over a large enough time frame and across a larger number of policies, its profit will average out very close to \$25,000. Insurance companies can therefore act as if they were risk neutral.

Now consider the situation from the perspective of policyholders. Each one faces a risk of losing \$500,000. Although this will only happen on average once in a thousand years, when it does happen it is catastrophic. The availability of insurance allows customers to trade this uncertain prospect for a certain yearly cost of \$525. Another way to think about this is to consider the situation of a person who suffers a loss in a given year. This loss is covered by the insurance company by, in effect, *using the revenue that it has collected from the other 999 customers*.[22] In other words, the 999 customers who did not sustain a loss collectively pay for the loss of the one who did. This feature of insurance is similar to a situation where potential claimants are individually assigned liability according to the risk their policies create rather than the actual costs they incur. It is this sense in which insurance is a form of collective responsibility whereby "innocent" individuals (non-claimants) bear some of the cost caused by "guilty" individuals (claimants).

An important difference between insurance and collective punishment, of course, is that members of the insurance risk pool enter it voluntarily. Thus, they willingly take on the obligation to contribute to costs incurred by others in the pool. The reason they are willing to do so is the mutuality of obligations that the arrangement entails.

But there is also a voluntary component in the context of liability for risk in the sense that potential injurers can always refrain from engaging in the risky activity, thereby avoiding any possible liability. This obviously would entail a cost in the form of the forgone benefit from the risky activity, but that is a choice that potential injurers have to make whenever they engage in the activity. Both situations—buying insurance and engaging in a risky activity—therefore involve a choice regarding whether or not to enter the "risk group."

[22] Actually, it will have received revenue from all 1000 customers, assuming that the claimant paid its premium.

One may object that the group punishment scheme described above will not always involve a voluntary choice to enter (or remain in) the risk group; it depends on the circumstances. Innocent people may sometimes find themselves in the wrong place at the wrong time, thus potentially being swept up in a dragnet. But in other cases, people either knowingly join a group that contains actual wrongdoers, or, when they learn about the presence of wrongdoers, choose to remain in the group anyway. In these cases, their "innocence" in the event that one of those wrongdoers commits a crime is subject to debate, as some of the examples of, and justifications for, group punishment suggested.

Another apparent difference between insurance and collective responsibility is that victims of accidental losses do not intentionally cause the harms in question whereas criminal offenders do.[23] However, our discussion of accidents revealed that victims of accidental losses often have the ability to take precautions aimed at avoiding or mitigating those losses. Indeed, the possibility of moral hazard is a legitimate concern of insurers, given that insurance reduces the incentive of policyholders to invest in precaution.[24] The logic is the same as the demonstration that strict tort liability (as a form of insurance) eliminates incentives for victims to invest in precaution. Insurance companies respond to this problem in a number of ways. One is by only offering partial coverage—that is, by requiring customers to pay deductibles in the event of a claim, thereby subjecting customers to at least some responsibility in the event of an accident. Another is to condition premiums on observable behaviors that are correlated with riskiness, such as one's past record of accidents.

A related problem is when some customers are inherently riskier in the way that they behave, which results in some people filing insurance claims more often than others. Although a person's "riskiness" is not generally observable, insurance companies respond to this adverse selection problem by using proxies of risk to classify customers into different risk groups.[25] One such strategy is *statistical discrimination*, which uses a person's observable characteristics that are known to be correlated with risk, like age or gender, to set premiums. This is not a

[23] Coleman (1992, pp. 223–224), for example, notes that insurance for criminal acts would be seen by most people as "deplorable.".

[24] See, for example, Shavell (1982) and Shavell (2004, Chapter 11).

[25] See Akerlof (1970) and Rothschild and Stiglitz (1976).

perfect metric, however, because it attributes to *all* members of a group the characteristics of the *average* member. Racial profiling is a particularly nefarious—and hence illegal—version of this strategy, and hence it has been subject to severe criticism, particularly in the context of law enforcement.

It is noteworthy that people object to statistical discrimination for the same reason that they object to group punishment. It is because they see it as assigning responsibility for harm to someone other than the person who actually caused it. The ability of individuals to opt out of groups that are potentially subject to statistical discrimination is one safeguard against widespread use of the practice.But when opting out of a "punishment group" is not practical (because other options are lacking) or possible (as in the case of racial or ethnic profiling), legal prohibitions are necessary and just, even though the practice may be efficient strictly on economic grounds.[26]

References

Adelstein, R. 2017. *The Exchange Order: Property and Liability as an Exchange System*. New York: Oxford Univ. Press.

Aeschylus. "Oresteia." In *Aeschylus I*, edited by D. Grene and R. Lattimore. Chicago: Univ. of Chicago Press, 1953.

Akerlof, G. 1970. The Market for 'Lemons': Quality Uncertainty and the Market Mechanism. *Quarterly Journal of Economics* 84: 488–500.

Buell, L. 1986. *New England Literary Culture*. Cambridge: Cambridge Univ. Press.

Coleman, J. 1992. *Risks and Wrongs*. Cambridge, UK: Cambridge Univ. Press.

Dillbary, J. 2021. The Case Against Collective Responsibility. *Boston College Law Review* 62: 391–452.

Dillbary, J., and T. Miceli. 2023. Of Sinners and Scapegoats: The Economics of Collective Responsibility. *Washington Univ. Law Review* 100: 1299–1351.

Dillbary, J. and T. Miceli. "Reformulating Detection in the Economic Model of Crime: Probability Scaling and Group Punishment," Working paper, 2024.

Friedman, D. 2000. *Law's Order: What Economics has to do with the Law and Why It Matters*. Princeton: Princeton Univ. Press.

Harries, J. "The *Senatus Consultum Silanianum:* Court Decisions and Judicial Severity in the Early Roman Empire." In *New Frontiers: Law and Society in*

[26] See Posner (2003, p. 689–690).

the Roman World, edited by P. du Plessis. Edinburgh: Edinburgh Univ. Press, 2013.

Hirshleifer, J., and J. Riley. 1992. *The Analytics of Uncertainty and Information*. New York: Cambridge Univ. Press.

Holmes, O.W. 1881[196]. *The Common Law*. Boston: Little Brown.

James, B. 2011. *Popular Crime: Reflections on the Celebration of Violence*. New York: Scribner.

Kahan, D. 1998. Social Meaning and the Economic Analysis of Crime. *Journal of Legal Studies* 27: 609–622.

Kandel, E., and E. Lazear. 1992. Peer Pressure and Partnerships. *Journal of Political Economy* 100: 801–817.

Levinson, D. 2003. Collective Sanctions. *Stanford University Law Review* 56: 345–428.

Levmore, S. 1995. Gomorrah to *Ybarra* and More: Overextraction and the Puzzle of Immoderate Group Liability. *Virginia Law Review* 81: 1561–1604.

Levmore, S. 1995. Rethinking Group Responsibility and Strategic Threats in Biblical Texts and Modern Law. *Chicago-Kent Law Review* 71: 85–121.

Miceli, T. 2010. A Model of Criminal Sanctions that Incorporates Both Deterrence and Incapacitation. *Economics Letters* 107: 205–207.

Miceli, T. 2019. *The Paradox of Punishment: Reflections on the Economics of Criminal Justice*. Cham, Switzerland: Palgrave Macmillan.

Miceli, T., and K. Segerson. 2007. Punishing the Innocent Along with the Guilty: The Economics of Individual Versus Group Punishment. *Journal of Legal Studies* 36: 81–106.

Miceli, T., K. Segerson, and D. Earnhart. 2022. The Role of Experience in Deterring Crime: A Theory of Specific Versus General Deterrence. *Economic Inquiry* 60: 1833–1853.

Mungan, M. 2018. Optimal Preventive Law Enforcement and Stopping Standards. *American Law and Economics Review* 20: 289–317.

Parisi, F., and G. Dari-Mattiacci. 2004. The Rise and Fall of Communal Liability in Ancient Law. *International Review of Law and Economics* 24: 489–505.

Posner, R. 1983. *The Economics of Justice*. Cambridge, MA: Harvard Univ. Press.

Posner, R. 2003. *Economic Analysis of Law*, 6th ed. New York: Aspen Publishers.

Rothschild, M., and J. Stiglitz. 1976. Equilibrium in Competitive Insurance Markets: An Essay on the Economics of Imperfect Information. *Quarterly Journal of Economics* 90: 629–650.

Shavell, S. 1982. On Liability and Insurance. *Bell Journal of Economics* 13: 120–132.

Shavell, S. 1987. A Model of Optimal Incapacitation. *American Economic Review* 77: 107–110.

Shavell, S. 2004. *Foundations of Economic Analysis of Law*. Cambridge, MA: Belknap Press.

Shavell, S. 2015. A Simple Model of Optimal Deterrence and Incapacitation. *International Review of Law and Economics* 42: 13–19.
Wood, M. 1998. *In Search of the Trojan War*. Berkeley, CA: Univ. of California Press.

PART IV

Defining Harm

"We are dealing with a problem of a reciprocal nature. To avoid the harm to *B* would be to inflict harm on *A*. The real question that has to be decided is, Should *A* be allowed to harm *B*, or should *B* be allowed to harm *A*? The problem is to avoid the more serious harm."

Ronald Coase (1960, p. 2)

CHAPTER 9

Reciprocal Causation

One of the messages of the previous parts has been that responsibility is a fluid concept that can serve many purposes. Harm, on the other hand, has been taken as a "fixed point" around which responsibility revolved. This part challenges that premise by calling into question the existence of a well-defined definition of "harm," and, concomitantly, a clearly-defined causal relation between the action (or inaction) of some individual (the injurer) and the harm suffered by another individual (the victim). As we have emphasized throughout, such a connection is the basis for the Pigovian approach to externalities, which depends on a technological relationship between A's action and B's harm. We also saw that the legal test for this connection—the "but-for" test—is backward-looking and fact-based, which makes it a seemingly irrefutable basis for determining the direction of causation, if not always the basis for actual responsibility.

However, a different approach to the problem of externalities has challenged this conventional view by arguing that the notion of causation as just described is not uniquely defined. The next section explicates that line of reasoning, and the remaining sections of this chapter, and Chap. 10, draw out its various implications.

T. J. Miceli, *Harm and Responsibility*,
https://doi.org/10.1007/978-3-031-74831-8_9

The Coase Theorem and the Arrow of Causation

An important contribution to the economic theory of externalities was offered in a seminal paper by Ronald Coase (Coase, 1960).[1] Coase's starting point was the Pigovian approach as laid out in Chap. 2 and discussed in prior chapters. Coase's critique was not that the Pigovian approach is wrong, but that it is incomplete. This point is best demonstrated by using one of Coase's examples: that of a farmer and rancher who occupy adjoining parcels of land, which results in crop damage caused by straying cattle. A numerical example, adapted from Coase (1960), is shown in Table 9.1.

The choice variable, the rancher's herd size (shown in column one), ranges from one to four. The second column shows the marginal benefit (profit) to the rancher of adding steers to the herd, ranging from \$40 for the first steer down to \$10 for the fourth one. The third column shows the marginal crop damage, which is a constant of \$15 per steer. The final column shows the net social benefit, which equals the total benefit minus the total cost for each possible herd size. Thus, for a herd of one, the net benefit is \$40 − \$15 = \$25; for a herd of two, it is (\$40 + \$30) − ((\$15 + \$15) = \$40; and so on. The herd size that maximizes the net gain, and hence is socially optimal, is three.[2]

According to the Pigovian approach to this problem, the rancher, whose cattle are the physical cause of the harm, will inefficiently increase

Table 9.1 Rancher-farmer dispute

Herd size	*Marginal benefit of additional steers*	*Marginal crop damage*	*Net social benefit*
1	\$40	\$15	\$25
2	30	15	40
3	20	15	45
4	10	15	40

Source Adapted from Coase (1960)

[1] See Medema (2020) for a discussion of the influence of this article on the economics profession over the past six decades.

[2] Another way to determine the optimal size is to continue adding steers as long as the marginal benefit exceeds the marginal cost. This is true for the first three steers but not for the fourth.

his herd to four (thereby maximizing his profit) unless he is made to pay for the damages sustained by the farmer. The optimal policy is therefore to impose a tax on the rancher equal to the marginal harm of $15 caused by each additional steer. When faced with this tax, the rancher will cap his herd at three, the socially optimal size, because his private return then coincides with the social return. The same efficient outcome could equally be achieved by strict tort liability or a criminal fine of the same amount. Obviously, the institutional details of these various remedies differ in ways we have described, with each having its advantages and disadvantages,[3] but the incentives effects would be the same. What they all have in common, however, is that the party causing the harm is responsible for it.

This is where Coase enters the debate. Coase's analysis of the externality problem begins by demonstrating that the causal direction implicit in the Pigovian approach as just described is in fact incomplete. We have already encountered versions of this argument at various points in our study. For example, in the context of product-related accidents, the question was whether the seller or the buyer caused the harm resulting from a defective product. Our answer was that both did in the sense that each had to participate in the transaction for the harm to materialize. If the seller had not offered the product for sale, or the buyer had opted not to purchase it, no accident would have occurred. The same logic is of course true here: crop damage from straying cattle requires both ranching and farming to happen in close proximity to one another. And although there is a literal sense in which the cattle cause the harm because they are the "active" agents, from a logical point of view the presence of cattle and crops are both causes of the damage. Both activities, for example, would satisfy the but-for test for causation. In the same vein, recall the quote from *The Great Gatsby* in which Jordan Baker defended her reckless driving by observing that other people will get out of her way, and that "it takes two to make an accident." Coase attributed this to what he called the "reciprocal nature" of causation, and he used it as the basis for opening a new perspective on the externality problem.

Returning to the rancher-farmer example, suppose that the rancher is *not* held responsible for the farmer's losses. Would the rancher necessarily expand his herd to four, as the Pigovian view maintains? The answer is no,

[3] See Komesar (1994) and Shavell (1993) on comparative institutional choice.

provided that the farmer and rancher can bargain with one another. To see why, let's suppose the rancher initially *does* expand the herd to four. This adds an additional $10 to his profit, but it also imposes crop damage of $15 on the farmer. Thus, there is room for a bargain whereby the farmer pays the rancher not to add the fourth steer. The actual payment would fall somewhere between $10 and 15, depending on the nature of bargaining, but in any case, both sides would benefit from the transaction, and net social benefits would increase as a result. No further reductions in the rancher's herd would be possible by this means, and so the herd would stabilize at three, the optimal size.

The fundamental difference between this scenario and the Pigovian approach is how legal rights are assigned. Under the latter, the farmer is cast as the "victim" of the external harm, and so has a right to be compensated for the harm caused by the rancher, who is cast as the "injurer." This can be equally accomplished by a tax or tort liability. Both reflect a casual direction running from the rancher to the farmer, and that dictates the assignment of responsibility to the rancher. In questioning the direction of causation, however, Coase showed that the efficient outcome can also be achieved by reversing the assignment of legal rights, and correspondingly, the roles of injurer and victim. He thereby demonstrated that efficiency can be achieved independently of the assignment of the direction of causation, and of legal responsibility for harm, provided that the parties have the ability to bargain around that assignment. This conclusion, which posits the irrelevance of the law regarding efficiency under the stated conditions, is known as the Coase Theorem.

One might object that this conclusion has little practical relevance because most externality settings do not admit the sort of bargaining that is necessary to achieve the optimal herd size in the scenario in which the rancher is not held legally responsible for the crop damage.[4] While it is true that bargaining is not possible in many, perhaps most cases of unwanted harm, I will argue in subsequent pages that the conclusion nevertheless has substantial policy relevance.

[4] But see Ellickson (1991).

Property Rules and Liability Rules

In preparation for that discussion, however, we first need to examine the insights of another seminal contribution to the law-and-economics literature—that provided by Calabresi and Melamed (1972). While Coase's analysis highlighted the importance of the *assignment* of legal rights in cases involving conflict, Calabresi and Melamed focused on the rules for *protecting* that assignment.[5] The rule is important because it determines the conditions under which any initial assignment can be altered or exchanged in the future.

The authors specifically distinguished between *property rules* and *liability rules*.[6] Under property rules, rights can only be exchanged on a consensual basis; that is, by mutually acceptable bargains. By contrast, under liability rules rights can be exchanged without the holder's consent provided that the acquirer is willing to pay financial compensation for the holder's loss (i.e., damages) in an amount set by a regulator or a court. The distinction is reflected in the farmer-rancher dispute by the difference between the Pigovian approach, which reflected a liability-rule transfer, and the Coasian bargaining approach, which reflected a property-rule transfer as a result of a consensual exchange. Both were able to achieve an efficient resolution of the dispute (i.e., the optimal herd size), but they did so in different ways: the liability-rule approach relied on coercive government intervention, while the property-rule approach relied on bargaining. Calabresi and Melamed argued that the latter is preferred whenever such transactions are feasible, while the former is preferred when transaction costs are so high as to make bargaining impractical.

It is important to emphasize, however, that, despite the absence of consent under a liability-rule approach, the irrelevance of the initial assignment of legal responsibility under the Coase Theorem extends to this case as well. This is true because non-consensual exchanges under liability rules can always replicate the outcome of consensual (Coasian) exchanges, regardless of how rights are initially assigned, provided that damages are accurately computed by the enforcer, whether that is a court or regulatory agency.

[5] Also see Kaplow and Shavell (1996) and Polinsky (1980).

[6] We will discuss a third *inalienability* rule below.

This point can be illustrated with two well-known externality cases. The first is *Boomer v. Atlantic Cement Company*,[7] which involved a suit filed by a group of landowners living in the vicinity of a cement plant. The plaintiffs sought an injunction to shut the plant down because of the smoke and noise that it caused. The court denied the request and allowed the factory to remain open, but it required the plant to pay damages to the plaintiffs in the amount of the harm they suffered. The court's ruling therefore implicitly awarded the plaintiffs the right to be free from the external harm (i.e., they won the suit), but it protected that right with a liability rule that allowed the factory to continue operating as long as it paid the specified damages. The court's reasoning was that issuing an injunction—i.e., protecting the plaintiffs' right with a property rule—would likely have forced the factory to shut down given the impracticality of a negotiated bargain between the plant and the plaintiffs, each of whom could have resisted a deal. In other words, high transaction costs would have prevented a Coasian bargain. By adopting liability-rule protection instead, the court allowed the possibility for the factory to stay open if it was willing to pay damages. The ruling in this case represents the classic Pigovian approach to externalities in the sense that it identified the cement plant as the cause of the harm and held it legally responsible in the form of a liability rule. And, as long as the damage assessment was set to reflect the full harm of the plaintiffs, the outcome would be efficient.

Consider next the case of *Spur Industries v. Del E. Webb Development Co.*,[8] which involved a plaintiff who sought an injunction to have a cattle feedlot shut down because of the foul odors emanating from it. Here, the plaintiff was a residential real estate developer whose business began to encroach on the feedlot, which had been operating for some time in a previously undeveloped area. In this case, the court ruled in favor of the feedlot and protected its right to continue operating with a liability rule. This allowed the developer to shut the feedlot down as long as it paid the latter's costs of relocating.

The court's ruling in *Spur* stands *Boomer* on its head. Both cases applied the Pigovian approach (i.e., employed a liability rule), but *Spur* reversed the direction of causation, which is to say, reversed the roles of

[7] 26 N.Y.2d 219, 309 N.Y.S.2d 312, 257 N.E.2d 870 (Court of Appeals of New York 1970).

[8] 494 P.2d 701 (Ariz. 1972).

the injurer and victim. Although the feedlot, like the rancher, was the *physical* cause of the harm because its activity produced the odors, it was the action of the developer moving within range of the smell that the court interpreted as the "legal" cause of the harm. Thus, the feedlot was cast as the "victim" by virtue of its having been there first, and the developer was cast as the "injurer" because its behavior precipitated the harm.[9] Thus, the developer was held legally responsible for the feedlot's "harm" and hence was forced to pay its moving costs.

In combination, the *Boomer* and *Spur* cases epitomize the reciprocal nature of causation. For purposes of legal policy, the implication is that there is a degree of freedom in assigning legal responsibility for harm. For example, the court in *Spur* could have held the feedlot responsible for the developer's losses—a decision that would have reflected the conventional Pigovian solution. If it had, the efficient outcome would also have been achieved, provided that the court accurately measured the developer's harm. The only difference would have been the direction of payment. Similarly, in *Boomer*, the court could have ordered the factory to shut down and assessed its cost on the landowners. Again, the efficient outcome would have been achievable as long as it measured that cost correctly.

The key consequence of the reciprocal nature of causation as exemplified by these cases is that it challenges the conventional meaning of harm and benefit. When we talk about externalities like pollution or criminal acts, there is an implicit notion that they are inherently harmful and hence need to be controlled because they are market failures. That is the chief purpose of law according to the conventional view. But economists have long recognized that harms can always be defined as forgone benefits, and benefits can similarly be defined as forgone harms. Thus, there is not a unique solution to the problem. The preceding discussion illustrates the consequences of that idea for lawmaking.

It is important to keep in mind, however, that the common-sense meaning of these terms—the way that most people understand harms and benefits—will stand in opposition to this purely academic view.[10] In the *Boomer* case, for example, most people would *not* view efforts by

[9] The *Spur* ruling thereby reflects the common law doctrine of "coming to the nuisance." See, for example, Wittman (1980).

[10] See, for example, Epstein (1973, p. 166), who defines causation based on force, compulsion, fright, or dangerous conditions.

the residents to shut the factory down, versus efforts by the factory to continue polluting, as equivalent in a moral or common-sense way, even if they can ultimately lead to the same outcome. The manner in which an outcome is achieved is also important. This divergence between how most people understand causation and the way that economists view it becomes especially pointed when applied to criminal law, as we will see shortly.

Trespass and Nuisance

First, however, we note that the primary common law doctrines that control a landowner's right to exclude others are trespass and nuisance. The generally accepted distinction between the two is that "trespass is an invasion of the plaintiff's interest in the exclusive possession of his land, while nuisance is an interference with his use and enjoyment of it."[11] Practically speaking, the difference is between someone physically walking across or building a structure on one's land (trespass) versus creating smoke or noise that permeates it (a nuisance). As for remedies, the granting of injunctive relief, backed by criminal sanctions (i.e., ejection) is virtually automatic for trespass. This reflects protection by a property rule. The remedy for nuisance is more complicated. Both an injunction and money damages (a liability rule) are available, but a plaintiff can only obtain relief if the harm is judged by a court to be "substantial" as determined by a reasonableness standard. In particular, "a reasonable person would conclude that the amount of harm done outweighs the benefits served by the conduct."[12] This, of course, is just a version of the Hand test for negligence.

The distinction between these remedies broadly conforms to the Calabresi-Melamed framework as described above to the extent that those acts constituting trespass tend to involve low transaction costs, while those constituting a nuisance tend to involve high transaction costs. Given the different context in which these doctrines are typically applied, this would seem to be the case. As noted, cases of trespass generally involve physical invasions of a person's property, and the unqualified right of the owner to oust the trespasser will presumably encourage the latter to seek out the

[11] Keeton et al. (1984, p. 622). Also see Merrill (1985).

[12] Keeton, et al. (1984, p. 630).

owner and negotiate a sale of an easement to continue the encroachment, which will only happen if the offending conduct is more valuable to the trespasser than to the owner.[13] The law therefore channels any exchange of rights into the market, where bargaining is feasible and mutual gain is assured.

By contrast, nuisances tend to involve high transaction costs because the infringement is more diffuse in nature, often affecting numerous owners over a large area.[14] Thus, negotiation between the injurer and victim(s) either to curtail or cease the activity will be difficult. The *Boomer* case epitomizes this situation, and the court therefore acted appropriately in opting to resolve that case with a liability rule.[15] As a general proposition, nuisance law therefore limits responsibility for harm more than does trespass law by permitting certain uses without assigning responsibility. This difference defines a boundary between voluntary exchange (under trespass law) and judicial intervention (under nuisance law) as the means of internalizing harms. The next section elaborates on how that boundary is determined.

The General Transaction Structure

At this point, it will be instructive to add a bit more structure to the preceding analysis by positioning the various arguments within a coherent framework that reflects the fundamental relationship between markets and law as alternative institutions for organizing and regulating economic activity. That framework, which combines the insights of Coase regarding the assignment of property rights, and Calabresi and Melamed regarding rules for protecting those rights, will be called the General Transaction

[13] A limit on the right to eject trespassers is the doctrine of adverse possession. See, for example, Miceli (2017, pp. 200).

[14] See, generally, Ellickson (1993).

[15] Interestingly, the *Spur* case, which the court also resolved with a liability rule, probably did not involve high transaction costs between the injurer and victim because there was only one of each, and the source of the harm (the feedlot) was easily identifiable. Some have therefore questioned the appropriateness of the court's use of a liability rule in that case (Coleman, 1988, Chapter 2, footnote 5).

Table 9.2 The General Transaction Structure

Rule:	*Assignment:*	
	Farmer	*Rancher*
Property	Farmer can enjoin straying cattle	Rancher is free to let cattle stray
Liability	Farmer can seek compensation for lost crops	Rancher can seek compensation for restraining cattle

Structure (GTS).[16] The framework is laid out schematically in Table 9.2 in the context of the farmer-rancher dispute.

Note that it involves two choices: the assignment of rights (i.e., who prevails in a legal dispute), and the rule protecting those rights. The table displays the outcome for each of the four possible combinations. The left column represents cases where the right is assigned to the farmer, and the right column represents cases where it is assigned to the rancher. In the top row, the assignment is protected by a property rule, and in the bottom row, the assignment is protected by a liability rule.

The idea behind this framework is to create an institutional setting in which resources will flow to their highest-valuing users in the most efficient way. When transaction costs are low, market exchange will be the best means of accomplishing this, and so property rules should govern any transfers of rights. In this case, the law plays a purely supporting role—specifically, it protects private property and enforces contracts. In other words, the law is a *complement* to the market.

When transaction costs are high, by contrast, market exchange will not ensure that resources will move to their highest valuers. This is when liability rules are preferred because they allow non-consensual exchanges as mediated by the court. Specifically, those who wish to acquire a right held by someone else can take that right without first seeking the holder's consent, but they must pay compensation as assessed by the court. In such a case, forced exchange replaces market exchange, with the price being set by the court rather than by mutual consent. Efficiency is still achievable, however, provided that the price accurately reflects the loss incurred by

[16] See Klevorick (1985), Coleman (1988, Chapter 2), and Miceli (2017, pp. 229–233) for a discussion of this framework, which draws its inspiration from the work of Coase (1960) and Calabresi and Melamed (1972).

the losing party. In this case, we would say that the law is a ***substitute*** for the market.

It is not a perfect substitute, however, precisely because courts will not always be able to measure losses accurately.[17] This will be especially true when subjective values are involved, by which we mean values not captured by markets. The damages awarded by the court in the *Boomer* case, for example, would have reflected reduced property values in the vicinity of the factory as measured by the reduction in what prospective buyers would have been willing to pay for the property. However, that amount would not necessarily have reflected the full loss suffered by existing residents.[18] While this creates the risk of inaccurately pricing rights (usually in the direction of underpricing them), with a resulting inefficiency in exchange, the offsetting benefit is that it overcomes sources of market failure that would otherwise impede the transfer of rights to more valuable uses.

In *Boomer*, for example, the large number of victims would have made bargaining between the factory and residents prohibitively costly, which likely would have resulted in the factory's having to shut down if owners were given the right protected by a property rule. The court's use of a damage remedy (liability rule) avoided that outcome, albeit at the risk of undervaluing the harm suffered by residents. However, given the very high value of the factory relative to the damages in that case, and the extreme unlikelihood of a voluntary resolution, that would seem to have been the proper solution. The same can be said of most externality settings, where high transaction costs generally preclude a voluntary resolution.

It's one thing to question the direction of causation in the context of harms that fall under the umbrella of nuisance or tort law, it's another to do that in the contexts of harms that are categorized as crimes. The next section extends the foregoing argument to that case.

[17] See Kaplow and Shavell (1996).

[18] This reflects the difference between willingness-to-accept versus willingness-to-pay measures of value. See, for example, Hovenkamp (1991).

Extending the Argument to Criminal Law: The Market-Bypass Model

The logic of the GTS is that exchange should occur within a market setting (i.e., consensually) whenever feasible, but that non-market exchange is acceptable when mediated by a properly structured and administered liability rule. It follows that consent is a sufficient but not a necessary condition for efficient exchange. Consent ensures efficiency because both parties anticipate a gain from trade, but efficient exchange does not require consent, nor that both parties remain unharmed. It does, however, require the court or some other enforcement authority, to mediate the exchange and to set the right "price."

Let us now recall that one of the enduring conundrums of the economic approach to law is that it fails to explain the co-existence of both tort and criminal law for regulating non-consensual exchanges. Chapter 3 offered some reasons based on enforcement problems; the GTS suggests a very different explanation.[19] I will motivate that explanation by considering the "efficient theft" paradox.

Consider a thief who steals someone's property. When he is caught, what should the remedy be? According to the Pigovian approach, it should equal the harm suffered by the victim, which is the lost value of the stolen property. In other words, the "price" should be set equal to the victim's loss, thereby fully internalizing the harm. Let us assume for current purposes that thieves are caught with certainty (so there is no enforcement problem), and that losses from theft are measured accurately (so there is no problem in setting the correct amount of liability). The result is that only efficient thefts will occur, which is consistent with the objective of maximizing exchange values. In this way, it would seem that property ends up in the hands of the highest valuer, which is what the theory prescribes. The fact that it happens by theft rather than consensual exchange is, from the perspective of efficiency, beside the point. All that matters is that the thief expects to pay damages equal to the lost value to the owner, which results in only efficient (if non-consensual) exchanges occurring.

The problem with this argument is that it legitimizes violations of the GTS by essentially allowing individuals to *transform property rules into*

[19] The following explanation was first suggested by Calabresi and Melamed (1972), and then elaborated on by Klevorick (1985) and Coleman (1988, Chapter 2).

liability rules. That is, it allows someone, at their will, to substitute a non-consensual exchange for a consensual one. Another way to say this is that it allows individuals to "bypass" the market as a means of acquiring valuable assets or rights. This is undesirable according to the GTS, however, because of the asserted superiority of market exchange over non-consensual exchange when voluntary transactions are possible. The main reason for this superiority, recall, is that market exchange under property rules guarantees mutual benefit by virtue of the requirement of consent, whereas forced exchange under liability rules does not because courts cannot always set prices correctly after the fact. The risk of mispricing will be especially high when the rights in question are not easily valued in monetary terms, as when it involves subjective values or constitutionally-protected rights. But even when accurate valuation is possible (as we assumed in the hypothetical example), coercive exchanges will nevertheless be seen by many as morally objectionable when consensual exchange is feasible, or when no exchange at all is the socially desirable objective (as with the case of certain constitutional rights).[20]

The point is that compensatory damages alone will not prevent unwanted exchanges in situations where market exchange is feasible, and so some additional punishment—a "kicker"—must be added on top of mere liability in order to completely discourage the coercive act. This is the purpose of criminal punishment within the framework of the GTS. According to this view, criminal sanctions are *not* merely Pigovian prices aimed at achieving optimal deterrence of harmful activities; they are penalties aimed at punishing those who engage in behaviors that violate the GTS.[21] Criminal law is, in other words, an overlay to the GTS rather than being a part of it; that is, it is a meta rule. It is, in fact, the means by which the GTS is enforced.

The fullest articulation of this so-called market bypass theory of criminal law is by Posner (1985),[22] who argues that.

> The major function of criminal law … is to prevent people from bypassing the system of voluntary, compensated exchange—the "market," explicit or

[20] One reason for this is that the taker will acquire all of the surplus from the exchange under a liability rule, whereas a market exchange would allow the seller to negotiate for a share of the surplus.

[21] See Cooter (1984).

[22] Also see Klevorick (1985).

implicit—in situations where, because transaction costs are low, the market is a more efficient method of allocating resources than forced exchange. (p. 1195)

This logic is most obviously relevant for those crimes that involve the acquisition of wealth—what Posner calls "acquisitive crimes" (p. 1196)—given that explicit markets for acquiring those same assets are readily available. More controversially, Posner extends this logic to crimes involving non-monetary assets or rights, arguing that violators in these cases (for example, perpetrators of violent crimes) are bypassing "implicit markets," by which he means markets "in friendship, love, respect" (p. 1197), which constitute the "currency" of personal relationships and establish the boundaries of mutual respect for the rights of other members of society. Really, this is just a way of clothing in economic language the purpose of criminal law as understood by most people; namely, that it exists to deter or punish wrongful conduct.

Beyond the goal of channeling exchange into the marketplace, criminal law also enforces rules prohibiting the exchange of rights that are deemed non-tradeable—so-called inalienable rights.[23] In this case, criminal sanctions prevent people from transforming so-called inalienability rules into property or liability rules. Such laws would forbid, for example, selling oneself into slavery or violating a person's right to vote or to exercise freedom of religion.

The broad scope of actual criminal law, encompassing as it does acts ranging from traffic infractions and business practices to theft of property and physical violence, would seem to accommodate both the Becker model of criminal sanctions as "prices" and the Posner model of criminal sanctions as "kickers."[24] Some criminal sanctions, like parking tickets, are logically (and uncontroversially) interpreted as prices aimed at regulating legitimate behavior, while others, like harsh prison terms, are best seen as punishments aimed at preventing definitely unacceptable behavior. Those acts that fall into the first category are those for which the imposition if harm is almost certainly not the primary goal of the offender but is rather a byproduct of some legitimate activity. However, as we have noted, tort law would generally be an inadequate means of controlling

[23] Calabresi and Melamed (1972).

[24] See Hylton (2005), Curry and Doyle (2016), and Miceli (2023) for efforts to develop a hybrid model of crime that unifies the Becker and Posner models.

these acts because the harm is dispersed or detection is difficult. Violations of traffic laws or regulatory controls on business are examples of this sort of crime. For these cases, interpreting sanctions as prices does not seem to be morally objectionable.

By contrast, acts that are primarily intended to confiscate wealth when consent is possible, or to inflict harm or deprive people of fundamental rights, are hard to justify in this way because they either bypass legitimate alternative mechanisms, or have little or no offsetting benefits (at least none that would be counted in welfare). For these acts, sanctions are purely aimed at punishment for the purpose of complete prevention.

Both the Becker and Posner models of crime are largely normative in nature, meaning that they prescribe enforcement policies aimed at maximizing some measure of social welfare. Actual criminal justice policies therefore often depart from the prescriptions of these models, in some cases rather dramatically. Most prominently, both models prescribe large sanctions, either as a means of minimizing enforcement costs (e.g., probability scaling in the Becker model), or to completely prevent certain non-consensual acts (e.g., kickers in the Posner model).[25]

Adelstein (2017, 1981) has offered a theory of criminal law that, by contrast, seeks to explain how the criminal justice system actually sets punishments. His model shares with the models of Becker and Posner the idea that crime is a form of non-consensual exchange, but it departs from those models in its focus on how the system achieves justice in individual cases rather than pursuing a broader goal of maximizing welfare. The system does this, Adelstein argues, by imposing punishments on offenders in proportion to the harm that they caused. The focus is therefore on setting the correct price after the fact, rather than on creating an efficient signal before the fact.

We have already observed that proportionality of punishments to harms is a deeply rooted norm in human history.[26] This ethic manifests itself in practice in the resistance of legislatures, prosecutors, and courts to impose unduly harsh punishments in relation to a defendant's crime or personal circumstances. The implication for the economic theory of crime is that harsh punishments in the service of deterrence will not be acceptable on fairness grounds. This particularly precludes both probability

[25] Indeed, in both models, the optimal sanction is maximal. See Miceli (2023).

[26] See, for example, Parisi and Dari-Mattiacci (2004) and Miceli (2019, Chapter 3).

scaling and group punishment practices as prescribed by the Becker model and its extensions, as well as efforts to steer exchange into voluntary channels by setting tough sanctions (kickers) according to the market-bypass model. As we have previously argued, this interplay between the objectives of ex ante deterrence and ex post fairness represents an ongoing source of debate in the determination of criminal justice policy.

References

Adelstein, R. 2017. *The Exchange Order: Property and Liability as an Exchange System.* New York: Oxford Univ. Press.

Calabresi, G., and A.D. Melamed. 1972. Property Rules, Liability Rules, and Inalienability: One View of the Cathedral. *Harvard Law Review* 85: 1089–1128.

Coase, R. 1960. The Problem of Social Cost. *Journal of Law and Economics* 3: 1–44.

Coleman, J. 1988. *Markets, Morals and the Law.* New York: Cambridge Univ Press.

Cooter, R. 1984. Prices and Sanctions. *Columbia Law Review* 84: 1523–1560.

Curry, P., and M. Doyle. 2016. Integrating Market Alternatives into the Economic Theory of Optimal Deterrence. *Economic Inquiry* 54: 1873–1883.

Ellickson, R. 1991. *Order Without Law: How Neighbors Settle Disputes.* Cambridge: Harvard Univ. Press.

Ellickson, R. 1993. Property in Land. *Yale Law Journal* 102: 1315–1400.

Epstein, R. 1973. A Theory of Strict Liability. *Journal of Legal Studies* 2: 151–204.

Hovenkamp, H. 1991. Legal policy and the endowment effect. *Journal of Legal Studies* 20: 225–247.

Hylton, K. 2005. The Theory of Criminal Penalties and the Economics of Criminal Law. *Review of Law and Economics* 1: 175–201.

Kaplow, L., and S. Shavell. 1996. Property Rules Versus Liability Rules. *Harvard Law Review* 109: 713–790.

Keeton, W., D. Dobbs, R. Keeton, and D. Owen. 1984. *Prosser and Keeton on Torts*, 5th ed. St. Paul, MN: West Publishing.

Klevorick, A. "On the Economic Theory of Crime." In *NOMOS XXVII: Criminal Justice*, edited by J. Pennock and J. Chapman. New York: New York Univ. Press, 1985.

Komesar, N. 1994. *Imperfect Alternatives: Choosing Institutions in Law, Economics, and Public Policy.* Chicago: Univ. of Chicago Press.

Medema, S. 2020. The Coase Theorem at Sixty. *Journal of Economic Literature* 58: 1045–1128.

Merrill, T. 1985. Trespass, Nuisance, and the Cost of Determining Property Rights. *Journal of Legal Studies* 14: 13–48.
Miceli, T. 2017. *The Economics Approach to Law*, 3rd ed. Stanford: Stanford Univ. Press.
Miceli, T. 2019. *The Paradox of Punishment: Reflections on the Economics of Criminal Justice*. Cham, Switzerland: Palgrave Macmillan.
Miceli, T. 2023. On Economic Theories of Criminal Punishment: Pricing, Prevention, or Proportionality? *American Law and Economics Review* 25: 1–26.
Parisi, F., and G. Dari-Mattiacci. 2004. The Rise and Fall of Communal Liability in Ancient Law. *International Review of Law and Economics* 24: 489–505.
Polinsky, A.M. 1980. On the Choice Between Property Rules and Liability Rules. *Economic Inquiry* 18: 233–246.
Posner, R. 1985. An economic theory of the criminal law. *Columbia Law Review* 85: 1193–1231.
Shavell, S. 1993. The Optimal Structure of Law Enforcement. *Journal of Law and Economics* 36: 255–287.
Wittman, D. 1980. First Come, First Served: An Economic Analysis Of 'Coming to the Nuisance.' *Journal of Legal Studies* 9: 557–568.

CHAPTER 10

The Meaning of Harm

The arguments in the previous chapter culminate in the following question: What is the meaning of harm? The need to ask this question is a consequence of the reciprocal nature of causation, which, recall, reflects the fundamental economic insight that a forgone benefit can be defined as a harm, and an avoided harm can be defined as a benefit. This chapter examines some of the implications of that idea.

Determining the Content of Criminal Law

One of the promises of the economic theory of law was that it would remove lawmaking and law enforcement from dependence on subjective notions of justice or morality and place it on firmer, objective grounds.[1] This quest is particularly relevant for criminal law, given that the major alternative to the economic theory is a moral theory.

In previous chapters, we have reviewed at length the basic elements of the economic theory of crime as first developed byBecker (1968) and extended by others. In so doing, we have taken as given that the function of the law is to control harmful activities, both by deterring such acts in

[1] See, for example, Posner (1990), particularly Chapters 11, 12, and 15; and Holmes's (1881) classic treatise on the common law, a major theme of which is to ground law in objective factors.

T. J. Miceli, *Harm and Responsibility*,
https://doi.org/10.1007/978-3-031-74831-8_10

the first place, and by punishing the perpetrators of those which were not deterred. Becker himself only referred to the content of the law in passing, as if it were self-evident: "Usually a belief that other members of society are harmed is the motivation behind outlawing or otherwise restricting an activity" (Becker 1968, p. 172). This is just an affirmation of the Pigovian basis for law enforcement; namely, to control harmful externalities. The unstated assumption, however, is that these harms are objectively determined and measurable, like the smoke emitted by a polluting factory or the physical injury suffered by a victim of assault.

As we have noted, one aspect of this theory that has particularly troubled some critics is its apparent allowance of so-called efficient crimes, meaning crimes for which the offender's gains from the proscribed act exceed the victim's harm. According to impeccable utilitarian logic, such acts enhance social welfare and hence are desirable, despite their non-consensual nature. This reasoning is of a piece with that employed in our analysis of the *Boomer* and *Spur* cases in the previous chapter, which involved the use of liability rules to compensate for harms under nuisance law. Recall that in both cases, the court effectively authorized "efficient thefts"—in *Boomer* it allowed the factory to infringe on the neighbors' right to health and safety without the latter's consent, and in *Spur* it allowed the developer to seize the feedlot's right to operate in its chosen locale. To be sure, the acquirers had to pay the price set by the court, but we argued that the acquisition was efficient (assuming the price was properly set), despite being non-consensual. How are these infringements, which were mediated by a court and hence "legal," any different from actual thefts that also result in "efficient" exchanges? The economic theory of law has no ready answer for this question, nor does it see the need for one.

Critics of that model, by contrast, have argued that the answer to this question is self-evident: that the gains of the offenders in cases of theft *should not be counted in social welfare*, thereby ruling out the possibility of an efficient crime. No less an economist than Nobelist George Stigler, in one of the earliest criticisms of fellow Nobelist Becker's model, said as much:

> The determination of [the social value of the gain to offenders] is not explained, and one is entitled to doubt its usefulness as an explanatory concept: what evidence is there that society sets a positive value upon the

> utility derived from a murder, rape, or arson? In fact, society has branded the utility derived from such activities as illicit. (Stigler 1970, p. 527)

Lewin and Trumbull (1990) expressed this same view based on the idea that "the term 'criminal' represents an implicit societal judgment that the conduct in question has no social value" (p. 280). But this argument just begs the question because it defines crimes to be those acts for which the gains to offenders should not count.

Other scholars have recognized the tautological nature of this argument. For example, Friedman (2000, p. 230) observed that.

> If instead of treating all benefits to everyone equally we first sort people into the deserving and the undeserving, the just and the unjust, the criminals and the victims, we are simply assuming our conclusions. Benefits to bad people don't count, so rules against bad people are automatically efficient. We cannot deduce moral conclusions from economics if we start the economics by assuming the moral conclusions.

Kaplow and Shavell (2002) likewise argued for a non-judgmental approach to welfare analysis, which includes counting the gains that offenders derive from their illicit acts, as well as the disutility that they suffer from punishment. Although they qualified their argument by acknowledging that "some may not wish to credit criminals' gains as part of social welfare" (p. 320, fn. 54), most modern theories refrain from making such judgments and simply count all gains and losses, thus letting the chips fall where they may.[2]

A fundamental problem with this approach, however, is that it does not come to terms with the issue of reciprocal causation as epitomized by the *Boomer* and *Spur* cases.[3] Economic models of crime, whether or not they count offenders' gains, universally begin by defining some "harm" that society wishes to control, and then proceed to derive an optimal enforcement policy aimed at achieving that objective. In other words, they take as given the direction of the arrow of causation and hence the

[2] Shavell (1985) addressed this issue in his model of crime by attaching a scaling factor to the offender's gain, which reflects the value that society attaches to the activity in question. Again, however, this approach just begs the question.

[3] The logic of the following argument was anticipated by Klevorick (1985, p. 300).

meaning of harm. Whether or not offender gains are counted affects the resulting enforcement policy quantitatively but not qualitatively.

As an illustration of this issue, let us return to the farmer-rancher conflict detailed in Table 9.1, and begin with the conventional view that "crop damage" is the harm society wishes to control. Also, for purposes of this discussion, we will discuss the situation using the language of criminal law, though we will assume (for now) that enforcement is perfect. Thus, ranchers whose cattle cause damage will be subject to a criminal fine which, according to the Pigovian approach, should be equated to the marginal crop damage of $15. As we saw, when faced with this sanction, the rancher will limit his herd size to three, for beyond that point, the marginal benefit of adding additional steers is less than the sanction. Thus, at a herd of three, the rancher's profit, which now coincides with the net social benefit, is maximized. So far, this corresponds to our earlier analysis of this case. But observe that, because crop damage is labeled as "illegal" in this scenario, the rancher rationally ends up committing "efficient crimes" by maintaining a herd of three and imposing $45 worth of harm on the farmer, for which he pays an equivalent fine.

Now consider the opposite assignment of legal rights, which imposes no responsibility for crop damage on the rancher—i.e., crop damage is now "legal." Thus, the rancher is free to increase his herd size to four without incurring a fine. For sake of the current argument, we will rule out Coasian bargaining between the farmer and rancher as a way of internalizing the harm in this case. Thus, the farmer has no lawful means of preventing the crop damage. Let us suppose, however, that he can take his own steps to reduce the herd by, say, killing cattle, which would obviously be considered "illegal" and subject to a fine. In this case, the optimal Pigovian fine would reflect lost profits of the rancher and so would coincide with the marginal benefit schedule in column two of Table 9.1.

Now, assuming that the rancher's herd starts out at its maximal size of four, the farmer would have to pay a fine of $10 for killing the first steer, $20 for killing the second, and so on up to a maximum fine of $40. Under this sanction schedule, the farmer will rationally kill only one steer because the benefit from each offense in the form of saved crop damage is equal to $15, which is greater than the cost of killing the first steer ($10) but less than the cost of killing the second ($20) and any subsequent steers. This single offense again constitutes an efficient crime because the benefit to the farmer in the form of saved crop loss exceeds the cost to the rancher in the form of lost profit. It therefore achieves the efficient herd size of three.

Given costless enforcement, both of the preceding assignments of rights, each enforced by a criminal fine, are efficient because they arrive at the optimal herd size of three, although from different directions. Thus, which activity is "criminalized" is irrelevant for efficiency, reflecting the reciprocal nature of the harm. Although we have ruled out Coasian bargaining between the parties as a solution to the externality, the assumption of zero enforcement costs effectively replicates the results of the Coase Theorem regarding the initial setting of criminal rights. In particular, either initial assignment of legal rights can achieve an efficient outcome, provided the criminal sanction (a form of liability rule) is equated to the harm. We are therefore replacing a consensual bargain with a non-consensual "criminal exchange" that achieves exactly the same outcome. In combination, these scenarios establish what we might call a second-order Coase Theorem with respect to "criminal exchanges," which may be stated as follows: regardless of how criminality is defined, an efficient allocation of resources will be achieved provided that fines are calibrated to the relevant social harm, which is determined by the loss suffered by the victim of the activity that is labeled as criminal.

As is true of the actual Coase Theorem, this conclusion is illustrative of the relative nature of the labels of offender and victim in settings where individuals have conflicting interests. Consequently, the definition of harm is also a relative concept that depends on the way in which legal rights are initially assigned. When crop damage is designated as a crime, any departure from zero loss is regarded as a social harm, while the gains received by the rancher in the act of imposing that loss (by increasing his herd) are "criminal gains" that may or may not be afforded legitimate status in social welfare, depending on one's position in the above ethical debate. Conversely, when killing cattle is designated as a crime, any action by the farmer to reduce the rancher's herd causes harm to the rancher, while the saved crop damage that results is a criminal gain which likewise may or may not be afforded legitimate status.

Figure 10.1, which generalizes the preceding example, depicts the situation schematically. The upper panel graphs the rancher's marginal benefit from adding cattle (labeled b), and the farmer's marginal crop loss (labeled l), as functions of the herd size, x. The optimal herd size, x^*, occurs at the intersection of the curves. The lower panel shows the two assignments of legal rights and the associated Pigovian sanctions required to achieve an efficient outcome under each assignment. Some "efficient crimes" are committed and some are deterred under both assignments, but in each case, the optimal herd size is achieved.

Importantly, the "l-curve" (marginal crop loss) represents the measure of harm under the assignment that designates crop damage as a crime, while the "b-curve" (marginal profit from increasing the herd size) represents the measure of harm under the assignment that designates killing cattle as a crime. Correspondingly, therefore, the other curve in each case measures the offender's benefit from committing the designated crime. The offender therefore commits the illegal act up to the point where the benefit equals the cost.

The preceding argument will strike many as being morally suspect, and of course, that is the point. I have suggested that one of the objectives of the economic model of crime was to divorce law enforcement policy from a reliance on morality, which is both inherently subjective and continually evolving. As Becker (1968, p. 170) observed, one of the aims of his model was to "dispense with special theories of anomie, psychological inadequacies, or inheritance of special traits and simply extend the economist's

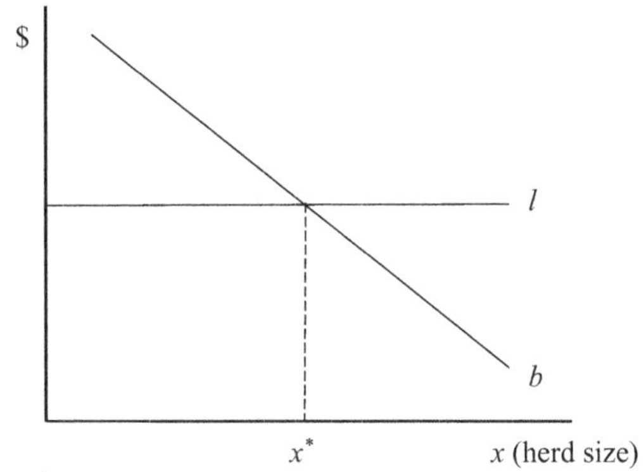

Crop damage is illegal, $s=l$	Efficient crimes committed	Crimes deterred
Killing cattle is illegal, $s=b$	Crimes deterred	Efficient crimes committed

Fig. 10.1 Defining legality and illegality in the rancher-farmer dispute

usual analysis of choice" to crime and punishment. The foregoing analysis, however, suggests this promise generally cannot be fulfilled. It is true that the Pigovian approach to criminal law prescribes an optimal structure for the *enforcement* of law (i.e., the pricing of crime), but it cannot offer a basis for determining the *content* of law as a consequence of reciprocal causation. It appears, therefore, that we have arrived at a point where, in the area of criminal law at least, rational choice theories and mathematical models must give way to morality, or some other social value, as the basis for defining harm.

Having said that, there are several qualifications to this "irrelevance" result with respect to the content of the law that might allow us to pin it down. One approach, suggested by criticisms of Coase's original demonstration of the irrelevance of property rights with respect to efficiency, is to appeal to enforcement costs. The idea is that property rights should be assigned so as to minimize the costs of enforcing the chosen assignment of rights.[4]

To see how this would work in the current example, suppose that the cost of detecting and punishing a violator, whether that involves crop damage or killing cattle, is \$3. The optimal fine in this case would therefore equal the external harm plus the enforcement costs; that is, the offender would be assessed the harm that he causes plus the cost of apprehending and punishing him.[5] Thus, under the scenario where crop damage is a crime, the optimal fine would equal to the marginal crop damage plus the fixed enforcement cost, or \$18 (=\$15 + \$3). Given the rancher's marginal benefit schedule, it would continue to be optimal for him to add three cattle to his herd, resulting in gross profit of \$90, crop damage of \$45, and enforcement costs of \$9. The net social gain in this case would therefore be \$36, which equals the net benefit of \$45 minus the total enforcement cost of \$9.

[4] See, for example, Cooter (1982, p. 14), who notes that when transaction costs are high, "the structure of law should be chosen so that transaction costs are minimized, because this will conserve resources used up by the bargaining process..." Fischel (1985) describes a similar standard for achieving efficient land use in the presence of externalities. He specifically proposes a "normal behavior standard" as the initial entitlement point such that any landowner who fails to adhere to that standard would be subject to a sanction. This structure is efficient, he argues, because it minimizes the transaction costs of inducing people to conform "to prevailing social standards of acceptable behavior" (p. 159). Also see Calabresi and Melamed (1972, p. 1093) and Miceli (2024).

[5] Becker (1968, p. 192).

Conversely, when killing cattle is a crime, the optimal sanction schedule would be given by the rancher's marginal benefit schedule with the \$3 enforcement cost added to each entry. Thus, the farmer's cost of killing cattle would range from \$13 for the first steer killed up to \$43 for the fourth. Given the farmer's constant marginal benefit of \$15 from preventing crop damage, the farmer would again only commit a single offense, resulting in herd size of three and total enforcement costs of \$3. The net social gain in this case would equal \$42, consisting of the net benefit of \$45 minus enforcement costs of \$3. The crucial point is that this value exceeds that from the previous scenario because of the lower enforcement costs in this case (\$3 versus \$9). In other words, the gross benefit is the same (\$45), but fewer offenses, and hence lower enforcement costs, are needed to achieve it in the current scenario. Thus, assigning legal entitlements so that crop damage is legal and killing cattle is illegal is optimal in this example.

The asymmetry here is due to the fact that the optimal herd size of three just happens to be closer to the maximal herd size than it is to zero. Thus, fewer "criminal exchanges" are needed to achieve that outcome when the entitlement is assigned to the rancher as opposed to the farmer, and as a result, total enforcement costs are lower in that case.

This example, of course, is a special case because, given the discrete nature of benefits, the enforcement cost of \$3 was small enough that it did not change the optimal crime rate under either assignment of rights. (This would have been the case for any enforcement cost between zero and \$5.) Thus, the optimal level of deterrence remained the same. Suppose instead that the enforcement cost is \$6, which is large enough that it *would* alter the optimal herd size. Specifically, when crop damage is a crime, the optimal fine would now be \$21 (=\$15 + \$6), and so the rancher would only add two cattle to his herd, resulting in a net social gain of \$28 = \$70 – \$30 – \$12. Conversely, when killing cattle is a crime, the optimal sanction would range from \$16 for the first offense up to \$46 for the fourth. In this case, the farmer would not find it optimal to kill *any* cattle; that is, complete deterrence is the optimal (second best) solution in this case. The result is a net social gain of \$40 = \$100 – \$60. Thus, it is again optimal not to criminalize crop damage but to criminalize killing cattle.

The preceding analysis, though a coherent economic argument, does not represent a particularly compelling basis for determining the content of the law. A second possible rationale concerns the ease with which the enforcer can measure the harm from a criminal act for purposes of setting the proper sanction. In the current example, both party's losses were assumed to be purely monetary and so easily measurable, but that will not always be case, particularly when the harm is a physical injury or involves the deprivation of a non-market right like freedom of speech. One solution in this case would be to award the disputed right to the party whose costs would be more easily measurable, thus avoiding the need for a court ever to have to undertake the more difficult measurement. The problem with this proposal, however, is that it would require the party who would suffer the non-monetary harm to commit an illegal act if it wanted to avoid that harm. In the *Boomer* case, for example, if the residents' harm from the pollution (e.g., long-term health risks) is more difficult to measure than the factory's loss from having to shut down, the proposed assignment would be to give the factory the right to operate. For most people, this would be the opposite of a just assignment in this case.

Calabresi and Melamed (1972) argued that in cases where the harm is not easily measurable, rights should in fact be protected by ***inalienability rules***, which would forbid any infringements. This does not dispense with the need to measure these losses, however, because some violations will inevitably occur, particularly given constitutional and ethical limits on sanctions. A more important objection to this proposal is that inalienability rules enshrine a particular assignment of rights that may turn out to be unjust as people's values change.

This last point—that laws need to vary over time and across cultures in response to changing values—is the primary reason why a purely objective or universally applicable theory of the content of law is not possible. While there will be broad agreement regarding the undesirability of certain acts based on widely-accepted notions of morality, in other cases it will be more difficult to reach a consensus. As Adelstein (2017, p. 172) observes:

> The definitions of crimes and the moral costs they impose in particular circumstances are strongly conditioned by the full range of a community's culture, attitudes, experiences, prejudices, religious beliefs, and historical past. Different communities may have different attitudes, and judge motives and behaviors accordingly. An act that might be honored as fulfilling a moral obligation in one community may be condemned as an immoral crime in another, to the mutual incomprehension.

A prominent example from U.S. history concerns segregation laws in the Post-Civil War era, which were eventually deemed unacceptable and thus overturned. One mechanism that precipitates such a change, and which signals evolving values, is when people systematically refuse to comply with laws that they deem to be unjust or out of touch with current moral standards. This type of non-compliance is epitomized by acts of civil disobedience, a subject to which we now turn.

Law Breaking as a Moral Act: Civil Disobedience

Civil disobedience is a principled act of law-breaking that is aimed at calling attention to an unjust law. Rawls (1971, p. 364) specifically defined it to be

> ...a public, nonviolent, conscientious yet political act contrary to the law usually done with the aim of bringing about a change in the law or policies of the government. By acting in this way one addresses the sense of justice of the majority of the community and declares that in one's considered opinion the principles of social cooperation among free and equal men are not being respected.

In Rawls's view, civil disobedience is undertaken with the aim of forcing "the majority to consider whether it wishes to...acknowledge the legitimate claims of the minority" (pp 366–367). In this way, it is an important tool of legal reformers seeking to act within the confines of a "nearly just society, one that is well-ordered for the most part but in which some serious violations of justice nevertheless do occur" (p. 363).[6]

The practice has a long history in human civilization,[7] but it was Henry David Thoreau who first brought it to prominence in the American social conscience when he spent a night in jail for refusing to pay taxes to a government that condoned slavery. He went on to write a celebrated essay defending his action, which has had an important influence on subsequent

[6] See Carbonara et al. (2012).

[7] An early example is found in Sophocles's play *Antigone*, when the title character defies an order by King Creon not to bury her dead brother. She says, "For me it was not Zeus who made that order. Nor did that Justice who lives with the gods below mark out such laws to hold among mankind. ...So not through fear of any man's proud spirit would I be likely to neglect these laws" (Sophocles 1954, p. 174). Also see Posner (1988, pp. 111–112).

generations of reformers, including Susan B. Anthony, Mahatma Gandhi, and Martin Luther King. In his essay, Thoreau posed the dilemma as follows: "Unjust laws exist: shall we be content to obey them, or shall we endeavor to amend them, and obey them until we have succeeded, or shall we transgress them at once?" (Thoreau 1965 [1849], p. 644). His answer was to break them at once. Rawls, by contrast, viewed civil disobedience as an option of last resort, to be used only "after the legal means of redress have proved of no avail" (p. 373).

In any event, the practice has attained a praiseworthy status in civil societies as a legitimate avenue by which a conscientious minority can express its strong disagreement with what it perceives to be an unjust law. As a result, violations are themselves considered to be moral acts when undertaken out of genuine conviction. Such actions, however, raise the question of how we can distinguish between true acts of civil disobedience from mere violations based on narrow self-interest—Becker's "efficient crimes." As we have already seen, any effort to distinguish them only begs the question of which gains should count in welfare. That is why economists generally do not seek to make such a distinction, opting instead to count all benefits and harms. One may quibble about how to attach a dollar measure to certain intangible harms and benefits, but the measurement problem is not itself a good reason to exclude these values from welfare. It does not, for example, prevent the inclusion of the value of a human life, or of various environmental resources, from consideration in debates about environmental policy.

By contrast, we have seen that those who embrace a moral theory of law would exclude a criminal's gains from social welfare because the law itself has decreed such acts as immoral. Dan Kahan, for example, observed that "as communities, [people] structure the criminal law to promote the meanings they approve of and to suppress the ones they dislike or fear." Further, "economic analyses that ignore these expressive evaluations produce unreliable predictions and uncompelling prescriptions" (Kahan, 1998, p. 610).[8]

Applying this logic to the straying-cattle example, when crop damage is a crime, the value of foregone cattle would not be counted in welfare; likewise, when killing cattle is a crime, crop damage would not be counted. Making such a choice is necessary because there is no neutral point; given

[8] Also see Cooter (1998) and Sunstein (1996).

the inherent incompatibility of the two activities, privileging one side necessarily harms the other. And as our analysis above showed, efficiency alone cannot provide an unambiguous answer.

On the other hand, those arguing for morality as a superior basis for favoring one activity over another offer no guidance as to how the competing values should be weighed, nor under what circumstances (if any) the existing assignment of rights can be adjusted or reformed. In particular, there appears to be no room in this view for Thoreau's contention that a truly moral course of action is sometimes to transgress at once what the offender sees as an unjust law. Under the economic theory, by contrast, rational non-compliance with the law, *for whatever reason*, is seen as a legitimate act (i.e., an efficient crime), provided one is willing to pay the price.

Further, as suggested above, systematic disobedience of a particular law can be an important signal that social values are in fact evolving with respect to that issue, and that legal reform may be warranted.[9] Repeal of Jim Crow laws during the Civil Rights era, and the decriminalization of medicinal or recreational use of certain drugs in more recent times, are examples of this evolutionary process. This perspective on legal reform, however, only makes sense if offenders' gains are counted as socially relevant.

Inalienable Rights, Moralisms, and Cancel Culture

We have already discussed the Calabresi and Melamed (1972) framework for protecting legal rights, or entitlements. That discussion specifically examined the choice between property rules, which mediate consensual exchanges of rights, and liability rules, which mediate non-consensual exchanges. We have argued that the latter serves as the basis for laws penalizing (or "pricing") non-consensual exchanges, whether viewed as torts or crimes. Additionally, we have seen that inalienability rules forbid the exchange of rights under any circumstances. Once an inalienable right is granted, the holder can neither sell it nor can anyone take it at a price set by the court. (In principle, the price or sanction should therefore be set infinitely high, as prescribed by the market-bypass theory.) Such rights

[9] See, for example, the analysis of Glaeser and Sunstein (2015).

are judged to be absolute and therefore not infringeable, as is the case of those rights enumerated in the Bill of Rights.

As mentioned, Calabresi and Melamed justified the categorization of certain rights as non-transferrable by arguing that their exchange would create external costs that are simply too hard to value in monetary terms. For example, being allowed to sell one's right to freedom, to vote, or to engage in free speech would create third-party costs to observers who would have principled objections to such exchanges, and it would be impossible to adequately measure those costs and compensate the various cost-bearers. The issue here is not just large numbers or the difficulty in identifying victims (though both of these problems may be present); it is, more fundamentally, the idea that certain values simply should not be made available for sale under any circumstances.[10]

What about more commonplace actions that merely "offend" someone but which do not infringe on a fundamental right? Calabresi and Melamed refer to these third-party costs as "moralisms," and note that they "are extremely common and greatly complicate the attainment of [economic efficiency]" (1972, p. 1101, note 30). The pervasiveness of moralisms and the concomitant desire to mitigate their effects shifts the problem from one of measurement to one of establishing a workable entitlement point. As the discussion of reciprocal causation made clear, there is no truly neutral assignment, or zero-cost point, in the presence of these sorts of externalities. Any assignment entails both harms and benefits because these concepts are only meaningful in relation to that initial assignment. The problem therefore amounts to asking what harms people should be expected to "tolerate" in a diverse society, and what harms they can reasonably seek to restrain or at least be compensated for having to endure.

As an example, consider recent debates about the issue of free speech versus hate speech. The First Amendment to the U.S. Constitution grants freedom of speech as an inalienable right, but the Supreme Court has recognized limits on that right, as when an utterance creates a "clear and present danger."[11] Thus, creating an imminent harm justifies a government restriction on certain speech, and if someone violates that restriction—for example, by shouting "fire" in a crowded theater—he or

[10] See, for example, Sandel (2012).

[11] *Schenck v. United States*, 249 U.S. 47 (1919).

she will be subject to a legal sanction. That sounds like a liability rule,[12] which implies that there is some scope for limiting or pricing speech if deemed sufficiently harmful. Most merely offensive utterances, however, do not rise to this level.

A fairly recent response to these more common moralisms is the phenomenon of "cancel culture," which is the practice of publicly shaming individuals, usually public figures, who have engaged in what some regard as socially or politically undesirable behavior. Although Steven Koh has argued that this is not a new practice—public shaming has long been a means of social control—its impact has been greatly amplified in recent times by the use of social media as its primary mechanism.[13] The objective of this form of social control is both to punish and deter the targeted behavior; in other words, to substitute informal for actual legal sanctions. The main difference is that there is no workable mechanism for calibrating the magnitude of the resulting sanctions to the harm it is aimed at controlling.[14] Nor is there anything like due process for the target of the cancelation.

Some legal scholars have argued that cancelation nevertheless potentially serves useful purposes: both to alert public authorities to potential crimes that may have escaped detection, and to impose punishments on those who have evaded legal responsibility, either because the offense was not an actual crime but still violated a social norm (like hate speech), or because a person's political power or social privilege allowed them to escape formal sanctioning (Koh 2022).

Offsetting these factors, however, is that many actions and behaviors targeted by cancelation have beneficial as well as harmful effects, and cancelation may lead to the censoring of speech that is potentially valuable. Nearly all political speech has this characteristic precisely because it involves issues that have cross-cutting effects, which is why courts grant the greatest latitude to political speech when defining the limits of freedom of speech.

With respect to the theme of this book, the most important problem with cancel culture is its susceptibility to fads and "groupthink." As we

[12] See, for example, Posner (2003, pp. 694–695), who likens such a limit to the Hand test for negligence.

[13] See Koh (2022).

[14] See Dillbary et al. (2024).

have argued, harm is only definable relative to some existing definition of rights, and how rights should be defined is constantly evolving based on prevailing political views, concepts of justice, and cultural norms. Some argue that in this sort of environment, unrestricted free speech is the best way to sort out competing perspectives, and cancel culture is merely the modern way that this sorting takes place. The pervasiveness of externalities in this context, however, casts doubt on whether that is a reasonable expectation. The next section develops an approach to this question in the context of a closely related issue—namely, the expression of identity. Following that, we revisit the issue of free speech.

Expression or Suppression of Identity

For many people, expressing their identity fundamentally defines their sense of self. This could involve expressions of gender, religious belief, or ethnic heritage. However, as Akerlof and Kranton (2000, p. 717) have recognized, "identity underlies a new type of externality. One person's actions can have meaning for and evoke responses in others."[15] In this sense, expression of identity presents the same economic problem as speech or any other externality-generating activity.

To develop an economic approach to this issue, consider two groups of people in society, each of whom derives happiness, or "utility," from expressing their own identity, but possibly suffers unhappiness, or "disutility," when members of the other group express theirs. Let I_1 be the expression of identity by a person in group one, and let I_2 the expression of identity by a person in group two, where I_i varies between 0 and 1. Specifically, $I_i = 1$ means a person in group i expresses his or her identity freely (maximally), while $I_i = 0$ means her or she is prevented from expressing it at all. Members of group one therefore enjoy the highest level of utility when $I_1 = 1$ and $I_2 = 0$; that is, when they can fully express their own identity while members of group 2 are prevented from expressing theirs. The same is true in reverse when $I_1 = 0$ and $I_2 = 1$.[16] Table 10.1 shows the utility levels (U_i) for members of each group as a function of the various combinations of I_1 and I_2, and Fig. 10.2 depicts

[15] Also see Carvalho (2013).

[16] If individuals derived no disutility from another person's expression, then the problem we are addressing goes away because free expression by everyone would be optimal.

the situation graphically, where I_1 is measured on the horizontal axis and I_2 is measured on the vertical axis.

The numbers in the table show that the joint optimum—the outcome that maximizes the sum of the (equally weighted) utilities—occurs when $I_1 = I_2 = ½$. In other words, each party has some rights of expression, but those rights are limited in recognition of the external effect. In the graph, the numbers in parentheses at each of the lettered points show the utility levels (U_1, U_2) based on the rankings in Table 10.1. Points A and B therefore represent the ideal outcomes for members of groups one and two, respectively. These represent asymmetric rights that allow full expression by members of one group coupled with full suppression

Table 10.1 Utility from expression of identity

I_1	I_2	U_1	U_2
1	0	4	−1
0	1	−1	4
1	1	1	1
0	0	1	1
½	½	2	2

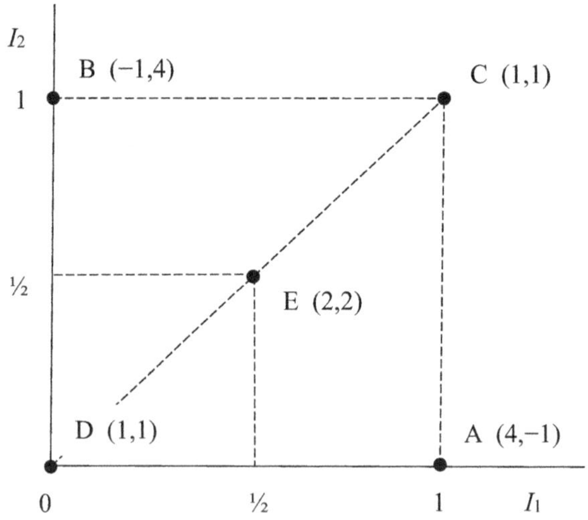

Fig. 10.2 Expression of identity

of members of the other group. By contrast, points along the diagonal represent equal rights ($I_1 = I_2$), ranging from free expression (point C) to full suppression (point D).

This situation is no different from any other externality problem owing to the inherent incompatibility of the rights of expression under consideration. In other words, it is not possible for those in group one to express their identities *without* harming those in group two, and vice versa.

A useful analogy, in view of the multi-lateral nature of the cost spillovers involved here, is the problem of neighborhood externalities in densely populated urban settings.[17] These arise because the value of any individual property depends, not only on the actions or characteristics of the owner of that property, but on the actions and characteristics of all property owners in the vicinity. Thus, for example, if one owner upgrades her property, it enhances her own property value but also that of her neighbors. Correspondingly, an owner's failure to maintain her property will lower her own property value but also that of her neighbors. The benefits and harms are therefore truly reciprocal in the Coasian sense.

Returning to the case of identity expression, we first ask, as a benchmark, what outcome the two types would reach if they were able to bargain in a Coasian fashion, as discussed in the context of the farmer-rancher dispute. Given the reciprocal nature of the harm, any increase in I above zero for one group benefits members of that group while simultaneously harming members of the other group. Thus, some mutual concessions would be necessary whereby each would agree to tolerate some amount of expression by the other (i.e., "live and let live"). One possible outcome is shown by point E in Fig. 10.1, which corresponds to $I_1 = I_2 = ½$. In fact, this represents the best the two groups can do in our example in the sense that it maximizes the joint level of utility.[18]

Such an outcome is not generally attainable without some government intervention, however, except perhaps in the case of close-knit groups or families where members explicitly or implicitly agree to refrain from excessively harmful levels of expression while tolerating moderate levels of expression by others. Enforcement in such a setting is generally by

[17] See Miceli (2011, pp. 40–42).

[18] This assumes that the utilities can be added, and that there is a (roughly) equal number of members of each group. If point E were reached by a actual bargaining, the parties would express their utility levels in monetary terms and would negotiate a mutually acceptable transaction.

informal means like peer pressure, and, in some cases, by the ability of members to exit the group or to be expelled.

In larger-scale settings involving strangers, however, such a voluntary outcome is not generally practical for a number of reasons, including large numbers, lack of a "currency" for bargaining (given that the harms and benefits are not easily monetizable), inability to exit, and the cost of detecting violators. Further, a well-organized sub-group may be able to exercise undue influence over the larger public opinion, especially in the age of social media. This can create a climate in which certain acts or beliefs are deemed "unacceptable" by the influencing group, and hence subject to public shaming and/or diminished economic opportunities for those holding the offensive beliefs. As we noted above, technology has actually enhanced the ability of small groups to exert this sort of influence, which is why the cancel-culture phenomenon tends to be driven by social media.

A political solution requires "capture" of the governmental apparatus by one of the groups. In that case, the group in charge will be able to put its preferred outcome into effect by legislation. In the above example, this will presumably result in points A or B being instituted, depending on which group is victorious. And since majorities are likely to shift over time, this sort of politically-driven outcome will probably oscillate between these two extremes.[19] Assuming equal time in power, we compute the average payoff for a member of each group in this setting to be $1.5 = (= (4 - 1)/2$. This is less than the per-person payoff of 2 from the hypothetical negotiated outcome corresponding to point E, at which each group agrees to less than full expression in every period. The negotiated solution is therefore better for everyone, but the political process is not well-suited to attain that outcome.

If a constitutional mandate requiring equal treatment were added, only outcomes along the diagonal line, reflecting the points for which $I_1 = I_2$, would be available. This would be a step in the right direction, but it would not fully resolve the conflict *because* any point on the segment CD would remain possible.

At one extreme is the outcome that would arise under the *minimal state*,[20] represented by point C, which entails free and full expression

[19] See, for example, Boettke and Thompson (2022).

[20] Nozick (1974).

by all members of society. In this scenario, all citizens have the right to choose I to maximize their own utility. The equilibrium outcome in this case is determined by Table 10.2, which shows the utility of a representative member of each group (as defined by Table 10.1) as a function of the choices made by both (all) individuals with respect to the expression of their identities.

Consider first the optimal behavior of members of group 1 in this setting. If they expect members of group 2 to choose $I_2 = 0$ (full suppression), members of group 1 will choose $I_1 = 1$ (full expression) because 4 > 1. And likewise, if they expect members of group 2 to choose $I_2 = 1$, they will again choose $I_1 = 1$ because 1 > −1. Thus, full expression ($I_1 = 1$) is the dominant strategy for members of group 1. And because the payoffs are symmetric, full expression will also be a dominant strategy for members of group 2. Thus, the unique Nash equilibrium is $I_1 = I_2 = 1$, as shown by the boldfaced entries in the lower right cell of the table.[21] This corresponds to point C in Fig. 10.2.

At the other extreme is a more interventionist, but still equal rights, regime in which the government gives each citizen the right to block expressions of identity by others if they deem them to be harmful. In this extreme cancel-culture scenario, members of a group in effect have the

Table 10.2
Equilibrium with free expression

		Member of group 2:	
		$I_2 = 0$	$I_2 = 1$
Member of group 1:	$I_1 = 0$	1, 1	−1, 4
	$I_1 = 1$	4, −1	**1, 1**

Table 10.3
Equilibrium with complete suppression

		Member of group 2:	
		$I_1 = 0$	$I_1 = 1$
Member of group 1:	$I_2 = 0$	**1, 1**	4, −1
	$I_2 = 1$	−1, 4	1, 1

[21] The game depicted in Table 1 is a Prisoner's Dilemma.

right to choose the level of expression by members *of the other group*. Table 10.3 shows the payoffs for this scenario, where members of group 1 can choose I_2 while members of group 2 can choose I_1. Proceeding as above, if members of group 1 expect members of group 2 to restrict I_1 to equal 0, they will likewise restrict I_2 to equal zero because $1 > -1$. Similarly, if they expect members of group 2 to choose $I_1 = 1$, they will again choose $I_2 = 0$ because $4 > 1$. Thus, full suppression ($I_2 = 0$) is the dominant strategy for members of group 1. Again, because the payoffs are symmetric, full suppression is also a dominant strategy for members of group 2. Thus, the unique Nash equilibrium in this case is $I_1 = I_2 = 0$, as shown by the boldfaced entries in the upper left cell of the table.[22] This complete-suppression outcome corresponds to point D in Fig. 10.2.

The preceding free-expression and full-suppression outcomes can be likened, respectively, to the "tragedy of the commons" and the "tragedy of the anti-commons."[23] Both represent inefficient departures from the compromise outcome represented by point E in Fig. 10.2. Given the hypothesized payoffs underlying these examples, the opposing outcomes yield the same level of utility for all parties, but this need not be the case. The comparison is similar to that between no liability and strict liability in accident settings, which, as we saw in Chap. 5, will not generally minimize accident costs when both injurers and victims can invest in precaution. In this case, a least-cost avoider rule would select one outcome as cost minimizing, but that would be case-specific. The same is true here. Generally, we would expect an intermediate solution to dominate both of these extremes.

Although Coasian bargaining as a means of achieving the compromise point E has been ruled out as impractical in most settings, something approximating it can perhaps be achieved by a well-designed regulatory regime that balances the interests of all parties. The key is to recognize the reciprocal nature of the harms and benefits—the fact that everyone is simultaneously an injurer and a victim.[24]

Returning to the neighborhood externality analogy, we note that well-designed zoning laws, which limit the freedom of landowners to those activities that do not impose undue harms on their neighbors, epitomize

[22] This game is also a Prisoner's Dilemma.

[23] See Heller (2008).

[24] See Miceli (2011, pp. 136–139).

this idea.[25] To quote Justice Holmes, it does this by achieving an "average reciprocity of advantage" across all owners.[26] In such a setting, victims of harm do not have a legitimate claim for compensation because, as Frank Michelman (1967, p. 1223) observes, "the disappointed claimant ought to be able to appreciate how such decisions might fit into a consistent practice which holds forth a lesser long run risk to people like him than would any consistent practice which is naturally suggested by the opposite decision."

Applying this logic in the current context is complicated by the fact that attaching monetary values to the harms arising from "moralisms" is daunting. Thus, a fully optimal solution is impractical. Nevertheless, it would seem that in most instances "corner solutions" like unrestricted freedom of expression or complete suppression will generally be inferior to an intermediate solution that allows some limited freedom, subject to reasonable restrictions that would apply equally to all. The next section applies this logic to limitations on speech.

Free Speech Revisited: The Marketplace of Ideas

The discussion of cancel culture above questioned the desirability of free speech as the best way to sort out conflicting ideas. Opposing this is the so-called marketplace of ideas, which is a powerful image often used to justify complete freedom of speech, or at least wide latitude in expressing one's views. The idea, again as stated by Justice Holmes, is that "…the best test of truth is the power of thought to get itself accepted in the competition of the market…"[27] The vigorous debate that an unrestricted marketplace of ideas fosters will ideally winnow out the most harmful or false ideas, thereby allowing the best and most productive ones to flourish and spread. This logic would seem to argue for essentially unrestricted free expression, like the outcome depicted by point C in Fig. 10.2. This is, however, an overly optimistic view of markets because of the externalities associated with ideas, which represent the content of speech.

[25] See White (1975) and Fischel (1985).

[26] See *Pennsylvania Coal v. Mahon*, 260 U.S. 393 (1922).

[27] *Abrams v. United States*, 250 U.S. 616 (1919), dissenting opinion. Also see Coase (1974) for a defense of a free market for ideas.

But ideas, like public goods, also have beneficial externalities because one person's good idea can be used by others without diminishing its quantity. This will tend to result in the under-supply or under-discovery of such ideas because originators cannot fully capture their value, which is why exclusive rights to profit from ideas, like patents and copyrights, have been created. These represent government-enforced monopolies designed to encourage the creation of useful ideas, though that protection is limited in both time and scope to balance the benefits against the costs of monopoly.[28]

Ideas can also be harmful: they can be false (so-called misinformation); they can offend people (like moralisms); or they can incite harmful behavior. These negative externalities may justify regulating speech for the same reason that pollution or straying cattle are regulated.[29] As noted above, the Supreme Court ruled that speech that creates a "clear and present danger" can be suppressed. This standard can be expressed in the familiar form of the Hand test—$B < PL$—where in the current context B is the cost of restricting the speech in question (i.e., the value of the speech to others), P is the probability of harm if the speech is allowed, and L is the resulting harm.[30] The argument for regulation therefore becomes stronger as the harm increases, as the harm becomes more likely, and as the value of the speech decreases.

In terms of Fig. 10.2, regulation of speech represents a movement down the diagonal from point C (unrestricted speech) to point E (some regulation). Movement all the way to point D (completely suppressed speech) would require a finding that the speech in question has little or no value, or that the risk of harm is very high (clear and present). Harsh limits on speech that expresses hate but has little redeeming value, or that is solely aimed to incite unrest, would seem to fit this description. At the other extreme, political speech is generally accorded a very high degree of protection because of the risk that regulating speech in the political arena will result in the suppression of legitimately valuable, if sometimes unpopular, ideas.

[28] See, for example, Blair and Cotter (2005).

[29] On this point, see Posner (2003, Chapter 28) and Cooter (2000, Chapter 13).

[30] Posner (2003, p. 694).

Defamation, which consists of the torts of libel and slander,[31] involves the infliction of damage to a person's reputation. In terms of regulation of speech, it generally falls in between the extremes of hate speech and political speech in that courts do hold speakers liable under certain circumstances. In terms of the above threshold test, one supposes that $B = 0$ for false statements, whereas $PL > 0$. (False but harmless statements would not be actionable.) Thus, there is no basis for protecting the speech in question. For statements that are false, however, there is an important distinction between plaintiffs who are public figures (e.g., politicians and entertainers) and those who are private figures. In order for the former to recover, they must show that the speaker knew the speech in question was false, or that the speaker had a "reckless disregard for the truth,"[32] which is close, if not identical, to an outright lie. Speakers are thus effectively shielded from responsibility for harm.

In the case of private figures, by contrast, parties alleging defamation have a lesser burden to meet. They must first prove that the statement is false (truth is always a defense), but beyond that, they generally also have to demonstrate that the speaker should have had "reasonable evidence" that the statement was true before making it.[33] That is, the speaker was negligent in ascertaining the truthfulness of speech. This is easier to prove because it doesn't require evidence about what the speaker *actually* knew, only what he or she *should have* known, which, as we have argued in other contexts, can often be proved by objective evidence. This distinction between private and public figures makes sense because the value of (truthful) information about public figures will be larger (almost by definition) than for private figures.

A caveat to the preceding argument again involves the relative nature of harm, particularly when it takes the form of insults that may induce mental suffering by a victim. As our earlier discussion of moralisms revealed, this type of harm is both hard to quantify—because it is often "in the eye of the beholder"—and pervasive in society. Consequently, the ability of law to control speech, even if it is deemed constitutional, is debatable. More importantly, there is no obvious initial entitlement point against which

[31] See, generally, Keeton et al. (1984, Chapter 19). Libel generally consists of written statements while slander is generally spoken.

[32] See *New York Times v. Sullivan*, 376 U.S. 254 (1964).

[33] Cooter (2000, p. 325).

harm can be gauged. It depends on the perceived distribution of rights at a particular time and place. This is what makes the marketplace-of-ideas justification for unrestricted speech difficult to apply as a universal standard in the modern world. As *The Economist* observed in a book review on free speech,

> Many groups, including families and friends, remain intact—and can absorb the nosiest of arguments—because of unspoken and often unconscious limits on the sayable, even the thinkable. That kind of informal system works best in smallish communities, ... In a digital universe of billions, incorporating many religions and ideologies, no such commonality exists.[34]

Finally, a argument often advanced against restrictions on speech is that free speech is an inalienable right that deserves categorical protection, along the lines of our discussion of side constraints in Chap. 2.[35] Certain rights, it is argued, should not be tradeable, and speech is one of them. However, when inalienable rights come into conflict, a hierarchy is needed, which necessarily requires the subordination of somebody's rights, as in the hate speech-free speech dichotomy. The balancing approach to conflicting rights at least allows an "interior solution," like point E in Fig. 10.2, which accords some value to the rights of all concerned parties, rather than forcing a corner solution that favors one group over another, like point A or B, which a hierarchical approach requires.

Victimless Crimes

It should by now be apparent that an important theme of this book is that the identities of "injurer" and "victim" are relative concepts that depend on the direction of the arrow of causation. What, then, are we to make of crimes in which there is no apparent victim—so-called victimless crimes? How does this seemingly oxymoronic concept fit within the foregoing framework? The usual examples of victimless crimes include gambling, prostitution, the use and trafficking in drugs, pornography, and the sale of human organs. All appear to involve some sort of mutually

[34] "The megaphone and the muzzle," *The Economist*, February 5, 2022, pp. 73–74.

[35] Turley (2024) makes such an argument.

beneficial exchange, and so on what grounds are they made illegal? What, specifically, is the nature of the harm and who are the victims?

Criminologists sometimes dispute the term "victimless," claiming that there are "indirect" victims, such as the offender's family and friends, or society in general.[36] Cooter and Ulen (1988, p. 509) have likewise argued that, although the victim is admittedly vague, "some crimes are defined for actions perceived to be harmful to society or to the social fabric." For this reason, these acts are sometimes called "public order crimes," meaning that they are somehow offenses against society in general. This evokes the tort law concept of a "public nuisance," which is defined to be "an act or omission 'which obstructs or causes inconvenience or damage to the public in the exercise of rights common to all'" (Keeton et al. 1984, p. 643). Here, though, the connotation is that the harm takes the form of disapproval of some behavior or activity rather than actual physical damage to persons or property.

In whatever way the concept is defined, the issue seems to be different from actions that are inherently risky or that create a dangerous condition, which, as we have discussed, are appropriately subject to legal control as a way of mitigating future harm. The harm from these "victimless" acts seems closer to (though still somewhat different from) Adelstein's "moral costs," which he defines to be the costs that "sympathetic observers experience at the plight" of crime victims (Adelstein 2017, p. 167).[37] In other words, they reflect moral outrage by non-participants about the acts in question, though not as a result of any actual harm incurred by these observers themselves. Rather, they are costs of disapproval which, because of their pervasiveness, are not generally controlled by legal means, but instead are subject to social controls, such as peer pressure, public shaming,[38] damage to reputation, ostracism, etc.

However, when a sufficiently large consensus emerges about the harmfulness of certain acts, they may be elevated to the level of crimes,

[36] See, for example, Walsh (2012).

[37] These costs are similar to what Michelman, in a different context, called "demoralization costs," by which he means the disutility that losers and their sympathizers feel when deprived of some theretofore enjoyed right without adequate compensation (Michelman 1967). Michelman was particularly referring to the taking or regulation of land, but the concept applies broadly to any tangible or intangible asset.

[38] See Etzioni (1999).

particularly if the "victims" (i.e., those offended by the activity in question) succeed in gaining control of the political apparatus. The morality-shaping (expressive) function of law, as discussed in Chap. 6, is relevant here. Perhaps this is an efficient way to deal with these costs when they become large enough, and agreement about their inappropriateness is broad enough. However, the definition of harm is subject to political vagaries, and, like moralisms, it therefore constitutes an evolving concept that reflects prevailing social mores. Think of Jim Crow laws, Prohibition, and the War on Drugs, all of which were eventually repealed or greatly scaled back as public opinion changed. And of course, there are always new "offenses" on the horizon that certain groups seek to have classified as crimes, if only to empower them.

As Cooter and Ulen (1988, p. 509) note, "No doubt the actions that are so perceived change from time to time so that there are variations in the kinds of actions that are believed to threaten the public at large." This suggests that the quest for an objective meaning of harm is ultimately illusive, and that only "when a strong ethical or political consensus has formed on an issue" can the law "pronounce confident judgment on the soundness of the legal decision resolving the issue" (Posner 1990, p. 313). The longer such a consensus remains in place, the more likely it is to crystalize into a universally-accepted belief, and hence become encoded in law. Short of that, however, public opinion, often driven by vocal minorities and amplified by social media, will dictate the definition of harm and the consequent assignment of responsibility.

Concluding Remarks

The conclusion that we have arrived at—that economic reasoning cannot offer a definitive theory of how to assign responsibility for harm, or even to uniquely define harm in the first place—may seem like an unsatisfying way to end our analysis. This should not be interpreted, however, as an admission that economics is ultimately unsuited to address the question of how to assign responsibility for harm. As we have noted, it is actually the manifestation of a fundamental economic insight: that an avoided harm can always be defined as a benefit, and a forgone benefit as a harm. There is, consequently, an unavoidable indeterminacy when it comes to defining harm. The situation is not unlike the difficulty modern physics has had in trying to explain the direction of the "arrow of time," which, despite being an obvious a part of people's everyday experience of reality, is not required or explained by most theories of physics.[39] The theories function equally well whether time runs forward or backward. The same thing can be said of harm—people know it when they experience it, but economic theory cannot define or explain it independently of a baseline definition of rights. However, once a baseline is put in place, economics can establish an efficient enforcement structure for protecting and exchanging rights.

In the end, this realization is both limiting and liberating. It is limiting in the sense that economics cannot fulfill the hope of providing a purely objective (i.e., value-free) theory of law. But it is liberating because it does not tether the economic approach to the pursuit of any particular concept of justice or morality for imposing legal responsibility. What it offers instead is a methodology for structuring responsibility in ways that can achieve the desired goal in the most efficient manner. And it is hard to imagine how anyone can object to this role for economic theory on the principle, noted by Posner (2003, p. 27), that wasting resources is itself unjust or immoral.

References

Adelstein, R. 2017. *The Exchange Order: Property and Liability as an Exchange System*. New York: Oxford Univ. Press.

Akerlof, G., and R. Kranton. 2000. Economics and Identity. *Quarterly Journal of Economics* 115: 715–753.

Becker, G. 1968. Crime and Punishment: An Economic Approach. *Journal of Political Economy* 76: 169–217.

Blair, R., and T. Cotter. 2005. *Intellectual Property: Economic and Legal Dimensions of Rights and Remedies*. New York: Cambridge Univ. Press.

Boettke, P., and H. Thompson. 2022. Identity and Off-diagonals: How Permanent Winning Coalitions Destroy Democratic Governance. *Public Choice* 191: 483–499.

Calabresi, G., and A.D. Melamed. 1972. Property rules, Liability Rules, and Inalienability: One View of the Cathedral. *Harvard Law Review* 85: 1089–1128.

Carbonara, E., F. Parisi, and G. von Wangenheim. 2012. Unjust Laws and Illegal Norms: One View of the Cathedral. *International Review of Law and Economics* 32: 285–299.

Carvalho, J. 2013. Veiling. *Quarterly Journal of Economics* 128: 337–370.

[39] See, for example, Hertog (2023, pp. 122–123).

Coase, R. 1974. The Market for Goods and the Market for Ideas. *American Economic Review* 64: 384–391.

Cooter, R. 1982. The Cost of Coase. *Journal of Legal Studies* 11: 1–33.

Cooter, R. 1998. Expressive Law and Economics. *Journal of Legal Studies* 27: 585–607.

Cooter, R. 2000. *The Strategic Constitution*. Princeton: Princeton Univ. Press.

Cooter, R., and T. Ulen. 1988. *Law and Economics*. Glenview, Ill: Scott Foresman and Co.

Dillbary, J., M. Iwasaki, and T. Miceli. "On the Inadequacy of a Purely Economic Theory of Crime," Working Paper, 2024.

Etzioni, A. 1999. Back to the Pillory? *The American Scholar* 68: 43–50.

Fischel, W. 1985. *The Economics of Zoning Laws: A Property Rights Approach*. Baltimore: Johns Hopkins Univ. Press.

Friedman, D. 2000. *Law's Order: What Economics Has to do with the Law and Why It Matters*. Princeton: Princeton Univ. Press.

Glaeser, E. and C. Sunstein. "A Theory of Civil Disobedience," NBER Working Paper No. 21338, 2015.

Heller, M. 2008. *The Gridlock Economy: How Too Much Ownership Wrecks Markets, Stops Innovation, and Costs Lives*. New York: Basic Books.

Hertog, T. 2023. *On the Origin of Time*. New York: Bantam Books.

Holmes, O.W. 1881[1963]. *The Common Law*. Boston: Little Brown.

Kahan, D. 1998. Social Meaning and the Economic Analysis of Crime. *Journal of Legal Studies* 27: 609–622.

Kaplow, L., and S. Shavell. 2002. *Fairness Versus Welfare*. Cambridge, MA: Harvard Univ. Press.

Keeton, W., D. Dobbs, R. Keeton, and D. Owen. 1984. *Prosser and Keeton on Torts*, 5th ed. St. Paul, MN: West Publishing.

Klevorick, A. "On the Economic Theory of Crime." In *NOMOS XXVII: Criminal Justice*, edited by J. Pennock and J. Chapman. New York: New York Univ. Press, 1985.

Koh, S. 2022. 'Cancel Culture' and Criminal Justice. *Hastings Law Journal* 74: 79–121.

Lewin, J., and W. Trumbull. 1990. The Social Value of Crime? *International Review of Law and Economics* 10: 271–284.

Miceli, T. 2011. *The Economic Theory of Eminent Domain: Private Property*. Public Use, New York: Cambridge Univ. Press.

Miceli, T. 2024. On the Impossibility of a Purely Objective Economic Theory of Crime. *Asian Journal of Law and Economics* 15: 209–219.

Michelman, F. 1967. Property, Utility, and Fairness: Comments on the Ethical Foundations of 'Just Compensation' Law. *Harvard Law Review* 80: 1165–1258.

Nozick, R. 1974. *Anarchy, State, and Utopia*. New York: Basic Books.

Posner, R. 1988. *Law and Literature: A Misunderstood Relation*. Cambridge, MA: Harvard Univ. Press.
Posner, R. 1990. *The Problems of Jurisprudence*. Cambridge, MA: Harvard Univ. Press.
Posner, R. 2003. *Economic Analysis of Law*, 6th ed. New York: Aspen Publishers.
Rawls, J. 1971. *A Theory of Justice*. Cambridge, MA: Belknap Press.
Sandel, M. 2012. *What Money Can't Buy: The Moral Limits of Markets*. New York: Farrar, Straus, and Giroux.
Shavell, S. 1985. Criminal Law and the Optimal Use of Nonmonetary Sanctions as Deterrents. *Columbia Law Review* 85: 1232–1262.
Sophocles. "Antigone." In *Sophocles I*, edited by D. Grene and R. Lattimore. Chicago: Univ. of Chicago Press, 1954.
Stigler, G. 1970. The Optimum Enforcement of Law. *Journal of Political Economy* 78: 345–355.
Sunstein, C. 1996. On the Expressive Function of Law. *University of Pennsylvania Law Review* 144: 2021–2053.
Thoreau, H. "Civil Disobedience." In *Walden and Other Writings of Henry David Thoreau*, edited by B. Atkinson. New York: Modern Library, 1849 [1965].
Turley, J. 2024. *The Indispensable Right*. New York: Simon & Schuster.
Walsh, A. 2012. *Criminology: The Essentials*. Thousand Oaks, CA: Sage Publications.
White, M. "Fiscal Zoning in Fragmented Metropolitan Areas." In *Fiscal Zoning and Land Use Controls*, edited by E. Mills. Lexington, MA: Lexington Books, 1975.

References

Adelstein, R. 1981. Institutional Function and Evolution in the Criminal Process. *Northwestern University Law Review* 76: 1–99.

__________. "Plea Bargaining: A Comparative Approach." In *The New Palgrave Dictionary of Law and Economics*, P. Newman, ed., New York: Stockton Press, 1998.

Adelstein, R. 2017. *The Exchange Order: Property and Liability as an Exchange System*. New York: Oxford Univ. Press.

Aeschylus. "Oresteia." In *Aeschylus I*, edited by D. Grene and R. Lattimore. Chicago: Univ. of Chicago Press, 1953.

Akerlof, G. 1970. The Market for 'Lemons': Quality Uncertainty and the Market Mechanism. *Quarterly Journal of Economics* 84: 488–500.

Akerlof, G., and R. Kranton. 2000. Economics and Identity. *Quarterly Journal of Economics* 115: 715–753.

Baird, D., R. Gertner, and R. Picker. 1994. *Game Theory and the Law*. Cambridge, MA: Harvard Univ. Press.

Baker, M. and T. Miceli. "Crime, Credible Enforcement, and Multiple Equilibria." *International Review of Law and Economics*, article 106030 (2021).

Beard, T. 1990. Bankruptcy and Care Choice. *Rand Journal of Economics* 21: 626–634.

Bebchuk, L. 1984. Litigation and Settlement Under Imperfect Information. *Rand Journal of Economics* 15: 404–415.

Bebchuk, L. 1988. Suing Solely to Extract a Settlement Offer. *Journal of Legal Studies* 17: 437–450.

Bebchuk, L. 1996. A New Theory Concerning the Credibility and Success of Threats to Sue. *Journal of Legal Studies* 25: 1–25.

T. J. Miceli, *Harm and Responsibility*,
https://doi.org/10.1007/978-3-031-74831-8

Beccaria, C. *On Crimes and Punishments*. Indianapolis, IN: Hackett Publishing Co, 1764 [1986].
Becker, G. 1968. Crime and Punishment: An Economic Approach. *Journal of Political Economy* 76: 169–217.
Becker, G., and G. Stigler. 1974. Law Enforcement, Malfeasance, and Compensation of Enforcers. *Journal of Legal Studies* 3: 1–18.
Bentham, J. *An Introduction to the Principles of Morals and Legislation*. New York: Oxford Univ. Press, 1780 [1970].
Blair, R., and T. Cotter. 2005. *Intellectual Property: Economic and Legal Dimensions of Rights and Remedies*. New York: Cambridge Univ. Press.
Boettke, P., and H. Thompson. 2022. Identity and Off-diagonals: How Permanent Winning Coalitions Destroy Democratic Governance. *Public Choice* 191: 483–499.
Brague, R. 2005. *The Law of God: The Philosophical History of an Idea*. Chicago: Univ. of Chicago Press.
Brooks, R. 2002. Liability and Organizational Choice. *Journal of Law and Economics* 45: 91–125.
Brown, J. 1973. Toward an Economic Theory of Liability. *Journal of Legal Studies* 2: 323–349.
Buell, L. 1986. *New England Literary Culture*. Cambridge: Cambridge Univ. Press.
Calabresi, G., and A.D. Melamed. 1972. Property Rules, Liability Rules, and Inalienability: One View of the Cathedral. *Harvard Law Review* 85: 1089–1128.
Carbonara, E., F. Parisi, and G. von Wangenheim. 2012. Unjust Laws and Illegal Norms: One View of the Cathedral. *International Review of Law and Economics* 32: 285–299.
Carvalho, J. 2013. Veiling. *Quarterly Journal of Economics* 128: 337–370.
Calabresi, G. 1970. *The Cost of Accidents: A Legal and Economic Analysis*. New Haven: Yale Univ. Press.
Calabresi, G., and A.D. Melamed. 1972. Property Rules, Liability Rules, and Inalienability: One View of the Cathedral. *Harvard Law Review* 85: 1089–1128.
Clarke, R. 2013. *A Natural History of Ghosts: 500 Years of Hunting for Proof*. New York: Penguin Books.
Coase, R. *The Firm, the Market, and the Law*, Chicago, Univ. of Chicago Press, 1988.
______. "The Problem of Social Cost." *Journal of Law and Economics*, 3 (1960), 1–44.
______. "The Market for Goods and the Market for Ideas." *American Economic Review* 64 (1974): 384–391.
______. "The Nature of the Firm." *Economica*, 4 (1937), 386–405.

Coleman, J. 1988. *Markets, Morals and the Law*. New York: Cambridge Univ. Press.
Coleman, J. 1992. *Risks and Wrongs*. Cambridge, UK: Cambridge Univ. Press.
Cooter, R. 1982. The Cost of Coase. *Journal of Legal Studies* 11: 1–33.
Cooter, R. 1984. Prices and Sanctions. *Columbia Law Review* 84: 1523–1560.
Cooter, R. 1985. Unity in Torts, Contracts, and Property: The Model of Precaution. *California Law Review* 73: 1–51.
Cooter, R. 1987. Torts as the Union of Liberty and Efficiency: An Essay on Causation. *Chicago-Kent Law Review* 73: 1–51.
Cooter, R. 1989. Punitive Damages for Deterrence: When and How Much? *Alabama Law Review* 40: 1143–1196.
Cooter, R. 1998. Expressive Law and Economics. *Journal of Legal Studies* 27: 585–607.
Cooter, R. 2000. *The Strategic Constitution*. Princeton: Princeton Univ. Press.
Cooter, R., and D. Rubinfeld. 1989. An Economic Analysis of Legal Disputes and Their Resolution. *Journal of Economic Literature* 27: 1067–1097.
Cooter, R. and T. Ulen. *Law and Economics*. Glenview, Ill.: Scott Foresman and Co, 1988.
Cosgel, M., and T. Miceli. 2018. The Price of Redemption: Sin, Penance, and Marginal Deterrence. *Journal of Economic Behavior and Organization* 156: 206–218.
Cosgel, M., and T. Miceli. 2019. Toward a Theory of Religious Belief and the Emergence of Law. *Journal of Institutional and Theoretical Economics* 175: 692–713.
Curry, P., and M. Doyle. 2016. Integrating Market Alternatives into the Economic Theory of Optimal Deterrence. *Economic Inquiry* 54: 1873–1883.
Dana, D. 2001. Rethinking the Puzzle of Escalating Penalties for Repeat Offenders. *Yale Law Journal* 110: 733–783.
Demsetz, H. 1972. When Does the Rule of Liability Matter? *Journal of Legal Studies* 1: 13–28.
Dharmapala, D., and N. Garoupa. 2004. Penalty Enhancement for Hate Crimes: An Economic Analysis. *American Law and Economics Review* 6: 185–207.
Dillbary, J. 2021. The Case Against Collective Responsibility. *Boston College Law Review* 62: 391–452.
Dillbary, J., and T. Miceli. 2023. Of Sinners and Scapegoats: The Economics of Collective Responsibility. *Washington Univ. Law Review* 100: 1299–1351.
________. "Reformulating Detection in the Economic Model of Crime: Probability Scaling and Group Punishment," Working paper, 2024.
Dillbary, J., M. Iwasaki, and T. Miceli. "On the Inadequacy of a Purely Economic Theory of Crime," Working Paper, 2024.
Dostoevsky, F. 1866[1956]. *Crime and Punishment*. New York: Random House.
Doyle, A.C. 1930. *The Complete Sherlock Holmes*, 2nd ed. New York: Doubleday.

Easterbrook, F. 1983. Criminal Procedure as a Market System. *Journal of Legal Studies* 12: 289–332.

Ehrman, B. 2018. *The Triumph of Christianity: How a Forbidden Religion Swept the World*. New York: Simon and Schuster.

Ekelund, R., R. Herbert, and R. Tollison. 1992. The Economics of Sin and Redemption: Purgatory as a Market-Pull Innovation? *Journal of Economic Behavior and Organization* 19: 1–15.

Ellickson, R. 1991. *Order Without Law: How Neighbors Settle Disputes*. Cambridge: Harvard Univ. Press.

Ellickson, R. 1993. Property in Land. *Yale Law Journal* 102: 1315–1400.

Epstein, R. 1973. A Theory of Strict Liability. *Journal of Legal Studies* 2: 151–204.

Epstein, R. 1980. *Modern Products Liability*. Westport, CT: Quorum Books.

Etzioni, A. 1999. Back to the Pillory? *The American Scholar* 68: 43–50.

Fischel, W. 1985. *The Economics of Zoning Laws: A Property Rights Approach*. Baltimore: Johns Hopkins Univ. Press.

Fitzgerald, F. 1995. *The Great Gatsby*. New York: Scribner Paperback Edition.

Frank, J. 1995. *Dostoevsky: The Miracle Years: 1865–1871*. Princeton: Princeton Univ. Press.

Frank, R. "A Theory of Moral Sentiments." In *Beyond Self Interest*, edited by J. Mansbridge. Chicago: Univ. of Chicago Press, 1990.

Frech, H. 1979. The Extended Coase Theorem and Long Run Equilibrium: The Non-Equivalence of Liability Rules and Property Rights. *Economic Inquiry* 17: 254–268.

Friedman, D. 2000. *Law's Order: What Economics Has to Do with the Law and Why It Matters*. Princeton: Princeton Univ. Press.

Friedman, L. 2004. *Law in America: A Short History*. New York: The Modern Library.

Friehe, T., and T. Miceli. 2014. Marginal Deterrence When Offenders Act Sequentially. *Economics Letters* 124: 523–525.

Friehe, T., and T. Miceli. 2018. On the ROLE of the Exclusionary Rule for Optimal Law Enforcement. *Journal of Public Economic Theory* 20: 757–767.

Furlong, W. 1987. A General Equilibrium Model of Crime Commission and Prevention. *Journal of Public Economics* 34: 87–103.

Garoupa, N. 1997. The Theory of Optimal Law Enforcement. *Journal of Economic Surveys* 11: 267–295.

Garoupa, N., and M. Obidzinski. 2011. The Scope of Punishment: An Economic Theory. *European Journal of Law and Economics* 31: 237–247.

Gladwell, M. 2013. *David and Goliath: Underdogs, Misfits, and the Art of Battling Giants*. New York: Little-Brown.

Glaeser, E., and S. Glendon. 1998. Incentives, Predestination, and Free Will. *Economic Inquiry* 36: 429–443.

Glaeser, E. and C. Sunstein. "A Theory of civil Disobedience," NBER Working Paper No. 21338, 2015.
Grady, M. 1983. A New Positive Economic Theory of Negligence. *Yale Law Journal* 92: 799–829.
Grady, M. 1988. Common Law Control of Strategic Behavior: Railroad Sparks and the Farmer. *Journal of Legal Studies* 17: 15–42.
Grossman, G., and M. Katz. 1983. Plea Bargaining and Social Welfare. *American Economic Review* 73: 749–757.
Harries, J. "The *Senatus Consultum Silanianum:* Court Decisions and Judicial Severity in the Early Roman Empire." In *New Frontiers: Law and Society in the Roman World*, edited by P. du Plessis. Edinburgh: Edinburgh Univ. Press, 2013.
Hart, H.L.A. 1961. *The Concept of Law*. Oxford: Oxford Univ. Press.
Hart, H.L.A. 1982. *Punishment and Responsibility*. London: Oxford Univ. Press.
Hay, B. 2005. Sting Operations, Undercover Agents, and Entrapment. *Missouri Law Review* 70: 387–431.
Heller, M. 2008. *The Gridlock Economy: How Too Much Ownership Wrecks Markets, Stops Innovation, and Costs Lives*. New York: Basic Books.
Hertog, T. 2023. *On the Origin of Time*. New York: Bantam Books.
Hirshleifer, J., and J. Riley. 1992. *The Analytics of Uncertainty and Information*. New York: Cambridge Univ. Press.
Holderness, C. 1989. The Assignment of Rights, Entry Effects, and the Allocation of Resources. *Journal of Legal Studies* 18: 181–189.
Holland, T. 2019. *Dominion: How the Christian Revolution Remade the World*. New York: Basic Books.
Holmes, O.W. 1897. The Path of the Law. *Harvard Law Review* 10: 457–478.
Holmes, O.W. 1881[1963]. *The Common Law*. Boston: Little Brown.
Horwitz, M. 1977. *The Transformation of American Law: 1780–1860*. Cambridge, MA: Harvard Univ. Press.
Hovenkamp, H. 1991. Legal Policy and the Endowment Effect. *Journal of Legal Studies* 20: 225–247.
Hylton, K. 1996. Optimal Law Enforcement and Victim Precaution. *Rand Journal of Economics* 27: 197–206.
Hylton, K. 2004. Slavery and Tort Law. *Boston University Law Review* 84: 1209–1255.
Hylton, K. 2005. The Theory of Criminal Penalties and the Economics of Criminal Law. *Review of Law and Economics* 1: 175–201.
Hylton, K. 2016. *Tort Law: A Modern Perspective*. New York: Cambridge Univ. Press.
Hylton, K., and T. Miceli. 2005. Should Tort Damages be Multiplied? *Journal of Law, Economics, and Organization* 21: 388–416.

Iannaccone, L. 1998. Introduction to the Economics of Religion. *Journal of Economic Literature* 36: 1465–1495.
Iannaccone, L., R. Finke, and R. Stark. 1997. Deregulating Religion: The Economics of Church and State. *Economic Inquiry* 35: 350–364.
James, B. 2011. *Popular Crime: Reflections on the Celebration of Violence.* New York: Scribner.
Johnson, D. 2016. *God in Watching You: How the Fear of God Makes Us Human.* New York: Oxford Univ. Press.
Kahan, D. 1998. Social Meaning and the Economic Analysis of Crime. *Journal of Legal Studies* 27: 609–622.
Kandel, E., and E. Lazear. 1992. Peer Pressure and Partnerships. *Journal of Political Economy* 100: 801–817.
Kaplow, L., and S. Shavell. 1996. Property Rules Versus Liability Rules. *Harvard Law Review* 109: 713–790.
Kaplow, L., and S. Shavell. 2002. *Fairness versus Welfare.* Cambridge, MA: Harvard Univ. Press.
Katz, L. 1987. *Bad Acts and Guilty Minds: Conundrums of the Criminal Law.* Chicago: Univ. of Chicago Press.
Keeton, W., D. Dobbs, R. Keeton, and D. Owen. 1984. *Prosser and Keeton on Torts*, 5th ed. St. Paul, MN: West Publishing.
Klevorick, A. "On the Economic Theory of Crime." In *NOMOS XXVII: Criminal Justice*, edited by J. Pennock and J. Chapman. New York: New York Univ. Press, 1985.
Koh, S. 2022. 'Cancel Culture' and Criminal Justice. *Hastings Law Journal* 74: 79–121.
Komesar, N. 1994. *Imperfect Alternatives: Choosing Institutions in Law, Economics, and Public Policy.* Chicago: Univ. of Chicago Press.
Landes, W. 1971. An Economic Analysis of Courts. *Journal of Legal Studies* 14: 61–107.
Landes, W., and R. Posner. 1973. Private Enforcement of Law. *Journal of Legal Studies* 4: 1–46.
Landes, W., and R. Posner. 1987. *The Economic Structure of Tort Law.* Cambridge, MA: Harvard Univ. Press.
Levinson, D. 2003. Collective Sanctions. *Stanford University Law Review* 56: 345–428.
Levmore, S. 1995. Gomorrah to *Ybarra* and More: Overextraction and the Puzzle of Immoderate Group Liability. *Virginia Law Review* 81: 1561–1604.
Levmore, S. 1995. Rethinking Group Responsibility and Strategic Threats in Biblical Texts and Modern Law. *Chicago-Kent Law Review* 71: 85–121.
Lewin, J., and W. Trumbull. 1990. The Social Value of Crime? *International Review of Law and Economics* 10: 271–284.

Lott, J. 1987. Should the Wealthy Be Able to "Buy Justice"? *Journal of Political Economy* 95: 1307–1316.

Madison, J. "The Federalist, 51." In *The Federalist Papers*, edited by L. Goldman. Oxford: Oxford Univ. Press, 2008.

Marino, A. 1991. Market Share Liability and Economic Efficiency. *Southern Economic Journal* 57: 667–675.

McAdams, R. 2017. *The Expressive Powers of Law: Theories and Limits*. Cambridge, MA: Harvard Univ. Press.

Medema, S. 2020. The Coase Theorem at Sixty. *Journal of Economic Literature* 58: 1045–1128.

Mercuro, N., and S. Medema. 2006. *Economics and the Law: From Posner to Post-Modernism*. Princeton: Princeton Univ. Press.

Merrill, T. 1985. Trespass, Nuisance, and the Cost of Determining Property Rights. *Journal of Legal Studies* 14: 13–48.

Miceli, T. 1990. Optimal Prosecution of Defendants Whose Guilt is Uncertain. *Journal of Law, Economics, and Organization* 6: 189–201.

Miceli, T. 1994. Do contingent Fees Promote Excessive Litigation? *Journal of Legal Studies* 23: 211–224.

Miceli, T. 1997. *Economics of the Law: Torts, Contracts, Property, Litigation*. New York: Oxford Univ. Press.

Miceli, T. 2007. Criminal Solicitation, Entrapment, and the Enforcement of Law. *International Review of Law and Economics* 27: 258–268.

Miceli, T. 2010. A Model of Criminal Sanctions That Incorporates Both Deterrence and Incapacitation. *Economics Letters* 107: 205–207.

Miceli, T. 2011. *The Economic Theory of Eminent Domain: Private Property, Public Use*. New York: Cambridge Univ. Press.

Miceli, T. 2012. Judicial Versus 'Natural' Selection of Legal Rules with an Application to Accident Law. *Journal of Institutional Economics* 8: 143–159.

Miceli, T. 2013. Escalating Penalties for Repeat Offenders: Why Are They So Hard to Explain? *Journal of Institutional and Theoretical Economics* 169: 587–604.

Miceli, T. 2015. Transaction-specific Investments and Organizational Choice: A Coase-to-Coase Theory. *Journal of Institutional Economics* 11: 283–299.

Miceli, T. 2017. *The Economics Approach to Law*, 3rd ed. Stanford: Stanford Univ. Press.

Miceli, T. 2018. On Proportionality of Punishments and the Economic Theory of Crime. *European Journal of Law and Economics* 46: 303–314.

Miceli, T. 2019. *The Paradox of Punishment: Reflections on the Economics of Criminal Justice*. Cham, Switzerland: Palgrave Macmillan.

Miceli, T. 2022. Counting Offenders' Gains? Economic and Moral Considerations in the Determination of Liability. *European Journal of Law and Economics* 54: 475–496.

Miceli, T. 2022. Of Coase, Cattle, and Crime: Why the Becker Model is Compatible with a Moral Theory of Law. *Review of Law and Economics* 18: 179–198.

Miceli, T. 2023. On Economic Theories of Criminal Punishment: Pricing, Prevention, or Proportionality? *American Law and Economics Review* 25: 1–26.

Miceli, T. 2023. Expressive Law and Escalating Penalties: Accounting for the Educational Function of Punishment. *Review of Law and Economics* 19: 245–262.

Miceli, T. 2024. On the Impossibility of a Purely Objective Economic Theory of Crime. *Asian Journal of Law and Economics* 15: 209–219.

Miceli, T., and M. Mungan. 2021. The Limit of Law: Factors Influencing the Decision to Make Harmful Acts Illegal. *Economics of Governance* 22: 293–307.

Miceli, T., and K. Segerson. 1991. Contingent Fees for Lawyers: The Impact on Litigation and Accident Prevention. *Journal of Legal Studies* 20: 381–399.

Miceli, T., and K. Segerson. 2003. A Note on Optimal Care by Wealth-Constrained Injurers. *International Review of Law and Economics* 23: 273–284.

Miceli, T., and K. Segerson. 2005. Do Exposure Suits Produce a Race to File? An economic analysis of a tort for risk. *Rand Journal of Economics* 36: 613–627.

Miceli, T., and K. Segerson. 2007. Punishing the Innocent Along with the Guilty: The Economics of Individual Versus Group Punishment. *Journal of Legal Studies* 36: 81–106.

Miceli, T., and K. Segerson. 2013. Liability Versus Regulation for Dangerous Products When Consumers Vary in Their Susceptibility to Harm and May Misperceive Risk. *Review of Law and Economics* 9: 341–356.

Miceli, T., K. Segerson, and D. Earnhart. 2022. The Role of Experience in Deterring Crime: A Theory of Specific Versus General Deterrence. *Economic Inquiry* 60: 1833–1853.

Miceli, T., K. Segerson, and S. Wang. 2015. Products Liability When Consumers Vary in Their Susceptibility to Harm and May Misperceive Risk. *Contemporary Economic Policy* 33: 468–476.

Miceli, T., and M. Stone. 2014. Piggyback Lawsuits and Deterrence: Can Frivolous Litigation Improve Welfare? *International Review of Law and Economics* 39: 49–57.

Michelman, F. 1967. Property, Utility, and Fairness: Comments on the Ethical Foundations of 'Just Compensation' Law. *Harvard Law Review* 80: 1165–1258.

Miller, P., and T. Johnson, eds. 1963. *A Sourcebook of Their Writings*. New York: Harper and Row.

Montesquieu, C. *The Spirit of Laws*. Berkeley: Univ. of California Press, 1748 [1977.
Mungan, M. 2010. Repeat Offenders: If They Learn We Punish Them More Severely. *International Review of Law and Economics* 30: 173–177.
Mungan, M. 2018. Optimal Preventive Law Enforcement and Stopping Standards. *American Law and Economics Review* 20: 289–317.
Murdock, G., and D. White. 1969. Standard Cross-Cultural Sample. *Ethnology* 8: 329–369.
Norenzayan, A. 2009. *Big Gods: How Religion Transformed Cooperation and Conflict*. Princeton: Princeton Univ. Press.
Nozick, R. 1974. *Anarchy, State, and Utopia*. New York: Basic Books.
Parisi, F., and G. Dari-Mattiacci. 2004. The Rise and Fall of Communal Liability in Ancient Law. *International Review of Law and Economics* 24: 489–505.
Parker, J. 1993. The economics of mens rea. *Virginia Law Review* 79: 741–811.
Pigou, A. 1920. *The Economics of Welfare*. London: MacMillan.
Png, I. 1986. Optimal Subsidies and Damages in the Presence of Legal Error. *International Review of Law and Economics* 6: 101–105.
Polinsky, A.M. 1980. On the Choice Between Property Rules and Liability Rules. *Economic Inquiry* 18: 233–246.
Polinsky, A.M., and Y. Che. 1991. Decoupling Liability: Optimal Incentives for Care and Litigation. *Rand Journal of Economics* 22: 562–570.
Polinsky, A.M., and W. Rogerson. 1983. Products Liability, Consumer Misperceptions, and Market Power. *Bell Journal of Economics* 14: 581–589.
Polinsky, A.M., and D. Rubinfeld. 1988. The Deterrent Effects of Settlements and Trials. *International Review of Law and Economics* 8: 109–116.
Polinsky, A. M. and S. Shavell. "The theory of public law enforcement." In *Handbook of Law and Economics*, edited by A. Polinsky and S. Shavell, Vol. 1, Amsterdam: Elsevier, North-Holland, 2007.
Posner, R. 1972. A Theory of Negligence. *Journal of Legal Studies* 1: 29–96.
Posner, R. 1983. *The Economics of Justice*. Cambridge, MA: Harvard Univ. Press.
Posner, R. 1985. An Economic Theory of the Criminal Law. *Columbia Law Review* 85: 1193–1231.
Posner, R. 1988. *Law and Literature: A Misunderstood Relation*. Cambridge, MA: Harvard Univ. Press.
Posner, R. 1990. *The Problems of Jurisprudence*. Cambridge, MA: Harvard Univ. Press.
Posner, R. 2003. *Economic Analysis of Law*, 6th ed. New York: Aspen Publishers.
Priest, G. 1977. The Common Law Process and the Selection of Efficient Laws. *Journal of Legal Studies* 6: 65–82.
Priest, G., and B. Klein. 1984. The Selection of Disputes for Litigation. *Journal of Legal Studies* 13: 1–55.
Rawls, J. 1971. *A Theory of Justice*. Cambridge, MA: Belknap Press.

Reinganum, J. 1988. Plea Bargaining and Prosecutorial Discretion. *American Economic Review* 78: 713–728.
Ringleb, A., and S. Wiggins. 1990. Liability and Large-Scale, Long-Term Hazards. *Journal of Political Economy* 98: 574–595.
Robinson, G. 1985. Probabilistic Causation and Compensation for Tortious Risk. *Journal of Legal Studies* 14: 779–798.
Rosenberg, D., and S. Shavell. 1985. A Model in Which Suits Are Brought for Their Nuisance Value. *International Review of Law and Economics* 5: 3–13.
Rothschild, M., and J. Stiglitz. 1976. Equilibrium in Competitive Insurance Markets: An Essay on the Economics of Imperfect Information. *Quarterly Journal of Economics* 90: 629–650.
Rubin, P. 1977. Why Is the Common Law Efficient? *Journal of Legal Studies* 6: 51–63.
Rubinfeld, D. and S. Schotchmer. "Contingent Fees." In *The New Palgrave Dictionary of Law and Economics*, edited by P. Newman. New York: Stockton Press, 1998.
Sandel, M. 2012. *What Money Can't Buy: The Moral Limits of Markets*. New York: Farrar, Straus, and Giroux.
Shavell, S. 1980. Strict Liability Versus Negligence. *Journal of Legal Studies* 9: 1–25.
Shavell, S. 1982. The Social Versus Private Incentive to Bring Suit in a Costly Legal System. *Journal of Legal Studies* 11: 333–339.
Shavell, S. 1982. On Liability and Insurance. *Bell Journal of Economics* 13: 120–132.
Shavell, S. 1985. Uncertainty Over Causation and the Determination of Civil Liability. *Journal of Law and Economics* 28: 587–609.
Shavell, S. 1985. Criminal Law and the Optimal Use of Nonmonetary Sanctions as Deterrents. *Columbia Law Review* 85: 1232–1262.
Shavell, S. 1986. The Judgment Proof Problem. *International Review of Law and Economics* 6: 45–58.
Shavell, S. 1987. *Economic Analysis of Accident Law*. Cambridge, MA: Harvard Univ. Press.
Shavell, S. 1987. A Model of Optimal Incapacitation. *American Economic Review* 77: 107–110.
Shavell, S. 1990. Deterrence and Punishment of Attempts. *Journal of Legal Studies* 19: 435–466.
Shavell, S. 1991. Individual Precautions to Prevent Theft: Private Versus Socially Optimal Behavior. *International Review of Law and Economics* 11: 123–132.
Shavell, S. 1992. A Note on Marginal Deterrence. *International Review of Law and Economics* 12: 345–355.
Shavell, S. 1993. The Optimal Structure of Law Enforcement. *Journal of Law and Economics* 36: 255–287.

Shavell, S. 1996. Any Frequency of Plaintiff Victory is Possible. *Journal of Legal Studies* 25: 493–501.

Shavell, S. 2002. Law Versus Morality as Regulators of Conduct. *American Law and Economics Review* 4: 227–257.

Iannaccone, L. 2004. *Foundations of Economic Analysis of Law*. Cambridge, MA: Belknap Press.

Iannaccone, L. 2015. A Simple Model of Optimal Deterrence and Incapacitation. *International Review of Law and Economics* 42: 13–19.

Smith, A. *A Theory of Moral Sentiments*. New York: Liberty Press, 1759 [1976].

Sophocles. "Antigone." In *Sophocles I*, edited by D. Grene and R. Lattimore. Chicago: Univ. of Chicago Press, 1954.

Spence, A.M. 1977. Consumer Misperceptions, Product Failure, and Producer Liability. *Review of Economic Studies* 44: 561–572.

Stark, R. *The Rise of Christianity: How an Obscure, Marginal Jesus Movement Became the Dominant Religious Force in the Western World in a Few Centuries*, San Francisco: Harper, 1996.

Stevenson, D. 2004. Entrapment and the Problem of Deterring Police Misconduct. *Connecticut Law Review* 37: 67–153.

Stigler, G. 1970. The Optimum Enforcement of Law. *Journal of Political Economy* 78: 345–355.

Sunstein, C. 1996. On the Expressive Function of Law. *University of Pennsylvania Law Review* 144: 2021–2053.

Thoreau, H. "Civil Disobedience." In *Walden and Other Writings of Henry David Thoreau*, edited by B. Atkinson. New York: Modern Library, 1849 [1965].

Tsvetanov, T., T. Miceli, and K. Segerson. 2021. Products Liability with Temptation Bias. *Journal of Economic Behavior and Organization* 186: 76–93.

Turley, J. 2024. *The Indispensable Right*. New York: Simon & Schuster.

Viscusi, W., J. Harrington, and J. Vernon. 2005. *Economics of Regulation and Antitrust*, 4th ed. Cambridge, MA: MIT Press.

Vitielo, M. 2004. Reforming Three-Strikes Excesses. *Washington University Law Quarterly* 82: 1–42.

Wade, N. 2006. *The Faith Instinct: How Religion Evolved and Why It Endures*. New York: Penguin Press.

Walsh, A. 2012. *Criminology: The Essentials*. Thousand Oaks, CA: Sage Publications.

Weber, M. *The Protestant Ethic and the Spirit of Capitalism*, translated by T. Parsons, New York: Dover Publications, 1958.

White, M. "Fiscal Zoning in Fragmented Metropolitan Areas." In *Fiscal Zoning and Land Use Controls*, edited by E. Mills. Lexington, MA: Lexington Books, 1975.

Wittman, D. 1980. First Come, First Served: An Economic Analysis of 'Coming to the Nuisance.' *Journal of Legal Studies* 9: 557–568.

Wittman, D. 1981. Optimal Pricing Of Sequential Inputs: Last Clear Chance, Mitigation of Damages, and Related Doctrines in the Law. *Journal of Legal Studies* 10: 65–91.

Wood, M. 1998. *In Search of the Trojan War*. Berkeley, CA: Univ. of California Press.

Index

T. J. Miceli, *Harm and Responsibility*,
https://doi.org/10.1007/978-3-031-74831-8

The manufacturer's authorised representative in the EU is Springer
Nature Customer Service Centre GmbH, Europaplatz 3, 69115 Heidelberg,
Germany. If you have any concerns regarding our products, please
contact ProductSafety@springernature.com

Printed and bound by CPI Group (UK) Ltd, Croydon, CR0 4YY
30/09/2026
02225583-0008